Personal Computers for Education

Personal Computers for Education

Alfred Bork
University of California, Irvine

HARPER & ROW, PUBLISHERS, New York
Cambridge, Philadelphia, San Francisco,
London, Mexico City, São Paulo, Singapore, Sydney

1817

Sponsoring Editor: John Willig
Project Editor: Mary Kennedy/Susan Goldfarb
Front Matter Design: Editing, Design & Production, Inc.
Text Design Adaptation: Robert Sugar
Cover Design: Sullivan Studios
Text Art: Vantage Art, Inc.
Production: Delia Tedoff
Compositor: ComCom Division of Haddon Craftsmen, Inc.
Printer and Binder: R. R. Donnelley & Sons Company

Personal Computers for Education

ISBN 0-06-040866-9

84 85 86 87 9 8 7 6 5 4 3 2 1

Contents

Preface

I began this book while I was on a leave of absence from the University of California, Irvine, working as a visiting faculty member at the University of Geneva during the last three months of 1982.

During my time at the University of Geneva, I was the guest of Bernard Levrat. He asked me to give a series of lectures, and those lectures, and discussions that followed with computer science faculty there, had considerable influence on the direction of this book.

The first version was recorded on tape in Geneva and transcribed in California. My wife, Annette, read this rough draft very carefully, making many stylistic changes. I also worked through the material again at that stage, so by the time I returned to California in 1983 most of the book was written.

This book arose out of the belief that it was important to have a book that covered all aspects of the computer in education in a serious way. The available books, it often seemed, were incomplete, stressing or favoring some uses over others and not giving a balanced presentation. Perhaps readers will feel the same about *this* book.

My attempt is to describe the uses of the computer in education in a nontrivial way and in a way that reflects overall high standards for what happens with computers. But I hope it is not a doctrinnaire position. I try not to rule out on general philosophical grounds certain ways of using the computer over other ways, but rather to consider each application on its own merits.

It is impossible in a book of this broad scope to acknowledge all the debts to many other people. My colleagues in the Educational Technology Center at Irvine, and in the earlier Physics Computer Development Project, certainly played major roles in guiding my thoughts. In the early days of our activities at Irvine, beginning about 1968, my colleagues were Richard Ballard and Joseph Marasco. Later Estelle Warner joined our group as a senior coder. Stephen Franklin came soon after. More recent colleagues have included Barry Kurtz, David Trowbridge, Ruth Von Blum, Werner Feibel, and Augusto Chioccariello.

The Educational Technology Center also had a very dedicated group of student programmers, and the success of our materials is due in part to these very competent men and women who have chosen to work with us, often giving up more financially rewarding jobs. Our first student programmer was David Robson, now at the Xerox Palo Alto Laboratory.

Many professional colleagues have also come to work with us for short periods of time. Our own work with the computer in science education has been particularly influenced by Arnold Arons during an association of many years. Arnold continues to work with us on current projects.

I have been very fortunate to have had an excellent secretary, Mary Doi, who also served as my typist for this book. Her contributions to our endeavors have been major, far beyond those of a highly capable typist.

These are indeed interesting times. The computer is just beginning the long process of changing our educational system. I feel fortunate to have been working in this area at such a time. Since my early experiments in using the computer in education while a faculty member at the University of Alaska in 1960, I have been convinced that the computer was eventually going to become the dominant delivery device in education. I see no reason to change that opinion.

Alfred Bork

Personal Computers for Education

chapter *1*

Introduction and Overview

● Computers in Schools, Universities, and Homes
● Order and Contents of This Book
● We Have Much to Learn
● Important Points

We stand at the beginning of a major revolution in the way people learn, a revolution that Eric Ashby called "the fourth revolution." At present, despite all the talk about computers in education, they are used relatively little in educational systems. However, we are moving rapidly toward a future when computers will comprise the dominant delivery system in education for almost all age levels in most subject areas. Not since the invention of the printing press has a technological device borne such implications for the learning process.

This book attempts to state the case for com-

puters in education, providing some understanding of their importance, and to review the many ways educational institutions can use computers. It addresses a very wide audience of those interested in education: teachers, administrators, university professors, educational decision makers, parents, future parents, and those interested in training within companies. The changes in education that are about to occur will affect all of us, and all of us need to understand them.

Currently education faces problems in many parts of the world, particularly in the United

1

States. I will not delineate these problems, because they have been discussed at length elsewhere. For example, a report released in 1983, "A Nation at Risk," was written by a committee appointed by the Secretary of Education of the United States. I argue that computers do provide some escapes from our current educational difficulties, perhaps the only ways possible.

A future with computers as the dominant educational delivery system seems inevitable for reasons both good and bad, many discussed in this book. But the computer is not always used in education in ways that are desirable. It remains to be seen whether such a future with computers leads to an improved educational system or to a deterioration in our already troubled current system. We can only strive for a better system of the future, trying to avoid some of the pitfalls. Unfortunately currently many mistakes are being made in computer use, with these mistakes being widely duplicated all over the country. I hope to show that some directions are ill advised and to suggest better alternatives.

This is *not* a history book. It doesn't start from counting on one's fingers and advance to the Cray supercomputer. Sometimes historical events are noteworthy, but only when relevant to today's situation. I have done research in the history of science, so it seems natural for me to include historical details. But to give an adequate view of the history would require a much larger book, and I do not think the space is warranted. What usually passes for "history" in many science and technology books, unfortunately, is a set of legends, dates, and names that have nothing to do with the real essence of intellectual history. So this book makes little pretense at providing historical details. Nor does it review older projects, except insofar as those projects are relevant to today's situation.

COMPUTERS IN SCHOOLS, UNIVERSITIES, AND HOMES

As of September 1983, there were approximately 350,000 computers in U.S. schools, amounting

to about four computers a school on the average. These computers are by no means equally distributed. Many schools, perhaps one-third of those in the country, still have no computer, while other schools, particularly those in more affluent districts, provide many computers for students. The number of computers per school is not remarkable. Estimates in England and Scotland indicate that in those countries, about three computers are available per school. By policy of the British government, *every* school should have at least one computer, and the government has assisted schools in their purchases.

It is harder to get data about home computers, but some estimates put the number of home computers in the United States at present at several million. With both home computers and school computers, the number purchased each year approximates the number already present, so both markets are growing extremely rapidly.

It is interesting to note that schools continue to buy computers in sizable numbers, even in a time of monumental financial problems. Parents themselves are demanding this. Middle-class parents in particular seem to feel that their children are receiving an inferior education unless computers are available. This reflects the fact that society currently sees computers as magical devices, ones people hope will solve the major social problems. So parents, being dissatisfied with their children's education, tend to think of computers as a solution, although they possess little knowledge of how they could be so. Hence they induce schools to purchase computers, and in some cases even raise the necessary funds. Parents also see computer skills as valuable for future jobs.

Unfortunately when computers arrive at these schools, often there is little understanding of how to use them. Teachers are seldom trained to use computers in education, and the few available training programs are often weak. Furthermore, in spite of assurances from computer vendors, very little good curriculum material using computers is currently available; much is poor. Therefore, the computer in the school is only too often a disaster rather than the educational boon anticipated. Teachers and administrators and finally students and parents should come to understand that the computer is no magic panacea but a tool that requires the same careful use as any other educational device.

ORDER AND CONTENTS OF THIS BOOK

The basic guiding principle in organizing this book is that *pedagogical issues* take precedence over *technical details,* such as the nature of the hardware. In other books about the computer in education, intended for wide general audiences, often this is not the case. Long discussions about the nature of computers, with many terms such as bits and bytes, occur very early. These books seem to give the impression that it is most important to learn all the vocabulary, whereas my own strong feeling is that teachers should consider pedagogical issues initially. If they have only limited time to read about computers in education, only the pedagogical issues need concern them.

The book is divided into three parts. In chapters 2 to 6 (the first part), I consider five modes of usage of the computer in education: learning about the computer, particularly about programming; computer literacy; the computer as an intellectual tool; computer-based learning, where the computer is used as an instructional device in any area; and the use of the computer as an aid in the management of learning. These five chapters give a panoramic view of the ways computers can be used with students. These modes should *not* be considered as alternatives in the sense that only one must be the "chosen" one. Rather, all these uses are important in education, and all should occur in most schools.

The second part, chapters 7 to 12, might be described as miscellaneous. This part covers the hardware issues, offering a background that is not necessary for many teachers. It also contemplates the psychological background, advantages, and disadvantages of using the computer

in education, and investigates details of the classroom situation. It concludes with two long chapters, of interest to selected readers, on how to produce computer-based learning materials. Not all teachers will become producers, but some will.

The third part, chapters 13 and 14, concentrates on the future. Today's computer technology is changing extremely rapidly, and even the rate of change is increasing. Any attempt to use the computer in education must consider the future, or material will soon be far out of date. Chapter 13 considers the future of computer hardware, while chapter 14 concentrates on educational futures. In a sense this organization is the reverse of that in parts I and II, but it seems appropriate to end the book with considerations of the long-range and profound effect of computers on education. Readers interested only in these long-range effects may prefer to read these two chapters closely.

A person who is trying to obtain a rapid overview of the role of the computer in education does not need to read the entire book. I recommend that such a reader look at chapters 4, 5, 7, 8, and 14. Chapter 3 on computer literacy is also recommended for this rapid overview.

Chapter 4 introduces the important notion of intellectual tools, and chapter 5 the notion of computer-based learning. These two notions will eventually become the most commonly used roles of the computer in learning, and so they furnish a good introduction to modes of usage. Chapter 7, concerning the advantages and disadvantages associated with computer use in education, and chapter 8, on evaluating computer materials, also give important introductions to the role of the computer in learning and of the criteria that can be used for selecting material. Chapter 14, on the future of our educational systems using computers, is recommended for all readers.

Both hardware chapters can be omitted by those with little time. Of the two, chapter 13 is the most important and can be read by itself.

WE HAVE MUCH TO LEARN

I wish to make it very clear that I do not regard the current situation of computers in education as final. The current uses of computers and the current materials are *all,* without exception, relatively primitive as compared with what will exist in a few years. In my optimistic moments I think we are as much as 20 percent of the way toward learning how to use computers effectively in education.

A number of things are needed to propel us into the future. First, we need much more educational research involving the computer, including research on the general nature of the learning process and how to assist it. We still have far to go, and any coherent national plan for the future must greatly emphasize such research.

We also need much more practice developing computer-based learning materials and using them in classes. This is particularly true in some of the more advanced techniques, such as those that combine the computer with the videodisc.

The difficulty is that we have much to learn within little time. The rush to use computers in education is accelerating continually, and it is increasingly controlled by commercial or other interests outside the educational sector. Hence our needs are great and our time is short.

IMPORTANT POINTS

The following important points are made a number of times in this book. I gather them here to further emphasize them and to put them in a single location for the reader with little time.

1. Learning rather than technology should be emphasized. The computer itself is not the main interest of this book. Rather, I stress the effective use of the computer in education. The computer is a means to an end, the end being to assist all students to learn efficiently and effectively. We should make our decisions not on technological grounds but on pedagogical grounds.

2. The future is more important than the present. In thinking about the influence of computers on education, we must look to the future, not to the present. This is important because of very rapid changes in the underlying technology. Planning based on today's technology is almost certain to be inadequate.

3. Over the next 25 years the computer will become the dominant delivery system in education. In most subject areas, more people of all ages will learn more things from computers than from lectures, textbooks, or other modes. In educational institutions the next 25 years may be a time of great turmoil.

4. The computer can be used in many different ways to aid students to learn. It is useless to debate which is the best way to employ the computer. Decisions should be made on pedagogical grounds. We should not decide in advance that there is only one way to use the computer.

5. Because the computer will become very important in education, our educational systems must change. Current educational systems, based on older technologies, will not be adequate. We must consider new possibilities of how learning will be organized.

6. We must encourage administrators, teachers, and parents to distinguish between good and bad learning material involving the computer. Much commercially available material is poor. To have better material, users must distinguish between good and bad; they must insist on better material. If teachers buy poor material, vendors will continue to supply it.

7. Not everyone needs to learn to program. As new powerful computer tools become widely available, most people will be users of these tools and will not be directly involved in programming. If programming is taught, it is more important for people to learn the details of programming style and the strategies of

software engineering than to learn the grammatical details of one or several languages.

8. The major learning advantage of the computer is that it is an *interactive* medium, allowing constant interaction between the student and the computer. Because of this, the learning experiences provided by the computer can be individualized to the needs of each student.

9. Major curriculum development is needed to make the computer more effective in education. We need a whole new range of courses and curricula that are based on the availability of this new and powerful learning device.

10. As new curricula are developed, training of teachers to use the new material will be important. Some of the new modules, particularly those intended for home and classroom use where teachers are not available, may be independent of teachers.

11. Computers are not necessarily desirable in educational contexts. Each use should be justified. They can be used to aid education, or they can lead to poorer education than our current modes. Some problems already exist, with inadequate teaching of programming and with poor computer-based learning material. We must not assume that because the computer is used, education is automatically improved.

12. Although the computer will become the dominant educational delivery system, it does not necessarily follow that the future educational system will be better than the current system. At present the quality of our learning future is in doubt. We probably have only a few years to assure a better future.

13. Contemporary education has many problems, as recent reports and studies have revealed. Wide use of the computer may be the only feasible solution to our current educational problems.

14. We still have much to learn about the learning process generally and with regard to computers. So humility is needed, a realization that our current strategies and techniques, even the most advanced, may not be eventually the most desirable. We must be prepared for new modes, new strategies, new course organizations.

I

MODES OF COMPUTER USAGE

In the next five chapters I examine different ways of using computers in an educational context—programming, computer literacy, intellectual tool, computer-based learning, and management.

Each of these computer uses has both advantages and disadvantages. All are important in some situations. They correspond to *different* pedagogical needs, and so they should *not* be considered as competing; that is, you are not asked to pick or choose among these various ways of using the computer. Unfortunately, books and papers often give users of computers in education, particularly novices, the false idea that they must make a choice. Indeed, many authors even argue the "superiority" of one usage over another.

All this prattle about "which to use" is unfortunate. We should decide which way to use the computer on *pedagogical* grounds, not on some philosophical prejudices developed in advance about where the computer will be effective and where it will not. Only additional empirical practice, not abstract decisions, can determine the best way to use the computer in a particular situation.

Readers are encouraged to consider each type of computer usage as presenting opportunities and possibilities. The classification scheme in these five chapters, the modes of computer usage in education, is to some extent arbitrary. All attempts to categorize are an imposed condition, not necessarily inherent in the discipline.

The types of usage described in this section are largely independent. A chapter not of great interest can be omitted, or chapters can be read out of order. Thus, if you are primarily interested in computer-based learning, proceed immediately to that chapter. A few types of usage are difficult to classify, and so are mentioned several times in different chapters.

chapter 2

Learning to Program

One way of using computers in education is to learn *about* the computer, partially about programming. Although it is not essential for all students, learning to program a computer is one of the most common uses of computers today in schools and universities, and many people learn to program outside of formal courses. At the high school level learning to program accounts for perhaps 80 percent of the current usage. At the university level the percentage is probably higher. Programming courses are beginning to appear even in junior high and elementary schools, although these courses are sometimes called computer literacy.

All these courses and informal learning modes introduce students to a computer programming language or languages. The learning units may be subject-matter dependent; a programming course for science students, for example, may differ from the same course for fine arts students. While learning to program is currently one of the dominant computer uses, as the computer becomes more widely used, this is likely to change.

Not enough competent programmers can be found in the United States; it is estimated that we are currently short about 100,000 programmers, and this shortage is increasing each year.

Therefore there is much pressure to teach programming.

However, programming experiences are not necessarily desirable. Despite the fact that learning to program is one of the more common persistent uses of computers today, many current programming courses are probably doing more harm than good. In many cases students inculcate a set of bad habits that are extremely difficult to overcome later. Initial programming habits, picked up during study of one's first programming language, can be overcome, but if they are very deep-rooted, the task is very difficult. This issue will be discussed further in this chapter.

WHAT IS PROGRAMMING?

I have been referring to programming, but you may find this term unfamiliar. The problem addressed by the writing of computer programs is primarily one of communication between a human being and a computer. Human beings have problems to solve. The problems could be numerical or they could deal with language or some other nonnumerical symbol system. The human being presumably knows how to solve the problem, or at least knows how to solve some related problem. But if the computer is to aid in the solution of this problem, humans must convey their intent to the computer.

Some type of "language" is used in all forms of communication. The term *language* has in this context a more general sense than is customary. When you speak of French or German or English, you are pointing to a language used for interpersonal communication among human beings. Human languages are not ideal for communicating with computers, however, primarily because they frequently entail a fair amount of ambiguity. Human-to-human communication can tolerate this ambiguity because of tacit agreements or because nonverbal communication is also present. But in communicating with a machine, *everything* is carried out in a literal fashion, so we need to be very precise and spe-

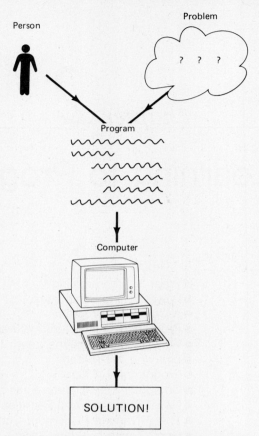

Figure 2.1 Programming allows communication between a person and a computer.

cific in describing the task to be carried out. Hence people have developed specialized languages, called programming languages, for person–machine communication.

Programming, then, is the communication activity by which the person "tells" the computer (not orally at this time) what it is to do. Anyone who wants the computer to *do* something must engage in this person–computer communication, using a well-defined computer language.

This prescription of the process to be carried out is stored in the computer in advance, before it is carried out, so that the instructions can be executed rapidly. This concept of *storing* the program inside the computer, suggested by

John von Neumann, is one of the computer's most important notions. The term *stored program computer* was an early descriptive term for the digital computer, what we now call the computer.

One way of viewing a program is as a specification for *transforming information,* accepting some information and producing some new information. The transformation rules are called algorithms.

PROGRAMMING LANGUAGES

We need a way to tell the computer what we want it to do. The basis for most descriptions to the computer of an activity to be carried out is a *programming language.* This is a special language that does not include ambiguities. Computer languages must have precise descriptions of the tasks to be performed.

A major aspect of the evolution of computers is the large number of different computer languages, some serving specialized purposes. This proliferation of languages started in the earliest days of computers and is continuing today. To the novice, it seems strange that we should have so many languages. As the French say, *c'est la vie;* all indications are that this situation will continue for a long time.

Hundreds, perhaps even thousands, of computer languages have been developed. No single list of languages can be complete. Many languages never see the light of day beyond their initial developer. Indeed, just what we should call a language is not entirely clear. Thus the term dialect enters. A dialect is a slight variant on a particular language, usually not considered a separate language. Most computer languages have dialects; two or more different implementations, or versions, of a language, perhaps used on different computers, may not be identical. A program that runs on one computer may not run on another though it purports to use the "same" language; or even worse, one program may produce different results on two computers.

To avoid this problem, computer language experts often attempt to keep various versions of a given language as close as possible. The process of discouraging dialects of a language is called standardization. Language designers and users formulate a set of standards for the language and require, legally if the name of the language has been copyrighted, that each version observes those standards.

It is not always easy to determine if a realization of a language on a computer, one implementation of the language, does match the standards. Perhaps the best way to determine this is to develop a large set of programs in the language, using all the features of the language, plus a specification of how those programs are to act. Such a collection of programs is called a validation suite; the collection could be very extensive. A validation suite for Ada, a recently developed language, is said to contain several thousand programs.

Various types of standardization are possible; a language can be standardized in just one country or internationally. I won't go into details. You should merely be aware that some languages are better standardized than others.

Table 2.1 cites the most widely used languages, their dates of development, whether

Original Information   Program   New Information

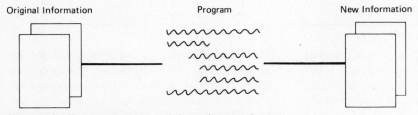

Figure 2.2 The computer as an information transformer.

Table 2.1 COMPUTER LANGUAGES

Language	First developed	Standardization attempts	Comments
Ada	Reference manual July 1980 Approved implementations 1983	Name copyrighted; validation suite.	Developed in competition sponsored by the U.S. Department of Defense.
ALGOL	1960 1968 (much modified)	ISO standard (international standard).	Popular mostly in Europe. Many relatives, such as Pascal.
APL	Iverson's 1962 book APL/360—1967	An effective (de facto) standard because of the IBM implementation, widely used.	Concise, very symbolic language.
BASIC	1965	Recent standardization efforts. Still varies widely.	Developed for student use at Dartmouth College.
COBOL	Initial design—1959 First running versions —1960	Several levels have been standardized since 1965.	Primarily used for business applications. Most commonly used programming language.
FORTRAN	1957 Latest version—1977	Several standardization efforts.	First successful "algebraic" language, allowing formulas.
LISP	1960	Many variants.	List programming language used in artificial intelligence.
Logo	1967	None.	Initially for junior high level. Turtle geometry added after initial use.
Pascal	1971	ISO standard.	Modern general-purpose language, ALGOL relative.
PL/I	1968—first IBM compiler	None.	Early attempt at a comprehensive language.
SNOBOL	1962	None.	Symbol (string) manipulating language.

there has been an attempt at standardization, and some other important information. While the list is by no means complete, these languages are probably used more than 95 percent of the time.

Not all programming languages are intended for the same purpose. Some of the languages are general, while others have been developed for specialized uses. Many earlier languages, from FORTRAN on, emphasized scientific calculations. More recently, there have been a variety of other special-purpose languages; however, the notion of general-purpose languages is still very important. Most programming is done in these languages.

The history of languages is reasonably straightforward. Early computer languages were close to the machine itself; these languages often were a simple transliteration of the actual code that the machine knew how to interpret, so they were often called machine language or sometimes native code. This type of computer language is almost never used by humans today. Rather, all computers work on the principle of language translators. That is, computers have a quite elaborate program that translates or interprets language more akin to human languages into one suitable for the machine, or native code. The program that does this translation is usually called a compiler or interpreter.

Native code differs greatly from one computer to another, so one purpose of the higher-level languages is to make it easier to move (transport) programs from one machine to another.

A COMPUTER PROGRAM

Just as with a natural language, a programming language has a grammar, a set of syntactical rules specifying the available expressions, which must be observed rigidly. The grammatical details will generally differ from language to language, even for apparently similar constructions. Many languages include English words, perhaps because most early programming languages were developed in English-speaking countries. Thus we find in a language like Pascal (from Switzerland) such words as READ, WRITE, CASE, FOR, WHILE, REPEAT, and

UNTIL, among others. A reader may be able to understand much of what is happening in a program simply by understanding English!

A computer program is (typically) a sequential collection of "sentences" or statements, each following the grammatical rules of the programming language. Each sentence contains information for the computer. You can think of these declarative sentences as fed to the computer one by one in sequential order; the computer then "executes" each sentence, or does what the sentence tells it to do.

Statement 1   (executed first)
Statement 2   (executed second)
Statement 3   (executed third)

Later I will indicate that this linear order of execution, each statement one by one, can be varied under certain circumstances. Normally statements in a program are executed sequentially.

Programming always occurs in some type of supporting environment consisting of programs to help the programmer. One component of the programming environment is an editor, which allows easy entry and modification of the program. An editor is a specialized form of word processor (see chapter 4, page 45). Thus if an error occurs in a line, perhaps because of incorrect typing, a good editor allows you to make the necessary change easily, without retyping the entire line. Most editors do not have any "knowledge" of the programming language being used, but a few recent ones do have such built-in "intelligence."

The editor is only one aspect of a *programming environment,* a set of facilities or computer

Program (User-oriented Language)

Program (Convenient Machine Form)

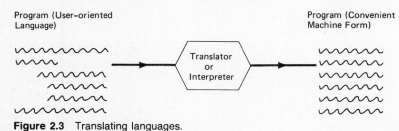

Figure 2.3 Translating languages.

programs to ease the task of programming. A computer program is also referred to as "software." Special programs to locate errors, called debugging, may also be available, for example.

The support environment for programming is provided with the computer. It is part of the *system software,* (the fundamental software usually supplied with the computer), rather than *applications* programs (the programs devised by each user).

PROGRAMMING STYLE— STRUCTURED PROGRAMMING

More important than the grammatical rules of a language, although it has received less attention until recently, is the *style,* the spirit, in which the language is used. Programming methodology is not necessarily inherent in the programming language, although some languages enforce stylistic aspects more than others. The critical stylistic question is whether the program can be easily understood.

You might wonder at first glance why style is important for computers. Offhand it would look as if computers wouldn't care. But *people* using the computers do care, particularly if a program needs to be modified later, almost always the case with any substantial program, or if it needs to be moved to different computers, again a common occurrence.

This movement of computer programs, called transporting or "porting" a program, is frequent because of the rapid evolution of computers. An institution or business that uses computers for numerous things is likely to acquire better computers as they become available— and that is frequently. An important economic issue is to be able to maintain the older programs and keep them running. Style alone does not ensure this, but by trying to make the program more readable, more easily understood, modifications for the new machine become easier.

Only in recent years have we learned about the importance of programming style. In the early days programmers worked with little previous programming experience, simply because the whole notion of writing programs for computers in any language was new. As we gained more experience and as some major programming projects failed, the important question of how to program to avoid difficulties was addressed. Now there is greater concern with these stylistic issues. But many old-fashioned programming texts have very little to say about style. The stylistic issues emphasized today are referred to as structured programming.

Structured programming is a loosely connected construct of ideas. Here, instead of attempting a full exposition, I discuss a number of important concepts in structured programming.

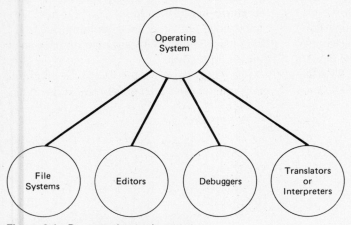

Figure 2.4 Programming environment.

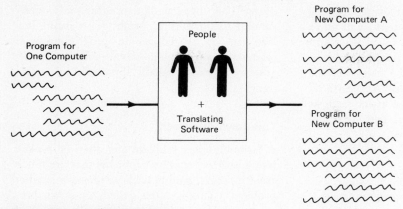

Figure 2.5   Transporting a program.

Readability

The first, most important issue with regard to programming style is that the program should be easy for people to *read*. You should be able to determine what will be accomplished as the computer carries out the program. A program should be easy to use to locate errors, change and improve, and move to other computers. In large programs it is estimated that the number of instructions that must be changed in the program's early years is about the same as the number of instructions in the entire program. And very often these changes must be made by someone who did not write the program. The ease with which programs are changed depends on the program's *readability*. Software must be reliable and adaptable.

Reading a program is different from writing one, and it is less studied, unfortunately. Nevertheless, it is very important to be able to *read* programs, particularly programs written by others, just as it is important to be able to read a story written by someone else. Reading and writing programs are *different* activities, with different skills involved. It takes practice to learn how to read a program, but it is much easier if a program is written with readability in mind.

Making reading easy encompasses a collection of ideas, many of them discussed in the next few pages. One important aspect is that the pro-

gram comprises two parts that need to be considered equally. One part of the program is a set of instructions for the computer—the algorithm. But equally important in programming, although not recognized at first, is the question of *data*.

Data

Data refers to the characters, words, sentences, paragraphs, numbers in various forms, and coded entities that are to be transformed, or changed, by the algorithm. The importance of data, and the need to specify data carefully within the computer program, has only gradually come to be understood. Yet it is now considered one of the most important aspects of structured programming.

Most good modern languages *require* that every data item, such as the name of something, be carefully specified within the program before that item is used. Planning the data structure is an important part of modern programming. So it must be stressed at an early stage in learning to program.

Certain data types will be inherent in the language; thus most languages with control over data allow the possibility of integers or characters as data types. But it is also important to provide programmers with the ability to define their *own* data types, as appropriate to the area under consideration.

In most modern programming languages the type of data and the data items will have *names,* identifiers for the data. Good programming practice insists that these names convey to the user, as far as possible, the nature of the data. Thus cryptic names such as "A," "Susan," or "X23" should be avoided. A name such as "Average" is better, because it tells us something about the named item.

Modularity

A critical idea of structured programming is *modularity,* whereby one writes not a long single program but instead a collection of smaller tasks or programs, each specifying a self-contained job for the computer to carry out. The basic unit, the smaller task, is often called a *procedure,* although the term subroutine or routine is also used. A modular program uses many procedures.

An individual procedure should be short, representing a single task. If it is, it will be possible to find out in which procedure any trouble occurs, pinning it down to only a few statements within the computer program. And it will be easier to modify the program if each procedure functions independently of the other procedures.

Procedure is a key notion in structured programming. The procedure is the basic unit of a modern program; the full program should be a collection of relatively small modules or procedures. This division of a program into many small procedures is important in programming. The use of procedures in programming is related to good problem-solving practice. It suggests an approach called "top-down" programming.

Top-down Approach

A large complex problem can often be broken into a series of smaller problems that are much easier to solve, simply because they *are* smaller problems. This is often called top-down programming; it contrasts with the older type of programming of simply writing the program line by line. With top-down programming an overall outline is written *first.* This outline is called the *main program.* The overall outline may be only a dozen or fifteen statements long, even for a very complex task. Each statement may be some type of subtask needed to complete the desired full task. Each subtask may correspond to a procedure, which in turn may depend on other procedures; thus we create an outline of the subtask, as well as the overall outline.

Procedures in top-down coding may also entail their own data, not available to any other procedures or other parts of the program. Indeed, good programming practice demands that the data be "known," or available, to as small a part of the program as possible; this makes it

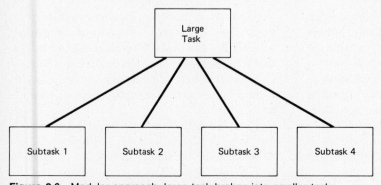

Figure 2.6 Modular approach: large task broken into smaller tasks.

easier to pin down possible errors. The computer scientist refers to the *scope* of data, or where within the program, and in which procedures, a particular data item can be used.

The term *outline* is probably familiar to you from writing activities. In the early stages of writing we generally prepare an outline of the composition first. But this term may be slightly misleading when applied to computer programs. The main program, or a procedure, may be more than a conventional outline; it may have decision points, places where different things are done under different circumstances.

Later in this chapter I will present a sample program for the simple task of taking an average. I have considered the process of preparing such a program from a top-down point of view, asking "What are the steps involved in taking an average?" One possible answer, among many, is shown in Figure 2.7.

Control Structures

Another important aspect of structured programming is the use of a set of facilities, statements in the language, that change the *order* of a calculation. With most programming languages the statements in a program are carried out one by one in the order in which they appear. But an important feature, facilities for repeating statements, allows us to alter this flow, executing statements in a different order.

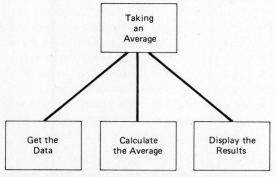

Figure 2.7 Top-down approach for taking an average.

A basic concept is repetition, a *loop*. In a loop in a program a given collection of statements, a subset of the program, (a *block*,) is to be executed (repeated) many times. The number of times the loop is executed may be set in advance or may depend on conditions that arise during the calculations. Thus the loop may continue until a variable takes a specified value. Furthermore, the testing on these conditions determining, for example, if the variable is zero, can occur either at the beginning, during, or at the end of the loop. Facilities available are language-dependent. Providing natural looping structures that are easy to understand is an important aspect of programming languages. Two examples are shown here.

```
Statement 1
Statement 2
        Do these next three statements 100 times:
                Statement 3
                Statement 4
                Statement 5
Statement 6
```

A loop executed a fixed number of times.

```
Statement 1
        While Time is less than 100, keep doing
these:
                Statement 2.1          (alters Time)
                Statement 2.2
        Statement 3 (Will be done when Time is equal
to or greater than 100)
```

The number of executions depends on calculations within the loop.

Another type of powerful control statement is the "If-then-else" statement. It works like a two-way switch. If the condition is satisfied, the THEN statements are carried out; if it is not satisfied, the ELSE statements are executed. The statement works the way a reader of English would expect.

Comments

A program should have many comments at many places in the program. These comments should explain to the reader what the program is doing. The comments aid humans; the computer ignores them.

Software Life Cycle

It is also important in programming to realize that designing and writing a program is part of a long process, with many stages. Thus the design activities that precede the programming itself are important and must be given full consideration. Furthermore, the issue of modifying the program—that is, first getting it to work properly and then improving it through usage and careful testing—goes on for the whole history of a major program. Even beginners should get some idea of the software life cycle, to plan for it carefully. In the armed services it is estimated that 80 percent or more of the cost of programming is concerned with the long-term maintenance of the program, so programming strategies must anticipate the life cycle.

Only some features of good modern structured programming have been covered, yet this is enough to give you an idea of the requirements of style in modern programming.

IMPORTANT STYLISTIC QUESTIONS

- Is the program easy to read?
- Is the data structure clearly specified?
- Is the program modular, with many separate pieces?
- Was the program designed by breaking a large problem into a series of smaller problems?
- Is the flow of control clearly indicated?

I cannot overstress programming style; the following quote illustrates this point.

It is important that students exercise good programming habits from the very start. . . . It is much easier to train a programmer properly than to eliminate bad habits once they become an established part of a programmer's view of solving problems.*

WHY SHOULD SOMEONE LEARN TO PROGRAM?

Often it seems taken as a fact of life that everyone should learn to program. Programming courses are springing up everywhere at all levels in schools. Some of these are disguised as computer literacy courses, a topic discussed in chapter 3. I question whether programming *is* valuable for computer literacy.

Often in teaching programming, it seems implicitly assumed that *everyone* will be a programmer in some distant future. Although this is a possibility, particularly if one interprets the word programmer very loosely, it does not seem a necessary or even likely conclusion.

While it is a fact that everyone will be a computer user, that is not to say that everyone will be a computer programmer. Many computer uses will not involve programming; increasingly powerful and elaborate applications packages, such as some that will be discussed in the next few chapters, may be the only contact most people will have with the computer. It should be clearly understood that in the *real* world, most people *use* programs rather than *write* them.

One argument often seen for teaching people to program is that it gives them "control" over the computer. Proponents of this viewpoint feel that someone who has not learned to program is "being controlled" by the computer. I argue that this is so much semantic nonsense. Students who make effective use of a word processor, or a spreadsheet, have precise control for getting the system to do what they wish. Any knowledge they might have of a simple com-

*College Board's Advanced Placement Computer Science Development Committee, *Teacher's Guide to Advanced Placement Courses in Computer Science,* (Princeton: Educational Testing Service, 1984).

puter language contributes nothing to their control of the computer in using such tools.

Another very different type of argument for learning programming may conceivably have some merit, but as yet it is mostly undemonstrated. The claim is that programming, *properly taught,* assists people either in problem solving or in more logical thinking, which is possibly the same thing. Some advocates of this viewpoint recommend a very different approach to programming than is normally taken, using artificial intelligence languages such as Prolog. In other cases, particularly those with strong emphasis on problem-solving, the structured languages such as Pascal may be recommended. More research is needed before it can be stated definitely that programming will in certain circumstances improve a person's problem-solving and logical reasoning capabilities.

The strong arguments *for* learning to program usually come because the student will need to program within some particular applications area later in life. Thus anyone who is going to study science should learn to program, as suggested at the end of chapter 3. Certainly a student who will study computer science needs a sound background in programming, a background not available in most schools at present. In the school system, only those students with a clear need should be taught to program.

Another reason to teach programming is if students need it for some intellectual capability —such as learning Logo to assist in further learning of mathematics.

If students *want* to learn to program, they should be given that opportunity. It may influence later career direction.

Programming is intimately related to particular disciplines, as just noted. Because of this, learning programming skills might be discipline-oriented, occurring within the teaching of mathematics, physics, or other areas. Generally, programming is taught as a separate course, but that is not necessarily the best method. However, there are dangers in learning to program in a particular discipline, if the course is taught by professionals who do not understand computer systems.

Educators must always ask what the students are expected to *do* with programming skills once they have them. We could teach a five-year-old to run a machine lathe, but it is not a wise thing to require in the educational process because it is not useful for such a student.

LEARNING TO PROGRAM

How does a student learn a programming language in class or informally? What methods are available to students and teachers? What are the advantages and disadvantages of various methods?

Students learn programming languages for a variety of purposes, and the answers to some of these questions may well be different if purposes differ. Someone may be learning a little bit about computers, just to become acquainted with them. On the other hand, a student may be studying a computer language with the aspiration of making a career of computer science, or of doing extensive work with a computer though his or her major interests lie elsewhere. The serious programmer, as in these last two cases, has a more rigid set of requirements to satisfy than the casual programmer.

The Grammatical Approach

Most programming languages still are learned in a way similar to the old way of teaching natural languages, through emphasis on grammar and vocabulary. The syntactical rules of the language (the grammar) are arranged in what seems to be "logical" fashion for the instructor or the author of the textbook. Students of the language (natural or computer) then learn these grammatical concepts one by one, including learning the special words or symbols that occur in the language.

The concept of a full program, using such a grammatical approach to a computer language, comes only after learning a grammar. Often students are required to learn all or most of the grammar rather quickly before using the language extensively. The emphasis is *not* on style. In a few cases people learn some grammar and then proceed to use extensively that subset of the total capability. Though the second procedure is, I believe, clearly desirable, it is uncommon.

The grammatical approach to learning a language, although by far the dominant one, has many negative aspects. It does *not* focus on programming itself, and it does *not* necessarily encourage the good habits of style that go under the collective name of structured programming. Though most available courses and books follow this grammatical approach, there are better ways to learn to program.

One sign of an outmoded approach to programming is the teaching of flowcharting. While flowcharting was widely used as a technique in the early days of programming, and indeed was emphasized in many courses, generally it is not consistent with modern structured approaches. The notion of starting at the "top," with the overall modules, and working down to details is inconsistent with the typical old-fashioned programming strategies that first worked with the details represented in flowcharts, graphical representation of the details. So a course that is still teaching flowcharting is not meeting modern standards.

Teachers should keep strongly in mind the fact that the main purpose in teaching programming is not to teach the grammatical details of a particular programming language. These should be regarded as the least important things, just the grubby mechanisms needed to implement programs, necessary details but not the heart of the programming activity. It is the stylistic issues that are fundamental. Far too many courses at all levels end up, from the student's point of view, as nothing but the syntax.

Examples

Another way of learning a computer language, a good though little-used way, is through a se-

ries of carefully chosen examples. The strategy is to start with full programs, which are then explained step by step, with the grammatical details introduced within the context of the example programs. These sample programs can be chosen from some area that is of interest to the learners, so they can see the relevance of the computer to their other interests immediately. Issues of good style can be illustrated easily with this approach. This method is somewhat like the newer ways of teaching natural language, where students are started immediately with full "dialogs" using the language.

The advantage to the example method is that the user begins immediately with the final application, the writing of programs, and thus recognizes the essentials of programming at once. If the programs are written in a good modular top-down style, the user also sees good practice right from the beginning. This method should be more prevalent, since it has many advantages. But few textbooks use this approach, as the textbook tradition, unfortunately, is the grammatical approach.

Introductory Facilities

A third way of learning a language relates to the example method. The user is supplied not just with the raw language but with a set of powerful facilities or capabilities within this language. These powerful facilities, picked because of their interest to beginning learners, lead very quickly to interesting ways to use the language. The facilities themselves are often usable alone, so that the user immediately has something to do, some interest, with the language.

The turtle geometry introduction to Logo, a set of drawing facilities, now almost universally used in teaching that language, is certainly the best known example of this approach. (Turtle geometry is discussed in chapter 4.) Other languages (UCSD Pascal, for example) have also adopted this approach. Perhaps most interesting about turtle geometry are its *visual* facilities. The simple initial commands, Forward (drawing a line) and Right (altering direction), lead very quickly to interesting pictures on the screen. Logo is discussed further in chapter 4.

The *Karel, The Robot* facility provides another example of this type of approach, offering the student again a collection of simple visual capabilities similar to turtle geometry. Students deal immediately with attractive and appealing output, much better than numerical output. In the Computer Power course, the quilting and cartooning programs partially carry out this graphic approach to programming, introducing programming through pictorial facilities.

Interactive Approaches

A more specialized fourth way of teaching a programming language is interactively. At least two interactive methods are possible: the immediate mode and the computer–based learning mode. The immediate mode works only with certain types of implementations of computer languages where a single statement of the language can be entered by the student, usually in an on-line mode with the student working directly at a computer display; the computer *immediately* executes just one statement right after it is entered. In languages where this is possible, students can enter a set of given statements one by one, observing what happens.

This might also be considered a controlled discovery mode. The instructor has specified the stimuli, but students are free to experiment and try new things. Thus students discover grammatical details through exploration rather than passively being told. This approach has been used for many years at Irvine and a similar method has been used with Logo at the Department of Artificial Intelligence at the University of Edinburgh. However, this strategy for learning a programming language is limited to certain languages and to certain realizations of those languages on particular computers.

Another type of interactive learning of the language is entirely different. This method involves using computer-based learning material as the environment for learning the language (see chapter 5). Relatively few examples of this way to learn programming are available, but eventually use of the computer as a device to learn about the computer will increase and many programming courses will be given primarily from the computer itself.

One example, although not a complete course, was developed by Kenneth Bowles in connection with the development of UCSD Pascal at the University of California, San Diego. Students take a series of on-line exams, directly at the computer, to demonstrate their progress through points in the course. All the exams in this course do not offer extensive help, but they have the *potential* for offering such assistance.

At the present time far too few competent instructors are available to teach programming in high schools and universities. Hence it would seem that computer-based learning material for learning computer languages, used directly by the student, will be increasingly important. Some of the material will be relatively simple to develop. More complex sections that can check student programs and offer detailed assistance will also be possible. Unfortunately, little such material is currently available, but the direction is a promising one.

Peer Learning

One seldom-stressed aspect of teaching programming is the question of whether an individual thrives better working alone or whether people learn to program more satisfactorily in groups. In actual practice in industry, most complex programming involves groups of people, because the programs are often too large for one individual to complete in reasonable time. Hence the ability of a person to work within a larger team is important in programming, and so it is interesting that some courses, such as Computer Power, employ this approach immediately in the learning process.

Peer influence, working with other students, is often a powerful learning aid, little exploited in our schools and universities. Peer learning means students help one another, their peers, in the learning process, and they learn to work together. Students can work together in groups to solve programming problems in a cooperative fashion.

Area Specialization

Another factor that should be considered in learning to program computers cuts across most of the methods discussed. The typical programming course throws together students with every type of background. The net result is that almost no common subject area can be found that can lead to meaningful programs. Often a desirable alternative is to teach programming *within some subject area,* where some common background can be assumed. Thus programming might be taught within a physics course with familiar physics examples. Not only can this become a highly meaningful activity with regard to learning to program, but it can contribute toward learning physics.

One Language or Many?

An interesting question in regard to learning to program is that of languages. Should students learn initially many different languages or is a single language enough? Students probably have a finite amount of time to devote to such study. Should students devote considerable amount of time to learning language A, or should they divide that time between languages A, B, and C? There seems to be some tendency, particularly in high school teacher training, to assume teachers need to be introduced to many languages, and so courses in a variety of languages are offered. Often this happens in environments where very little is said or emphasized about good programming style. While good universities abandoned the type of computer science curriculum composed of one language course after another many years ago, it has been adopted in some high schools.

The notion that a student is better off learning a bit of Pascal, a bit of BASIC, and a bit of Logo, and perhaps other languages, rather than

a sound introduction to a single language based on modern programming habits is *not* reasonable. Teaching kids many languages is particularly bad when teachers themselves often have little previous experience with computers. But learning *two* languages simultaneously in some depth is useful in some circumstances.

Richard Dennis of the School of Education at the University of Illinois, experienced in training teachers to use computers, summed this up well at a recent meeting: *"Children should not collect languages!"*

PROGRAMMING EXAMPLE

This book is not a textbook on a programming language. Nevertheless, to understand some of the issues of learning to program, I use an example of a program, discussed from a structured programming point of view. In this section I will "read" the program, illustrating some features of the programming language Pascal.

A computer program always *does* something! In the example under discussion, an average is being taken. While this simple task does not require a computer program unless there is a lot of data, it is used as an illustration. To write a program that embodies a strategy for carrying out an operation—an algorithm—the program developer knows how to take an average. It is necessary for the programmer to understand the algorithm.

To take an average, we gather together a collection of numbers, add these numbers, and then divide by the number of numbers. The result, if it is to be useful, must be transmitted to a person.

Here is the Pascal program for taking an average.

In the first line the program declares that it *is* a program. The *name* is an English word, Average, telling what the program does. That is, the program is *not* named XYZ42, MYPROGRAM, or GEORGE—none of these names is sufficiently descriptive to tell what the program does. The program ends with END, followed by

```
PROGRAM Average;                          PROCEDURE FindAverage;
                                          BEGIN {Average}
VAR     NumberOfItems: INTEGER;                 Result := 0;
        Item: INTEGER;                          FOR Item := 1 TO NumberOfItems DO
        Data: ARRAY [1..100] OF REAL;                 Result := Result + Data[Item];
        Result: REAL;                           Result := Result / NumberOfItems {THE
                                                    AVERAGE}
PROCEDURE GetData;                        END; {Average}
BEGIN {Data Entry}
      WRITE ('Please enter the number of date   PROCEDURE DisplayResults;
        items ');                         BEGIN {DisplayResults}
      READLN (NumberOfItems);                   WRITELN; WRITELN ('The average is ',
      WRITE ('Please enter the data ');           Result)
      FOR Item := 1 TO NumberOfItems DO   END; {DisplayResults}
            READ(Data[Item])
END; {Data Entry}                         BEGIN {Main program}
                                                GetData;
                                                FindAverage;
                                                DisplayResults
                                          END {Main program}.
```

Pascal program for taking an average.

a period. Every Pascal program ends with a period.

A structural outline of the program may be of use at this point. While the details are omitted, this "outline" shows the program's features.

```
PROGRAM     Name
      {Data Specification}
            {This data can be used anywhere in
            the program}
      {Subprograms—Procedures and Functions}
            {May have some data of their own}
BEGIN
      {Main Program}
END.
```

The program, as shown in the outline, starts with some specification of the structure of the data, proceeds with several procedures (subprograms), and ends with the "main program," the program that the computer actually executes.

Let's examine first the main program and then the data. In a good structured program using a language such as Pascal, the main program usually shows the main steps of the full program. That is, a reader of the main program should have, even without seeing the rest of the program, a good overall idea of how the program works. In this case we have a simple main program, since taking the average is a simple calculation. Only three steps occur in the main program—getting the data, taking the average, and displaying the results. Note that each of the identifiers—the names—used in the main program is recognizable. You can tell what each means by reading it, because the identifiers are meaningful to a reader of English.

The use of uppercase and lowercase characters in the identifiers is not required. It is done just to make the program more readable. Some Pascals allow underscores separating a multiple-word identifier such as those used here.

The three identifiers in the main program are procedure calls. When the program is executed, the computer starts with the main program and so first encounters GetData. It finds it has a procedure called that, and then it executes that procedure. It then returns to the main program, encounters FindAverage, looks for this procedure, executes it, and finally does the same with the third procedure.

This is a simple main program. A good structured main program should *not* be long. A typical rule of thumb, although obviously one that depends on the computer, is that the whole main program or any procedure or function should fit on the computer screen at one time. No logical decision tests occur in this main program, an oddity as compared to "real life" programs, the ones that really do something useful.

Another program aspect that should be examined early when reading a program is the data, defined at several places in the program. As mentioned earlier, good modern programming style demands that the data items be carefully specified. Many modern languages, such as Pascal, require this. Almost always some data is defined right after the "PROGRAM" statement at the beginning of a Pascal program. It may also be specified within any procedure. Variables and other identifiers specified within a procedure can *only* be used in that procedure or within procedures that are defined inside that procedure. Some of the data is *global,* known to the entire program, and some of the data is *local,* known only to parts of the program. The area of the program over which the data is "known" is its *scope.* Good programming practice suggests that the scope for each variable be

as limited as possible; errors will then be easier to locate.

Since this is a simple program, the data items are relatively simple. Again, the identifiers for variables should give a clear understanding of the nature of the variable. Thus you will probably have already determined that NumberOfItems refers to the number of things to be added up in obtaining the average, Item to the particular piece of data, and Result to the value calculated.

Associated with each variable is a *type,* describing the nature of the variable. The types of variables in the average program are *integers* (whole numbers), *real* numbers (decimal numbers), and *arrays* (collections of data of the same type). Modern structured languages *insist* that the type of every variable is fully specified. For a small program such as this, that seems a bother, and it is! Remember, this is only a sample program. "Real" programs are longer, and the careful specification of all variable types is an aid in avoiding errors in those programs and in later modifications. Languages in which variables must be specified, as in most modern languages, are said to have *strong typing.*

One particular data type used is an *array.* An array is a collection of data entities of the same type. In this case the array is called Data and each entity in Data is a real number. One hundred storage locations have been allocated to Data, so if more data is required, the program would have to be modified. One *particular* item

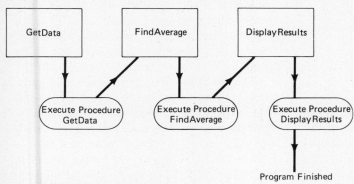

Figure 2.8 Calling procedures.

in the array can be referred to by the use of brackets. Thus

    Data[17]

refers to the seventeenth element in the array. The use of brackets to specify items in an array is a peculiarity of Pascal. Many other languages use ordinary parentheses for describing a component of an array.

Let us now get to some of the details of the syntax of Pascal, as shown in the average program. In each procedure there is a BEGIN and an END. These work like giant parentheses, grouping the material together. BEGINs and ENDs are used in a number of places in Pascal. The material within a BEGIN and an END is referred to as a *block*. Indentation is designed to make the programs easier to read. (As with the other terminology mentioned, readers not familiar with programming should *not* feel they need to learn these terms. They may be useful for some readers.)

A second grammatical feature is the use of the semicolon to separate statements. Semicolons are used differently in different languages. No semicolon occurs before each END; BEGIN and END define the block, so the semicolon, a further separator, is not needed. Some structured languages, such as Ada, require semicolons at these locations.

The next grammatical aspect is the control statement, such as the FOR statement. FOR sets up a *loop,* a series of operations that are to be repeated many times. Thus in the first procedure, GetData, the instructions within the loop will be repeated as many times as there are numbers of items, each time storing the next data item in the array Data. Pascal has other forms of control statements, which repeat a set of instructions a number of times, depending on calculations made while the instructions are being carried out.

Any statement has a particular syntax that must be followed. Computer programming languages, which aim at precise ways of saying things, have a precise syntax or grammar associated with each statement. It might be interesting for you to see one way in which syntax can be specified. Wirth, the developer of Pascal, uses diagrams to specify the syntax of Pascal. I show one for the FOR statement on page 26, without further explanation.

Finally, our Pascal program allows READing data (entering data) and WRITEing data. These statements allow the computer to communicate with the external world. In some languages, such as ALGOL and Ada, reading and writing statements are not part of the language; instead there are standard "packages" of such statements, special input and output commands, perhaps different for different purposes.

Note that variables are in the READ and WRITE statements. The variable for the WRITE statement shows what is to be written; for the READ statement, where the number accepted by the program will be stored within the computer. A variable can be thought of as an identifier for a mailbox slot, and the memory of the computer as a series of such slots; memory will be discussed further later. In the program there is a minor variant on the READ and WRITE statements—some statements have "LN" at the end. These indicate that the output device, probably a TV-like screen or a typewriter, is to start a new line *after* doing the indicated operation, READing or WRITEing.

COMPUTER POWER AS AN EXAMPLE OF A PROGRAMMING COURSE

One example of a course for learning about programming is the Computer Power course, developed by Michael Moshell, Robert Aiken, William Baird, Gould Smith, and Carl Gregory at the University of Tennessee.* It is, I believe, one of the best programming courses available for use at the high school level.

*University of Tennessee (Michael Moshell, Project Director), *Computer Power: A First Course in Using the Computer* (New York: McGraw-Hill, 1982).

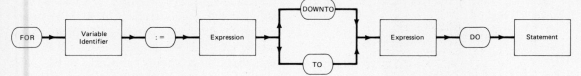

Figure 2.9 Syntax for FOR loop.

The course's approach is to start with Rascal, a subset of Pascal, and with an interpretive implementation of that subset. By interpretive I mean that the computer executes statements as soon as they are received, so feedback to the student is rapid. Rascal lacks some of the features of Pascal, such as semicolons at the ends of some lines. Students work with Rascal during the first quarter and graduate to full Pascal in the second quarter.

The course emphasizes the notions of modern structured programming, including top-down approaches, which are discussed in detail. They are made possible because the notion of the *procedure* is introduced very early in the course. Students work in groups part of the time, and the problems of coding in grouplike environments are stressed. The course emphasizes actual use of the computer, so it can be described as "hands-on." In addition to students writing programs on their own, including projects spanning some weeks, they also modify existing programs, which is a useful learning device.

The Computer Power course uses graphics and sound heavily, particularly in the early stages. But the graphic strategies are different from those used with Logo (see pages 48–52 for a description of Logo graphics). Students are supplied with a "quilting" program and with a set of cartoon characters. The quilting program allows them to design colorful patterns, like bright quilts, learning something about the computer in the process. Students can manipulate the cartoons, so their early programs lead quickly to animation sequences. This should be motivating to both junior high and high school students.

In addition to a complete student textbook and associated programs on disc, an extensive teacher guide is available. Ideally the teacher should be in the role of a "helper," not in the role of a "teller." But in practice this will probably be difficult to maintain. The difficulty with the Computer Power course, as with most teaching of programming in elementary and secondary schools, is that few teachers will have the background to do full justice to such a course.

NEW LANGUAGES AND FACILITIES FOR INTRODUCTORY PROGRAMMING

New types of languages and facilities for learning to program have been developed in recent years. While they are not interesting by themselves, they are interesting because they indicate a set of possibilities that need to be explored much further and more systematically. The tactics are different in different cases, but the aim is to enhance the introductory programming experience, the first experience, of a student.

Simple Structured Languages

The first category, perhaps most important from a long-range point of view, is special languages for the beginning programmer emphasizing the features of good modern programming stressed earlier in this chapter. Many of these languages might be described as subsets, or parts, of Pascal-like languages. The language of this type that has received the most attention in Europe is COMAL, used in a number of European countries. The language Rascal, just mentioned, is primarily a Pascal subset.

Although they do not exactly fit this category, a number of small-machine Pascals are subsets and so might be considered as simplified initial languages. Interpretive implementation,

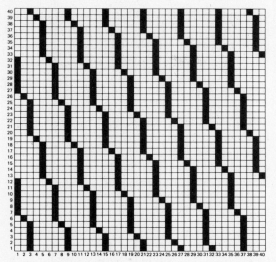 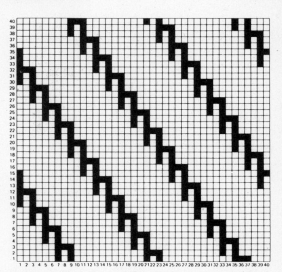

Figure 2.10 Two quilting patterns from the Computer Power course. [*Source:* University of Tennessee (Michael Moshell, Project Director), *Computer Power: A First Course in Using the Computer* (New York: McGraw-Hill, 1982).]

working line-by-line, and perhaps "hiding" such features as the editor, compiler, and interpreter, facilitate the progress of the beginning programmer.

Facilities Similar to Logo Turtle Graphics

A number of developments have taken the turtle facilities (see chapter 4), isolated them from the rest of Logo or embedded them in other languages, and then made them available. Some facilities even use the name Logo, which is unfortunate, as it confuses the nonexpert. However, nothing prevents such deception in advertising at present. The best-known facility of this kind is known as Delta Drawing; the turtle graphics capability is provided. Since it is relatively easy to write a program that provides turtle graphics, soon the market probably will be flooded with such programs, and it will be up to the user to understand that they are not actually Logo.

Turtle graphics are an interesting visual introduction to computing, if they are handled properly. But facilities beyond turtle graphics themselves, such as the ability to define procedures and then to use them within programs, must be available, if users are to get at even the rudiments of modular design.

At least one approach to Pascal, that in Kenneth Bowles' book, uses the turtle in the early stages. Turtles are *not* restricted to Logo!*

Other Visually Oriented Introductions

A third possibility for a visual introduction to programming is to develop other visual facilities similar to those in turtle geometry, which would appeal to the beginning programmer. This is more of a curriculum issue than a language issue, and could be done with almost any language. The Computer Power material does have some visual facilities, the quilting and cartooning programs, as indicated.

Perhaps the best example of this kind is *Karel, The Robot,* which is an introduction to structured programming and to Pascal. The robot's environment is more complex than the visual environment of the turtle. It was developed initially with university students in mind, but now is suggested for secondary school.

*Kenneth L. Bowles, *Problem Solving Using Pascal* (New York: Springer-Verlag, 1977).

Karel, The Robot has problems. The "graphics," in the versions I have seen, were developed for nongraphic terminals. Hence the visual information is crude compared to other visual capabilities for beginning programming. Initially the program ran in a large-computer environment and was moved later to personal computers; this probably hurt the graphics capability. But the visual approach with the robot is an interesting one.

Many more facilities of this kind need to be developed. I am certain that other equally exciting visual possibilities could be used in the same way. In the next few years designers will undoubtedly create many such pleasant introductory facilities, perhaps coupled with simplified structured languages, easing the task of teaching programming.

THE ADVANCED PLACEMENT COMPUTER COURSE

A very interesting new development is the proposed Advanced Placement exam in computer science for high school students, and the associated suggested course. As with other A.P. courses, it reflects university standards. From the standpoint of computer science departments in the United States and elsewhere, there is nothing surprising whatsoever about this course. It covers what these departments teach to first-year students and what they recommend to other students and teachers, just as with Advanced Placement courses in other academic areas. Looking at the exam from the standpoint of what already exists in most high schools, it is a very drastic but entirely reasonable change.

The Advanced Placement exam will be an important factor in helping us to improve the teaching of programming in school systems. The entire computer science program in schools must be geared in this direction, not just a final course for a few advanced students. If the students have not received an early structured introduction to programming, they will have developed bad habits which are very difficult to overcome. Schools will have to face the difficult problem of who will teach an Advanced Placement course. It will be difficult to persuade those fully qualified to teach such a course to stay with the school system, because a whole range of other positions will be open to them.

The Educational Testing Service has at least two publications concerning the Advanced Placement computer science examination.* One, perhaps written for high school students who will take the exam, looks primarily at the examination itself and outlines a generic course to help prepare for the exam. The other publication outlines for high school teachers and administrators two specific courses for preparation for the exam and has good references to Pascal texts that would be satisfactory for such a program. I urge readers who are seriously involved in teaching programming in schools at any level to look at these two publications.

DON'T TEACH OR LEARN BASIC

It is no secret that at the present time BASIC is the most commonly taught language in high schools and even in many colleges and universities. Yet the better universities, particularly in courses for computer science majors, avoid BASIC "like the plague." Almost all of these universities offer students Pascal or some similar language as the first programming language.

Anyone who may be at some future time a serious programmer is done no favor if taught BASIC as the first language. It is not impossible to teach good structured programming in BASIC; it is simply extremely difficult and so very seldom done, because of BASIC's limitations as a language. BASIC was developed many years ago when knowledge about how to program was much more primitive than at pre-

*College Board, *Advanced Placement Course Description: Computer Science* (Princeton: Educational Testing Service, 1984); College Board's Advanced Placement Computer Science Development Committee, *Teacher's Guide to Advanced Placement Courses in Computer Science* (Princeton: Educational Testing Service, 1984).

sent; it is no discredit to its inventors that they did not anticipate everything that has since happened.

Seymour Papert in *Mindstorms* compares BASIC with the old-fashioned "QWERTY" keyboard. He goes on to comment:

> Today, and in fact for several years now, the cost of computer memory has fallen to the point where any remaining economic advantages of using BASIC are insignificant. Yet in most high schools, the language remains almost synonymous with programming, despite the existence of other computer languages that are demonstrably easier to learn and are richer in the intellectual benefits that can come from learning them. The situation is paradoxical. The computer revolution has scarcely begun but is already breeding its own conservatism. . . . Programs in BASIC require so labyrinthine a structure that in fact only the most motivated and brilliant (mathematical) children do learn to use it for more than trivial ends.*

Why is the language BASIC so widely taught if almost all BASIC courses are disasters from the standpoint of students' future programming careers? First among many answers is simply habit; a lot of people have seen other people learn BASIC, and so it has become the "thing to do." Second, it is the language most commonly available on small personal computers. Indeed, for a while it was the *only* language. Now most personal computers offer Pascal at a slight additional charge (the amount varies from machine to machine). Undoubtedly the widespread availability of the BASICs on small machines has led to its widespread usage. Further, many high school teachers, with very limited programming experience, know *only* BASIC.

BASIC has the reputation of being "easy" to learn. My own experience, having taught many languages over many years, including almost all

the common ones, shows that how easy or hard it is to learn a programming language depends more on the way it is taught than on the language itself. If a teacher is intent, for example, on a grammatical approach, and insists that students learn *everything* about the grammar right away, then BASIC is indeed easier than a language like PL/I or APL, which has complex and extensive grammatical rules. But this approach is not reasonable.

This difference in ease of initial learning stems only from attempting to teach first the full rules of the language. If students learn only a subset, suitable for a given application, then the differences between subsets taught for the same application for different languages is likely to be minor.

On page 30, for example, are programs in five different languages, all working a simple physics problem, a mass on a spring bobbing up and down. I won't explain the programs, except to say that X is the position of the body, V its velocity, and T the time. Notice that these programs all look quite similar. Comparing from program to program, many lines have only slight differences. In no real sense is one program "easier" than any of the others.

The arguments for teaching BASIC because of the widespread availability of BASIC are similar to the "arguments" for an exclusive diet of junk foods: they are easy to get and everyone is using them! In fact, it is a good analogy to describe BASIC as the junk food of computer programming languages. The analogy works even further. If a person has spent a lot of time eating only junk food, it is difficult for the person to resume a normal diet. The same situation obtains with BASIC. One can fairly say that BASIC *poisons* many students, producing bad habits that are extremely difficult to overcome, if they can be overcome at all.

The set of structured programming habits is very unlikely to develop within any BASIC course I have ever seen. I repeat that it is not impossible, but extremely unlikely, to teach these within BASIC. Many universities now

---

*Seymour Papert, *Mindstorms* (New York: Basic Books, 1980), pp. 34, 35.

```
            1.1   T = 0
            1.2   X = 1
            1.3   V = 0
            1.4   D = .1
    JOSS    1.5   X = X + V*D
            1.6   V = V − X*D
            1.7   T = T + D
            1.8   TYPE T,X
            1.9   IF T<3, TO STEP 1.5
```

```
            110   LET T=0
            120   LET X=1
            130   LET V=0
            140   LET D=.1
            150   LET X=X+V*D
    BASIC   160   LET V=V−X*D
            170   LET T=T+D
            180   PRINT T;X
            190   IF T<3 THEN 150
            200   END
```

```
                  T=0.
                  X=1.
                  V=0.
                  D=.1
            10    X=X+V*D
                  V=V−X*D
    FORTRAN       T=T+D
                  WRITE (6, 70) T,X
                  IF (T−3.) 10, 10, 14
            14    STOP
            70    FORMAT (F10.2, F12.4)
                  END
```

```
                  ▽ HARMONIC
            [1]   T←0
            [2]   X←1
            [3]   V←0
            [4]   D←0.1
            [5]   CALCULATE:X←X+V×D
    APL     [6]   V←V−X×D
            [7]   T←T+D
            [8]   T,X
            [9]   →CALCULATE×T<3
                  ▽
```

```
            OSCILLATOR: PROCEDURE OPTIONS (MAIN);
                    T = 0; X = 1;V = 0;D = .1;
    PL/I    CALCULATE:    X = X + V*D; V = V − X*D; T = T + D;
                    PUT SKIP DATA (T, X);
                    IF T <3 THEN GO TO CALCULATE;
            END OSCILLATOR;
```

recognize that students who learned BASIC programming in high school have a difficult time mastering the computer science curriculum. This handicap is recognized too in the recent prototype College Board Advanced Placement test in computers just described, available from Educational Testing Service.

Even major defenders of BASIC admit that most BASIC courses are extremely poor and fail to promulgate the ideas of modern programming. They claim that it need not be taught this way. That is true, but it is very difficult to see that it will be taught any other way in the near future.

Believing that the "new" BASIC specified by the BASIC standards committee will cure many of the problems is merely grasping at straws. While this new BASIC does allow reasonable subroutines and does have better control structures, it still ignores the problem of data, and it still is easy to use in the old nonstructured fashion. Furthermore, it exists on extremely few machines. At the moment it is imaginary, not a real language.

I conclude with a quotation from a major figure in contemporary computer science, Edsger Dijkstra:

> It is practically impossible to teach good programming to students that have a prior exposure to BASIC: as potential programmers they are mentally mutilated beyond hope of regeneration.*

Dijkstra often makes strong comments about aspects of computer science. But this violent quote seems necessary to shake people from the complacency of their favorite junk food, BASIC. My very strong recommendation is *"DON'T TEACH BASIC!"*

*Edsger W. Dijkstra, "How Do We Tell Truths That Might Hurt?", *Sigplan Notices,* vol. 17, no. 5 (May 1982), p. 14.

chapter 3

Computer Literacy

A second way to use computers in classrooms goes under the name of *computer literacy.* This "new literacy" is frequently mentioned and discussed in educational literature. The term computer awareness is also used, often with a similar set of meanings.

Almost everyone favors computer literacy. It is like motherhood used to be, something broadly assumed to be desirable. Many courses are springing up in elementary, junior high, and high schools, and universities that use the name computer literacy or an equivalent. School districts are developing awareness and literacy cur-

ricula, often covering many years for each student.

But an examination of these courses and related books quickly shows that however popular the terminology may be, there is little agreement as to what computer literacy should be. Everyone has a different definition.

Some people argue that the whole computer literacy "movement" is only a fad that will soon pass. This remains to be seen. At the moment, at least, computer literacy must be counted as a possible mode of computer use in class, one that may receive increasing attention in school systems and universities in the next few years. Indeed, many courses in computer literacy or segments for use in other courses are appearing or about to be released by publishers. Many school districts and state departments of education are instituting requirements for computer literacy; in some cases computer literacy is required for all students.

LITERACY

The term computer literacy is clearly based on the older term, literacy. While my purpose is not to look at the history of that term, it is worth noting what literacy itself means: the ability to read at some minimum level and probably also the ability to write at a minimum level. Most people agree that reading is almost essential for everyone in the modern world. Anyone who cannot read has problems getting a job and in most other endeavors of modern society. Being illiterate is a distinct handicap. Most modern countries pride themselves on their citizens' high rate of literacy.

Even in this instance the term literacy may imply different conditions. Does it include writing as well as reading? What level of reading is required? How is this level specified? These questions are quite specific, unlike some of the questions that are raised in speaking of computer literacy.

Other uses of the term literacy have evolved over the years. For example, we speak of mathematical literacy, scientific literacy, and others. These adjectives change the term's specific meaning. Thus mathematical literacy implies that people cannot comfortably survive in the modern world without at least some minimal mathematical competencies. In dealing with change, purchasing, maintaining bankbooks, ascertaining benefits from salaries, preparing or checking income tax forms, and other such activities, to be able to perform simple arithmetic, or to use devices which perform it, is essential. A person who cannot do arithmetic is at a distinct disadvantage in our society; but this is changing as calculators and computers become more common.

Likewise, in a society where science is of major significance in decision making, everybody should have some understanding of its nature. So we speak of scientific literacy. Here literacy is probably at a lower level than for reading, writing, and mathematics. Still, many, including myself, would argue that scientific literacy merits greater emphasis.

A DEFINITION OF COMPUTER LITERACY

The term computer literacy can be considered to mean the minimum knowledge, know-how, familiarity, capabilities, abilities, and so forth, about computers essential for a person to function well in the contemporary world. The term computer awareness is similar but designates a lower level of capability.

Much of what I say in this book about computer literacy is oriented toward the citizen of the future, although computers are already very pervasive in our society. To live an everyday life in today's world often means to contact computer-based systems. Thus, with a Mastercard or Visa card, the computer is sure to generate the monthly statement. Awareness of the computer's role in producing statements may not help credit card users, but knowing if errors in billing are attributable to a computer, a programmer, or a person who enters the data, may be valuable. Almost all students today will *use* computers during their lifetime or will be affected by them. They will need to know about the computer as an effective tool for their future activities.

In the future, we can anticipate much greater exposure to computers for almost everyone in our society. Computers are rapidly increasing in numbers and, even more important, in types of applications. So computer literacy is often future-oriented, based on predictions of how computers are likely to be used in everyday life five, ten, or fifteen years from the present. In this orientation toward the future, computer literacy differs significantly from literacy as applied to reading and writing; it is already clear that reading and writing are critical for the "good life."

It is perhaps computer literacy's orientation toward the future that generates some of the confusion and multiple definitions. Given the difficulty of predicting the future, some people retreat to the past. Thus some computer literacy courses cover such things as punched cards, even though chances are exceedingly small that this historical beginning of the computer is likely to bear upon the life of any student today. Computer literacy courses with authentic future orientation will have very little or even nothing to say about cards!

Another unwarranted aspect of some computer literacy courses is a strong belief that vocabulary (in itself) implies knowledge. A common belief in the magical power of words imparts the feeling that if students can only utter the word, they must be knowledgeable about the area. Science as commonly taught in the elementary schools suffers from this misfortune, as can be seen by examining science tests. To define formally a "central processing unit" or any other bit of vocabulary relating to computers falls short, in my view, of any fundamental knowledge of computer literacy. Rather, it is merely incidental verbal information of no great use to students. Ten years from now central processing units will probably be quite different from those we know today. But it is easy to test for vocabulary, and so it tends to be part of many courses.

One fairly elaborate attempt to define computer literacy was carried out by a group at the University of Minnesota. Researchers there began with a large survey. The group generated a long list of factors they thought should be associated with computer literacy in categories such as applications, impact, software, and hardware, but many of these appear to require rote memorization. For example, students are expected to give a definition of an algorithm. It is hard to imagine this really contributes toward literacy, because it is the usual regurgitation process, memorizing vocabulary. Computer literacy as defined by this study, with too much emphasis on the recall of miscellaneous information, does not put enough emphasis on what students can actually *do*. The "survey" approach is inadequate to the problem.

COMPUTER LITERACY FOR WHOM?

Another way computer literacy differs from earlier forms of literacy is that it is much more *subject-dependent*— dependent on the individual's background—than reading and writing, mathematics, or science literacy. Perhaps this is a reflection of the newness of the area and its changing nature, but it also may be a more fundamental issue, reflecting that even people with some common interests will use computers in quite different ways.

To explore the notions of computer literacy, suppose we look at two individuals, a tenth-grade pupil and a junior high school science teacher. I claim that computer literacy for these two individuals, while having some overlap, will also differ considerably, because each can be expected to use the computer very differently in the next few years. The teacher, for example, needs to understand fully the educational role of the computer; the pupil does not.

So training in computer literacy for these two individuals should undoubtedly be very different. The curriculum will surely differ. This book may serve as an introduction to computer literacy for teachers—instructional computer literacy—since it treats the attitudes and information about computers and that will become more and more essential for teachers. It is *not* a computer literacy text for the tenth-grade pupil. In the next section I consider computer literacy from the student's point of view.

ESSENTIAL INGREDIENTS OF COMPUTER LITERACY FOR STUDENTS

I now mention features critical to computer literacy, some of them for everyone, and some of them subject-matter dependent. Particular emphasis is on students in primary and secondary schools.

Social Implications of the Computer

Probably the most important aspect of computer literacy, as well as the most difficult to learn and for which to develop curriculum material, is the social implications of computers. What will be the effect of computers on society? These issues are all of utmost import, with no uniformly accepted points of view. Everyone in our society should be sensitized to the issue of the effects of computers, so comprehending social implications should be a critical part of every computer literacy program. Computer literacy will change the values of our society.

Even at an advanced college level such courses are not easy to teach because of their concern with values. A common approach is to assemble a collection of readings, with small-group as well as larger class discussions about these readings. It is also important for students to write about the issue of computers and society, either directly or with computer mail or conferencing, the use of the computer to exchange information electronically. In such a system students can compose documents to be read later by others.

Another tactic I have found useful in such courses is field investigations made by small groups of students. Thus the class might be asked to investigate computer stores and other retail computer outlets. The teacher may suggest some topics for study. Individuals or groups visit these stores, after first developing their objectives for the visit. Both oral and written reports are useful.

The difficulty is to avoid the situation in which students pick up some vocabulary about computers but have no real understanding of the role of computers in society. Students should become sensitive to the societal and ethical issues involved in computer use.

Strengths and Weaknesses of Computers

Related to social implications is the matter of aiding people to understand what the computer is good for and what it is not good for. Computers are often pictured as magical devices, devices that can do anything. Or, conversely, they are pictured as an evil influence in society, certain to lead to horrible consequences. Many science fiction films portray the computer as evil, perhaps unintentionally. In Arthur C. Clarke's *2001: A Space Odyssey,* the computer murders the crew members in an attempt to protect the spaceship's mission.

What is needed is a rational rather than an emotional understanding of strengths. This rational attitude needs to be oriented toward application; applications are discussed in more detail later.

This consideration of strengths and weaknesses must deal with more than the computer alone; it should touch on the complex interactions between science and technology and society. Any technology, including the computer, can have both good and bad effects. Students need to understand that the computer alone is not "good" or "bad." Rather, the effect of computers depends on whether the computer is used in reasonable or unreasonable ways. Although difficult to convey, this aspect of computer literacy is very important.

Ability to Learn More About Computers

As the computer is a dynamic device, growing in capabilities as well as in uses, no single course or program in computer literacy can ever hope to cover everything students will need to know. Hence, educators must encourage the attitude and ability of continually learning about computers. The sources of information available and trends about where the computer is going should be stressed.

This issue is to some extent an attitudinal one. A computer literacy course or program must avoid completely the notion that everything is "known" about computers. Rather, the fact that little is known and that computers and their applications are changing very rapidly must be emphasized.

Just as with social implications of computers, it is not easy to structure learning experiences that deal with this topic. The same approaches mentioned earlier—reading, small-group and full-class discussions, writing, computer conferencing, field investigations—will also be useful. Reading by itself, or a lecture by itself, is likely to be of little value in building the desired attitudes.

Common Applications

A good computer literacy background should involve the student in the common applications of computers, including those in that student's main areas of interest. In addition, some computer applications are so pervasive that all programs in computer literacy should include them. I will discuss some of the common applications in the next few pages.

Word Processors   Perhaps the best example of an application that will be important for everyone in our society in a relatively short period of time is word processing, the use of the computer to write and modify letters, papers, and other documents. With the advent of home computers, word processing will probably soon be universal in our society. So word processing is an essential ingredient of computer literacy.

The basic notion of word processing is to provide a way to store documents and, even more important, to revise documents efficiently. Users sit at a personal computer with a keyboard very much like that of a typewriter. What users type appears not on a sheet of paper but on a televisionlike screen. The distinct advantage of word processing over ordinary typing is the ease of altering or modifying the material before reaching any "paper stage." A simple typing error can be corrected immediately by backspacing over the incorrect letters and re-

typing. Errors not noticed immediately are also easy to correct. No retyping of "good" material is needed. Material can be inserted or sections already typed can be moved from one place to another automatically, just as in the old cutting and pasting method of rewriting. This ability to change the text and thus to rewrite easily gives word processing its power. Segments of documents—for example, paragraphs in a legal letter—can also be stored and a document assembled by pulling together some of these segments as well as additional material specific to the situation.

Word processing is not common in homes, because inexpensive high-quality printers are still uncommon. But good printers are coming down in cost. Word processing will be a major application for home computing. Furthermore, it is likely to be very important for schools, particularly in learning to read and write, when combined with other aids. So it qualifies as a present common application important for computer literacy. Learning to type might be considered one aspect of learning to use a word processor. See chapter 4 for further discussion of word processing.

Spreadsheets   Another computer application becoming more and more common at present, although perhaps it does not have as much potential for students as word processing, is the use of mathematical spreadsheets on personal computers. Spreadsheets are tables of numbers, often financial data. They usually go under the name of VisiCalc™, the original spreadsheet program; Multiplan, SuperCalc, and Lotus 1-2-3 are variants. The notion entails tables of numbers, with row and column headings; some of these numbers depend on others in defined ways. For example, one column might be the sum of two other columns. Changing a number in one column will also change the sum. Complex formulas describing this dependence are possible, so changes can be propagated through the set of numbers.

Spreadsheet programs had initial successes in

businesses, both large and small. The availability of VisiCalc is the reason many small computers were sold to businesses, and VisiCalc-like programs are available on many small computers. Spreadsheet implications for home use include budgeting and checkbook balancing. Hence it is a good candidate for most computer literacy studies. Some spreadsheet programs were developed particularly for students, at a variety of levels. More can be expected to appear.

The November 1, 1982, issue of *Software News* suggests that over 300,000 electronic spreadsheet programs have been sold. Datapro claims that over 500,000 spreadsheet programs have been sold since VisiCalc was introduced in October 1979. Probably no other applications program has been distributed in this quantity. (See chapter 4 for further information.)

Personal Data Systems A third application common enough to justify including it in computer literacy programs is personal note taking or personal filing systems. Computers can store, classify, and handle information in many ways advantageous to a particular user's applications. Several such systems are already on the market, with their initial sales heaviest in small business applications. The potential for wider use is good. Students would find these systems useful in developing good study habits.

Other Application Areas Many applications will be area-dependent, and so will be needed for computer literacy for particular groups of students but not for others. As this book is addressed to teachers and administrators, it discusses computer-based learning and computers as intellectual tools. Both are important in education. These uses could be important in other areas of computer literacy as well.

The need to introduce students to relevant computer-based applications may slowly vanish. Today systems like word processors, spreadsheets, and personal filing systems must be "learned" by the user, either in courses or by studying the manuals and books. But as we become more skillful at relating computers to people, making computers easier to use, it will become easier for *anyone* with no previous training to use application programs such as word processing programs. The complete novice, or the experienced user, will be able to sit at the machine and begin immediately to use any program. Any necessary instruction will continuously be given directly at the computer display, relevant to the needs of each person. So formal teaching of this aspect of computer literacy may be only temporary, needed until software becomes more user-friendly.

Knowledge of Programming

One of the most controversial issues of computer literacy is its relationship to programming. Some advocates of computer literacy recommend teaching everyone programming; many so-called computer literacy courses are indistinguishable from programming courses. There is a trend toward calling a low-level programming course, where students are expected to learn only a smidgen, a computer literacy course. Learning to program is discussed in some detail in chapter 2.

Recently a school district in my area proposed a new "computer literacy" program. The notion, not uncommon, was to "expose" students beginning at the fifth grade to a series of programming languages. In each case the exposure was brief. As I mentioned earlier, I contend that a program of this type is of little value. It is similar to spending a week on Latin, a week on French, and a week on German, and then claiming "foreign language literacy."

This situation is reminiscent of what has been recurrent in the sciences, where, particularly in high schools and universities, watered-down, inferior versions of courses are offered to nonmajors as "enrichment" or "liberal education" courses. These courses are seldom of much value. In many cases they are positively harmful, as they give a false view of the nature of science. Only rarely in the sciences has a course been developed *particularly* for nonmajors. A similar situation exists in computer literacy—many existing courses use the name computer literacy as an "in" name for a "let's learn to program" course. Many books with "computer literacy" in their titles are primarily programming texts, usually low-level.

I want to emphasize the fundamental and clear distinction between these two kinds of courses, programming and computer literacy. Learning to program gives only one view of how to use the computer, a view that is often positively misleading. Learning a few simple programming commands does not give a feeling for the power of the computer. Educators should clearly distinguish between a programming course and a computer literacy course, between learning to program and learning to be computer-literate.

The vast majority of people who use computers will *not* be using the low-level, general-purpose languages currently available. They may, of course, use word processors and spreadsheets, or their later more sophisticated successors, but their activities will bear little resemblance to current programming activities. To me the argument for teaching programming in computer literacy programs is weak.

Some aspects of programming *should,* however, be part of many computer literacy courses or, perhaps better, be part of subject area courses. Students *should* understand that programming is essential to operate the computer and that they can use application programs only because someone already programmed the application.

The stylistic features of programming might be covered, including the notion of algorithms, processes for the computer to carry out, and the notions of programming style mentioned in the last chapter. But it is entirely unnecessary that students aspiring to computer literacy go into detail of the grammatical structure of one particular language. If a language *is* involved in a computer-literacy program, it should be language appropriate to the needs and interests of each individual learner to facilitate rapid progress into modes exciting for him or her. And it should be a modern language, as discussed in the last chapter.

Of utmost importance is *programming style,* a concept of what distinguishes good programs from bad programs. The features of modern structured programming are sufficiently important to suggest careful study. The ideas of modular programming are closely related to problem solving in all areas; they supersede the grubby details of any one computer language. That is, students should understand top-down structure and the notion of modular programming; these concepts are much more important than such grammatical details as the syntax of a "for" loop. The relevant issues were examined in chapter 2.

If any programming is taught as a computer literacy activity, the "grammatical" approach should probably be avoided. An applications-oriented approach, with examples related to students' area of interest, is a good way for most people to start programming.

A possible hidden danger may be present when programming is taught within a computer literacy course. Often people who have learned a small amount of programming have a very distorted view of a computer's capabilities. Students tend to assume the capabilities they have been exposed to are the *total* capabilities. As an example, think of a student who has seen only numerical programming, with no manipulation of collections of characters or strings; this student may believe that computers use *only* numbers. So a little bit of programming can be quite misleading.

Critical Attitude

Courses should stress the importance of a *critical* attitude toward computers and their applications. Students should not display a blind acceptance of technology, but should always question its usefulness.

COMPONENTS OF A COMPUTER LITERACY PROGRAM

- Social implications of the computer
- Strengths and weaknesses of computers
- Ability to learn more about computers
- Common applications
- Aspects of programming, particularly style
- Critical attitude

MISSING ITEMS OF DUBIOUS VALUE

In this discussion I have suggested that various items are *not* necessary in computer literacy courses and programs. Unfortunately these items and others that could well be missing are often stressed.

You will have perhaps noted that no description of *hardware,* the physical composition of the computer, is suggested in the components of a computer literacy program. At the level of such a course, "hardware" often becomes mere vocabulary, verbal definitions of words, particularly if the course is taught without computers. For most students it is of no value to have memorized definitions for such items as CPU, byte, bus, register, word, port, interface, memory, back plane, card case, motherboard. Operational understanding of some of these terms may be useful in some cases, but even so, the question of how much must be known about hardware is one that deserves careful consideration. An analogy with a car or TV is appropriate; intelligent usage does not demand extensive knowledge of how each works.

I have also stressed that extensive programming experience need not be part of computer literacy. In some cases *no* programming may be desirable. Style should be stressed, not details. As mentioned, BASIC should be avoided.

Programming a computer is only one way to use it, and not the way of most users. Far more people already use word processors and spreadsheets and get bank statements than program a computer. A small amount of programming can give a very misleading view of the nature of the computer.

AN EXAMPLE OF A COMPUTER LITERACY COURSE

In these chapters about various ways to use computers in education, I have pointed to good examples. Unfortunately, I do not consider any current computer literacy course entirely desirable. Indeed, there is a question of whether computer literacy should be a course at all; perhaps it should be a part of a variety of other courses.

Nevertheless, I mention a computer literacy course that, although it has serious flaws, represents one possible direction educators might take. This course was developed by the British Broadcasting Company (BBC) in the United Kingdom, and it is called The Computer Program. It is a series of ten video programs, with associated print materials, using a small computer. It follows some of the ideas I have already discussed.

The general strategy of the course is to follow a person, Chris, as he learns more about the nature of computers. The video material, in the BBC tradition, is well made. Some social issues are stressed. The major difficulty with this course is that it teaches a bit of simpleminded BASIC programming in each sequence, starting with such things as input/output and RUN; BASIC's primitive "routine" capability does not enter until the eighth videotape. The BBC computer manufactured by Acorn, now widely used in schools in the United Kingdom, is assumed as the basis of practical work associated with the video materials.

SHOULD COMPUTER LITERACY INVOLVE COMPUTERS?

If the main object of a course is to teach programming, there is usually no question that the computer will be an essential component. On the other hand, for computer literacy the question of whether computers are or are not used is debatable. Some computer literacy programs do not use computers.

The definition of and attitudes toward computer literacy developed in this chapter strongly suggest that active use of computers should occur in a computer literacy course. If students are to become familiar with the computer to understand something of its potential, there must be more than talk, reading, or films. None of these convey the full nature of an interactive personal computer. Only hands-on experience gives the direct exposure necessary. This exposure may be limited, it may occur in groups, but it is an essential ingredient of a computer literacy course.

IS COMPUTER LITERACY A SEPARATE COURSE?

One issue I have not addressed is whether I am talking about a distinct course, something labeled computer literacy and taught as a unit, or whether activities connected with computer literacy could better happen within other classes taken by students, or outside of school entirely. Perhaps readers assumed I was talking about a course of some type because that is the way we frequently think about learning, given our current organization of schools. The question deserves serious attention.

I believe that many important parts of computer literacy are clearly better learned in other classes, or perhaps even in nonclassroom environments, such as public libraries, shopping malls, and homes. Thus students should encounter word processing in environments where a sizable amount of writing is to be done, such as an English class with papers required. In such situations students see a meaningful application relevant to what they have been doing, and the computer is not presented as an isolated device. Through such use students can be led to see that word processing has applications beyond one particular class, and a number of other classes would use it. Likewise, spreadsheets and graphic capabilities should be introduced in arithmetic, mathematics, and science contexts where they serve a purpose. Databases should probably be a part of sociology courses, political

science courses, and other courses where data is important. Paint programs will find a natural home within art or industrial design classes.

> It has been said that the problem of the computerized society will be solved by teaching computers and programming to everyone. The real problem is elsewhere. . . . How should we educate and train people to make the best use of these increasingly powerful tools? There lies the real challenge for education.*

On the other hand, some aspects of computer literacy may be difficult to fit into other class structures. Perhaps the most important of these, as emphasized earlier, is that of the social consequences of the computer in our society, its possible long-range effects. While a discussion of this might take place within certain other courses, the topic does not have a completely natural fit with existing courses and so might need to be some type of separate "mini-course," or several such courses at different levels.

COMPUTER LITERACY FOR SCIENCE AND ENGINEERING—A CURRICULUM

This section presents a brief outline of a proposed computer literacy curriculum, aimed at students who will eventually become mathematics, science, or engineering students. This curriculum was initially prepared by the author for an International Federation of Information Processing working group (TC3, Deflt, June 1983) concerning informatics (computer and information science) for all students at the university level. I found it necessary to begin before the university level, with very young children.

In the early stages no one knows what eventual career a child will pursue. Therefore, much of the following outline for grades 1 through 12 might well work as a general com-

*J. Hebenstreit, "Computers in Education—The Next Step" (Paper delivered at International Federation of Information Processing TC3 Conference, Delft, The Netherlands, June 1983).

puter literacy plan. Some exceptions might occur with some of the courses in grades 9 through 12. In particular, I would not recommend that all students be required to take a strong modern programming course. It is not reasonable to expect everyone to become a skilled programmer. Most users of computers will use applications-oriented tools, powerful tools designed for particular needs, as will be described in the next chapter.

Many aspects of "computer literacy" as described in this outline fit into other courses in the school and university. In this proposed program the child begins to use the computer immediately in preschool. Some of the programs discussed, those that already exist, are also described in chapter 5. Others need to be developed. This outline is only intended to be suggestive and is likely to be useful only for a few years. But everything suggested is practical, given what we already know about computers in education. This outline is very different from the vast majority of computer literacy programs now available, for reasons already discussed.

GRADE 0–PRESCHOOL

Writing to Read, or some similar program. A phonics-based beginning reading program, supported by IBM. See chapter 5.

GRADES 1–6

Reading and prewriting, writing, and postwriting activities, based on word processing and associated systems developed for young children.
Computer-based learning in arithmetic.
- Students proceed at their own pace.
- Intuition and approximation are stressed, with less drill than in current courses.

GRADES 3–8

Science literacy via computer-based learning material and associated intellectual tools.
- Stresses the nature of science, placing students in situations where they must behave like scientists.
- Mostly available now from the Educational Technology Center.
- Most of it used at home or in public libraries.
Computer-based learning in mathematics and algebra.
- Powerful intellectual tools available (spreadsheets, Logo, Boxer, newly developed controllable worlds for algebra).
Further use of word processing.
School publications, communication with others, via computers and networks.

GRADES 9–12

Computer-based learning in mathematics.
- Through calculus.
- Again, emphasis on developing insight.
- Mastery based—all students learn to mastery level.
- More powerful tools.
Modern programming course.
- Satisfies advanced placement requirements.
- Emphasis on structured programming.
- Probably Pascal (Ada and Module II are also possibilities).
- Emphasis on graphics.
Social and ethical consequences of computers.
- Emphasis on values.
- Future oriented.
- Difficult course to develop, but essential.
Within physics, chemistry, and biology courses.
- Use of computer as a tool wherever possible.
- Student programming to solve problems. See chapter 4, page 44.
- Special intellectual tools available, including graphics.
- Brief introduction to numerical methods, where needed.
- Advanced computer-based versions, beyond first year, available.

UNIVERSITY

All science, math and engineering courses use computers in many modes.

- Tools, computer-based learning, intuition building.
- Tests include topics on use of computer.
- Most testing is done directly on-line.
- Subject matter restructured (new texts) to allow use of computer.
- Example: Feynman-like approach to beginning mechanics involving programming.
- Continue emphasis on composition skills, with more advanced tools.

Numerical methods course—second or third year.
- Emphasize modern methods.
- Use math packages for routine calculations.
- Emphasize graphics.

Social and ethical consequences of computers—fourth year.
- More advanced than earlier course.
- Explorations of the future.

Software engineering—third year.
- Curriculum similar to that of the Open University, United Kingdom.

Specialized computer application courses.
- CAD/CAM (Computer Aided Design/Computer Aided Manufacturing), for example.

Advanced research methods involving computers, related to each discipline.

COMPUTER LITERACY—THE ELEPHANT

Perhaps computer literacy, defined differently by different people, is something like the proverbial elephant inspected by a group of blind men. Each gives a different report of the nature of the animal. But a nagging question occurs: Is there an elephant there at all? That is, it might turn out that computer literacy is a play on words. Or perhaps the "elephant" of computer literacy is evolving rapidly in time, with parts of it disappearing as computers improve.

The "literacy" idea is being adapted to more and more areas. In the long run, we should all ask if it is relevant to computers. As computers become more common everywhere in our society, more humane, easier to use, they will require less and less special introduction and special handling. It may be that the need for computer literacy will eventually vanish, except for the sociological and value issues, particularly as computers much more adapted to the human condition evolve. But this is by no means certain.

Perhaps an elephant is there. Perhaps the elephant has only a finite life. Perhaps parts of it are immortal.

Intellectual Tools

The term intellectual tool is relatively new in our society. But humans' use of tools of all types dates at least from the stone age. Indeed, until recently the ability to use tools was believed to distinguish human beings from other living creatures. Now we know that other species also use tools; however, no living form uses tools to the extent and variety human beings do.

The word *tool* raises in most minds the concept of a mechanical device; indeed, most objects we commonly denote as tools are mechanisms of one kind or another. Thus the hammer and screwdriver are tools for building.

We can think of a mechanical tool as a device to focus or increase human muscular power or, more generally, to increase ability to do mechanical tasks. The prototype tool of this kind might be the lever or the pulley or, among more modern tools, the farm tractor. Farm tractors allow farmers to plow and cultivate far more land than would be possible without them.

Just as we can speak of mechanical tools as extenders of human physical powers, we can also speak of intellectual tools as extenders of the human intellect. These tools expand the power of our minds.

The notion of an intellectual tool is also not new. People have used devices to extend their intellect for very long periods of time. Cutting notches in a tree to remember the number of times some important event has occurred or to keep track of weather patterns over time is an intellectual tool. Certainly writing is an extremely important intellectual tool, although historians disagree as to whether it has helped or hindered human beings. Some believe it was a powerful step forward, but not everyone accepts this opinion. Books are intellectual tools. The calculator quickly became a very important and pervasive intellectual tool. Almost all students in science and mathematics now have hand-held calculators.

The computer is already expanding human intellect in many different ways; it is potentially the most powerful of all intellectual tools. And as an intellectual tool, we can expect the computer to have important applications in education.

While some powerful computer tools may have relatively little use in learning, others, such as word processing, have very strong implications for education as well as applications in everyday life.

One caution is necessary. Most people think of tools in a positive sense. Yet tools, whether they are mechanical or intellectual, can be used in good and bad ways. Thus we must not assume that *every* use of a tool, computer or other, is inevitably good. This type of computer application should be viewed with the same critical attention given to other computer uses. Consider only what use a computer tool could have been to a Hitler, extending his control.

I do not believe that an intellectual tool, completely by itself, is necessarily a useful device in education. Indeed, most computer tools must be set into an instructional matrix, some way of learning about the material. The failure of many tools in classrooms has been due to educators ignoring this fact. Once a few exceptional teachers are able to use the tool well within class, it is then often assumed that everyone will be able

to do so. But often a very different situation obtains in the ordinary classroom. It is only if we carefully consider the full educational situation involving each tool, and sometimes develop extensive associated curriculum material with and without the computer, that we can make effective use of the tool.

TYPES OF INTELLECTUAL TOOLS

It is desirable to distinguish between several types of intellectual tools in thinking about how the computer serves as such a tool. First, we have *general-purpose* intellectual tools, which help amplify our intellect in ways not specific to a particular discipline. Intellectual tools to help the reasoning process are valuable in almost every area of human endeavor.

On the other hand, some intellectual tools used in learning are specific to a circumscribed discipline. That is, they help expand intellectual capabilities in that discipline within a defined channel. In the next section I give computer-based examples of both these types of intellectual tools for aiding learning. As with all classifications, it is sometimes difficult to know exactly where an application belongs.

Another distinction is useful in considering different intellectual tools. Students will be supplied some tools, while they will generate or create others. With supplied tools for the computer, someone else has programmed a general-purpose computer tool available to the student. For tools specific to restricted applications, users themselves may need to code the tool, or write the computer program.

So intellectual tool usage often does involve students as programmers, working in some programming language. But the purposes differ from programming activities noted in chapter 2, where students learn programming for the sake of learning programming, just to become more competent in use of computers or for future job possibilities. Here students are programming with a specific purpose related to particular intellectual tools.

I will provide some examples of computers as an intellectual tool. The next section considers word processing, spreadsheets, and paint programs, mentioned in chapter 3. Later in this chapter two examples of tools will be considered in more detail. One, Logo, exemplifies both a general intellectual tool and also a tool specifically for teaching mathematics. Therefore it functions as both types of intellectual tools mentioned. Logo is also a full-scale computer language, and so could serve with a programming course. But it is not a fully modern language.

The second example of computers as intellectual tools is based on an approach used for over twenty years to teach beginning physics. The student writes programs to aid in learning mechanics. The computer allows a new approach to mechanics, with a quite different pedagogical ordering from the traditional approach in beginning physics. However, many people using this approach use it only as an add-on to a traditional introduction to mechanics.

EXAMPLES OF INTELLECTUAL TOOLS

Word Processing Systems

One of the most important computer tools is *word processing*. The basic facility allows the user to enter, modify, maintain, and print textual documents.

Let us suppose that a fifteen-year-old student with a home word processor (not an unlikely possibility for the immediate future) must write a paper for a history course. First, the student may gather ideas; a sophisticated word processing system may help the student with these prewriting activities, perhaps by asking a few critical questions. A sophisticated word processing system will also encourage the student to organize these ideas, perhaps develop outlines of the material, but such systems are still rare. The student may refer to those outlines as the material is written.

In the writing activity our student begins to type paragraphs. Immediate typing errors, such as simple mistyping of letters, can be corrected right away, if they are noticed soon. Letters, words, or lines can be retyped at this stage. The student does not need to worry about the ends of lines because the system splits text at word boundaries, which are the ends of words; this speeds up typing.

After the paper has been typed, spelling correctors, grammar aids, stylistic advisors and other elements of a "writer's workbench," both computer-based and other, can be used to aid the student evaluate and improve the composition. This process is called postwriting, or rewriting. It is easy to make many changes. Letters, words, sentences, or sections can be deleted, added to, or moved from one place to another. New sections can be inserted and the material can be rearranged.

Finally, the student can control the printed copy in various ways, such as line length, spacing, and other formats. Or perhaps the material will be viewed by others directly at the computer screen.

The actual act of writing is such a laborious process for many young children that they cannot be expected to revise a composition many times. But with a child-directed word processing system, these difficulties can be overcome. Some modes of teaching reading and writing have beginning students using computers and typewriters, where they can immediately produce a credible product and, with the use of word processing, can easily modify that product.

Another set of powerful intellectual tools related to word processing and again aiding the reading and writing process is the collection of ideas developed by Ted Nelson under the name of Hypertext. These have received a partial implementation at Brown University, but have not been fully implemented, to the best of my knowledge.

One of the basic notions of Hypertext is to allow you to look at text at a variety of depths. One might imagine, for example, that the person reading a book displayed on the screen has a lever. When the lever is in one position, the screen contains only an outline of an entire book. As the lever is moved, more and more of the book will be accessible; with the lever in the other extreme position, the reader could work through the entire book.

This is only one Hypertext idea. Another set of ideas relates to being able to establish cross references in computer-stored text, for both individual and for group use. This is the phase that Andreas Van Dam and his colleagues implemented in the project at Brown University.

One consequence of the widespread availability of word processing is that typing, probably learned directly at the computer, will be an important skill for everyone. New rationally constructed keyboards may aid the process, leading to faster typing.

The potential for an intellectual tool, such as word processors with associated programs, to aid writing and reading is great. But, as with many of the areas mentioned in this book, extensive curriculum development will be needed to realize the possibilities.

Electronic Spreadsheets

VisiCalc™, or the spreadsheet-type program more generally, is one of the most widely used computer applications. Although spreadsheets are not primarily for education—so far spreadsheets are used mainly in business—they are used in some educational environments, and they should be discussed in computer literacy courses. Educational use of electronic spreadsheets and related programs is likely to grow.

The spreadsheet is a chart, typically a two-dimensional one, containing both verbal information and numbers. The descriptive headings, verbal information, are usually at the top and left, although this is not necessarily the case. Headings at the top might be years, for example, and headings down the side might be cities; the data in the chart could show populations of different cities in different years.

A simple chart of this kind, containing only numerical data, does not utilize the major strength of spreadsheet programs. Rather, in most applications some of the data in the chart will be *dependent* on other data. Thus a given number may be a sum of several other numbers in the chart, or a column may contain a percentage of the values in some other column. The spreadsheet program does not, in the case of dependent data, store the actual number; rather it keeps the *rule* or formula for computing that number. Thus when one of the data numbers is changed, the numbers that depend on that number through formula also change. For example, if the chart shows payments on a loan, and the interest rate is changed, then all the payments would change instantly. By allowing the user to play with the possibilities, to see what happens instantly as variables change, spreadsheets offer help in decision making.

In addition to the central capabilities—headings, independent data, and formulas—spreadsheet programs can control this information in various ways. Thus the format of the data can be specified, formulas can be easily repeated when they are used over and over, printouts can be requested. Although the details differ from one sheet to another, spreadsheet products are quite similar.

Paint Programs

Another interesting intellectual tool, very different from others discussed, provides a range of artistic capabilities. With such a "paint" program the user can create simple or complex drawings, perhaps combined with textual elements. Not only are built-in objects available to the computer artists, both two- and three-dimensional in some cases, but objects can typically be drawn through "pads," surfaces which allow the user to draw on the pad in the usual fashion. The drawing appears on the computer screen. Various "brushstrokes" (textures of lines) may be available. The objects can be changed in size, shape, and orientation, can be

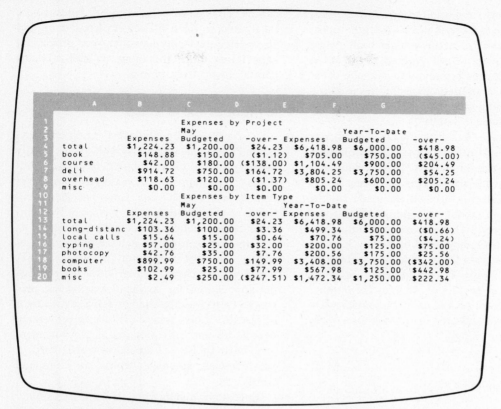

Figure 4.1 A spreadsheet display.

reflected in complex ways to display various types of symmetry, and can be combined. Some of the programs are intended for very young children. One such paint program was developed and is widely used at the Capital Children's Museum in Washington, D.C. Such capabilities have also been developed for use by professional artists and designers. Thus, Grace Hertlein has used such capabilities for textile design and other artistic endeavors.

Simulation Languages

Simulating a physical or social system of some kind, whether by some type of mechanical model (waves in a tank) or by means of a computer, is not a new idea. Simulations are often powerful tools in educational activities. In some cases students will be supplied with a prepared program. In other cases they may use the standard programming languages to prepare the simulation, the languages referred to in chapter 2. In still other cases, special languages have been developed to make the task of creating such a simulation easier. The advantage of being able to simulate a particular situation is that one can "play" with the various factors which determine that situation and so can study the results of the changes that are made.

It should be emphasized that these special languages are highly dependent on the type of simulation. Thus those simulations that have careful mathematical descriptions and can be described in terms of mathematical equations must be specified in a different type of language than used for specifying nonmathematical simulations. For any simulation where time-dependent factors, such as rates of change, are important, very powerful mathematical tools called differential equations are required. It is not too difficult to get even beginners to use such equations, if proper simulation capabilities are used or if the learning material explains what is happening in sufficient detail.

One language of this type is DYNAMO, developed by Jay Forrester at the Massachusetts Institute of Technology. DYNAMO came into great prominence a few years ago when it was used as a basis for predictions made by the "Club of Rome" about the coming difficulties of Western society.* One educational simulation with DYNAMO, developed by Nancy Roberts at Lesley College in Cambridge, Massachusetts, involved the study of a flu epidemic. Students could alter various factors, such as the number of people a given person came in contact with, and see how that affected the propagation of the disease.

Other Examples

Graphics programs, for use in science and mathematics classes or for business, are another example of intellectual tools. Often numbers are easier to understand if they are presented in graphic or pictorial form, such as pie charts, histograms, or in other ways. Such visual information is helpful to both students and professionals.

Another computer-based intellectual tool is *electronic mail,* the ability to send computer-stored messages from one place to another. The message might be entered with a word processor. As with ordinary mail, the users do not need to be using their computers at the same time; a message entered at one time will usually be read later. A more complex example of the same procedure is *computer conferencing,* where not only can messages be sent, but they

*Donella H. Meadows, *The Limits to Growth: A Report for the Club of Rome's Project on the Predicament of Mankind* (New York: Universe Books, 1972).

can be classified in different ways, votes can be taken, and so forth. Better electronic mail and conferencing systems may offer word processing capabilities, since the input to such systems comes mostly from typing.

INTRODUCTION TO LOGO

Logo, developed by Wallace Feurzig and Seymour Papert, starting about 1967, was initially used by junior high school mathematics students. As it happened, I visited the first Logo course, in Massachusetts. Logo has the potential to be one of the most important of the computer-based intellectual tools for education.

Logo is a computer language that resembles slightly another computer language, LISP, which was developed primarily for list processing applications for Artificial Intelligence programs. Logo was preceded by JOSS, a precursor of BASIC. Logo was a distinct improvement over JOSS and still remains an improvement over most BASICs. Like JOSS and BASIC, it uses English language words as command words.

Logo took a step forward from these older languages by adding a simple graphics capability, the "turtle," some years after the original language was developed. This picture-drawing capability has become almost synonymous with Logo and is a distinguishing characteristic. Indeed, many people not well acquainted with Logo think turtle geometry *is* Logo. Turtle geometry has been advertised and used in languages and programs other than Logo because in its simplest form it is almost independent of the language. But Logo proponents regard it as an integral part of the language.

Turtle Geometry

Only two turtle geometry commands, FORWARD and RIGHT, need be introduced initially to students. Both are graphic. The turtle can be either a mechanical turtle that moves across the floor in response to these two commands, or it can be, as in most situations, a line drawing on the computer screen that is generated as indicated by the two commands.

The turtle is a device whose *state* is specified by two quantities. The first quantity is the *location* on the screen. The second quantity is the current *heading* or direction of the turtle.

When the turtle receives a forward command, it moves forward a certain amount in the direction it is pointing in. A typical command would be:

FORWARD 50

In this case the turtle would move forward 50 units. The command

FORWARD 100

would move the turtle forward twice as far. Initially these numbers have no absolute meaning to the user, and, indeed, the user learns what they mean by experimenting and observing the results. The actual distance is dependent on the size of the screen. Units of distance are not emphasized. An early task might be to measure the screen size in "Logo units." Typically, when the turtle does move forward some distance it draws a line. Different versions of Logo differ somewhat as to how they indicate on the screen the direction the turtle is heading, but an arrowhead is common.

A second command might look like this:

RIGHT 25

The turtle does not advance but rather changes its *heading*. Again, the number used, 25, is not

usually explained immediately to the student; rather, trial and error may be involved in determining the meaning of the number. But the experienced user sees immediately that we are dealing with angles. The change in heading, the turning, is always from the latest position and heading. RIGHT means counterclockwise, the student sees.

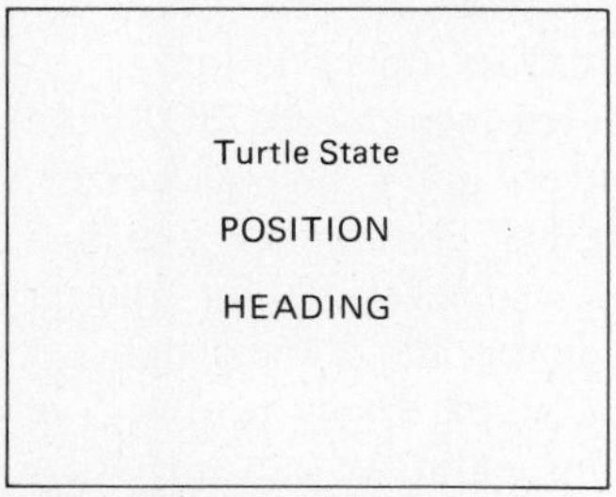

As mentioned, these two commands are the basis for much of the early work in both turtle geometry and Logo. The typical sequence of events for early use of Logo, beginning with turtle geometry, goes something like this. First, the two commands are introduced to students, perhaps by the teacher, through examples. Then the students are encouraged to "play" with these commands, trying different numbers and trying to draw whatever interests them or a picture suggested by the teacher. FORWARD and RIGHT are effective drawing tools, similar to an artist's capabilities. That is, an artist can move charcoal or pen a certain distance forward, then turn it, and so forth, in a similar fashion.

Logo Procedures

More explicit student tasks are introduced about this time. A typical first task with Logo is to draw a square. Ideally the student is not told how to draw the square but is asked to do it by a discovery process, trial and error. The emphasis on "do-it-yourself," learning by doing, is an important component of the Logo philosophy, though unfortunately this approach is not always followed. A learner must, by experience, get some understanding of the nature of the numbers in the command RIGHT, although still not necessarily with any explicit terminology; thus, the concept of "angle" need not be explicitly introduced.

Students may discover that to draw a square they need a sequence of commands like this:

FORWARD 50
RIGHT 90

Figure 4.2 The turtle.

FORWARD 50
RIGHT 90
FORWARD 50
RIGHT 90
FORWARD 50
RIGHT 90

After these commands the screen (assumed initially clear) looks like Figure 4.3. Remember, this sequence of commands should not be presented to the student; rather, the student, in a good Logo introduction, must generate this series of commands through a discovery process. This process may be dependent on the age of the student. When students have done this, they have written a *program,* the first purposeful program typically seen in Logo.

The next task might be to draw a triangle. Here, some discussion of the nature of a triangle is essential, usually from the teacher. At MIT students march around in triangles, using body motion as a clue as to which Logo commands are needed. Initial attempts usually do not succeed. Most students succeed only if they work toward drawing an equilateral triangle, with all sides the same length. To do this they must learn the magic "120" to turn the heading, FORWARD 120. Interestingly, teachers and more advanced students will often try "60" as the first angle, not realizing that the turtle is not measuring the same angle they are thinking of!

At this point it becomes a little harder to anticipate the typical beginning Logo learning sequence, because some divergence occurs.

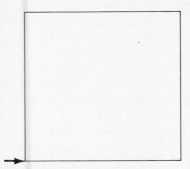

Figure 4.3 A Logo square.

Often, however, the next idea introduced is that the turtle can "learn" a sequence of commands and assign a new name to it. Thus a student might define a command called BOX. In order to BOX, the sequence typed would look something like this:

TO BOX
FORWARD 50
RIGHT 90
FORWARD 50
RIGHT 90
FORWARD 50
RIGHT 90
FORWARD 50
RIGHT 90
END

A similar procedure would be followed with triangles. Each student can build up a set of facilities, user commands Logo will recognize, to be used in other programs. At this point the idea of *programs* or procedures enters the discussion. The critical Logo word is "TO."

This idea, the ability to "teach the system," entails storing a *procedure* or subprogram (for example, BOX) in a conveniently available "personal computer library." The student might also define a procedure called "TRIANGLE." Logo makes this very easy; it assumes user storage of procedures as a fundamental capability. Note, too, that this idea is introduced to the student very early, as it should be in any modern approach to programming. In chapter 2 I stressed the notion of the subprogram or procedure as a key idea in structured programming. That Logo introduces it so early is to its credit. Note that the names are descriptive English words, not initials or abbreviations.

The two procedures introduced, BOX and TRIANGLE, however, are a bit specialized. Looking at the RIGHT commands, you find that the angles there are necessary for squares and triangles. On the other hand, the distance is strictly arbitrary; each box drawn is always of the same size. At this point we can introduce students to the important notion of a *variable,* allowing different size boxes.

An interactive system, such as Logo, allows experimentation with variables, an easy approach to introducing them even at an early level. Initially students might try commands like

```
Make S = 100
FORWARD S
```

Then they can proceed to a new procedure that looks like this:

```
TO SQUARE :SIDE
FORWARD :SIDE
RIGHT 90
FORWARD :SIDE
RIGHT 90
FORWARD : SIDE
RIGHT 90
FORWARD :SIDE
RIGHT 90
END
```

The word "TO" announces that a procedure is to be specified; the student is teaching the computer "to" do something. "END" announces that the procedure is complete. SQUARE is now available for use. At least one Logo dialect uses the word "BUILD" instead of TO. As mentioned, Logo is *not* a standardized language, and all Logos are slightly different.

Thus the student can now type

```
SQUARE 50
SQUARE 100
```

when the turtle is in its initial position and get a picture looking like Figure 4.3. Likewise, the following program can teach the turtle to draw a triangle of any size, like the one in Figure 4.4.

```
TO TRIANGLE :SIDE
FORWARD :SIDE
RIGHT 120
```

```
FORWARD :SIDE
RIGHT 120
FORWARD :SIDE
RIGHT 120
END
```

You may have noticed that these procedures, **SQUARE** and **TRIANGLE**, are rather repetitive. In **SQUARE** the sequence

```
FORWARD :SIDE
RIGHT 90
```

occurs four times. So it is not too surprising that Logo has a way of representing this by means of a *loop* (see page 17). Here is an equivalent program for SQUARE, one that will work just like the one we have seen:

```
TO SQUARE : SIDE
REPEAT 4 [FORWARD :SIDE RIGHT 90]
END
```

Procedures become *tools* to use within other programs. A good language introduction will therefore use them at once, as I noted in chapter 2.

Middle school students might now be asked to draw a house, or some similar object. A simple house can be put together rather easily with squares and triangles, a square for the house itself and for the windows and doors, and a triangle for the roof; so the tools just introduced, **BOX** and **TRIANGLE**, serve a new purpose. Drawing a house working only with FOR-

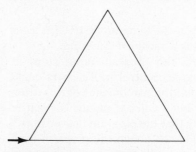

Figure 4.4 A Logo triangle.

WARD and RIGHT is a much more difficult job, so this task reasonably *encourages* the use of procedures. The house would be "improved" if a "RECTANGLE" procedure was used, rather than just BOX.

Another task often presented to the student is that of drawing a person. Again the procedures already defined are very useful. Thus the problems presented lend themselves naturally to a modular approach.

Logo and Recursion

Another programming idea often introduced early in learning Logo is recursion: A procedure "calls" *itself.* Recursion was at one time considered an advanced notion, but some (not all) authorities now recommend its use early even within a simplified programming language. Nevertheless this remains controversial, and many feel its early inclusion is not justified. Recursion is not an easy concept for many students, and is probably not worth the time required, I believe.

An early introduction to recursion in Logo is drawing a circle. The usual program is rather "funny," and perhaps students should not be taught it, because it is a "never-ending" program! Here's the program:

```
TO CIRCLE
FORWARD 5
RIGHT 5
CIRCLE
END
```

The fact that the program CIRCLE *calls itself* makes this a recursive program.

As indicated, this program never stops! It needs some way to control it. Teachers could use this as a point for introducing control structures in Logo, but I will not pursue the matter further. (To say that the program "never stops" is not quite right. Although the program itself has no built-in way of stopping on any actual computer, eventually it *will* stop on most computers and produce a program error. This is because each time CIRCLE is invoked, some storage is used up; eventually storage is exhausted!)

The earliest learning of Logo did not begin with these drawing activities; no graphic capabilities were available initially. In the class I observed many years ago, the early programs were all language-manipulating ones, such as reversing the letters in a word, writing a word in "pig latin" form, making a "triangle" out of a word, like this:

```
C
CO
COW
```

and similar tasks. From the start Logo's developers tried to avoid beginning with numerical calculations or trivial tasks. Creation, discovery, and learning were emphasized.

Logo has powerful list processing capabilities inherited from LISP, and these are often introduced along with the word manipulation programs.*

LOGO AND PROCEDURES

One of Logo's main advantages with regard to modular programming is the way it treats the procedures that are defined by the user. Each of these procedures is automatically accessible to that user; from the user's point of view it appears that the language has been extended to contain a new command. Thus when a command such as BOX is employed, each time the user uses the disc on which that command has been specified, that command will be available as if it were part of the language. This can be done in other languages only if the user knows where to find things, names of files. Hence Logo

*For details, see, for example, Daniel Watt, *Learning with Logo* (New York: McGraw-Hill, 1983), and Sylvia Weir, *Logo as a Teaching Tool* (New York: Harper & Row, 1984).

has not only the "immediate" capabilities of an interpreted language—the ability to execute single commands and so see the effect right away —but also the automatic library capability, which is a powerful tool for the beginning programmer. A few other languages, such as APL and Speakeasy, also can be extended, but Speakeasy is a rare language, not accessible to beginners. These automatic library facilities are one of Logo's most important properties as both a programming language and an intellectual tool.

Logo procedures behave very much like what APL calls functions. In APL a collection of functions is, possibly with associated data, present in something called a *workspace*. All the functions within the workspace (APL calls these functions but they behave like both procedures and functions in other programming languages) are available to any program that uses that workspace. Thus as in Logo, a set of special environments can be built up. APL goes further than Logo in this regard, because the workspaces can also contain data of arbitrary complexity—values of variables of any type, for example. These are stored too when the workspace is stored.

LOGO AS AN INTELLECTUAL TOOL

Logo has been highly recommended as an intellectual tool, both in the sense of a general tool applicable across many areas and as a specific intellectual tool for learning certain parts of mathematics.

Many suggestions concerning the use of Logo as a general computer-based tool are common to programming languages. One important issue in programming as a developer of powerful intellectual tools is the notion of breaking a large problem into smaller problems. When students are asked to draw a house in Logo, in a well-taught class they are encouraged to think of this as a set of subproblems. That is, drawing a house entails a series of smaller drawing activities, drawing the outline of the house, the

doors, the windows, and the roof. Each of these is a subtask, and so the larger task of drawing the house has been segmented into subtasks or pieces. Furthermore, students already *know* how to solve the subtasks because they have already learned to draw a square, or rectangle, and a triangle.

Making small problems out of a large problem is the essence of good modern programming, as well as a basic tool of problem solving. Hence it can be classified as an important general intellectual tool. Several factors make it possible for Logo to introduce this tool at an earlier age than most other languages. First, the language is graphically appealing, an advantage with young children. Second, it has a strong subrouting capability, the ability to define procedures easily, upon which the common ways of teaching the language rely heavily. In some languages the student's ability to form procedures is primitive, and their use is considered "an advanced" feature rather than something taught almost immediately. In a good modern structured programming approach to a language, whether taught for programming or as an intellectual tool, the subroutine or procedure is an essential and extremely important *early* tool. Until quite recently, Logo was available to a younger group of students than other programming languages, and some of the competing languages, such as BASIC, lack the structured programming capabilities of Logo.

Logo can also introduce other important intellectual tools for problem solving, in that writing a computer program *is* a problem-solving activity. These other aspects, as discussed in chapter 2, are less related to Logo and its properties than those already discussed, as they are more generally the features of good programming and good problem solving. Whether good modern top-down programming strategies are stressed by experienced users of Logo may well depend on how the language is initially used. Accomplishing these goals depends on the nature of the course involved.

Logo is also known as an important intellectual tool in teaching mathematics. Seymour Papert, one of Logo's developers, likes to tell this story: In American high schools it is difficult to learn French. Counselors tell students they should not take the course because it is tough. Some good students who do take it and have considerable trouble are said by their teachers not to have language aptitude. So only a small group of high school students in the United States develop a good functional knowledge of French.

Yet in France, where every three-year-old child learns to speak French, there is no talk of language aptitude or the subject being difficult! The incentive is greater too, we must admit.

The moral is that a natural environment exists for learning French, a "Frenchland." In other environments it is more difficult to learn French. In a similar way Papert likes to talk about a "Mathland," a natural environment in which to learn mathematics. Logo was an attempt to realize one such natural environment, at least for some areas of mathematics.

In geometry, Logo's drawing capabilities and the turtle could make the language an important intellectual tool. But there have been relatively few experiments in teaching Logo geometry in the schools. At the university level Harold Abelson and Andrea di Sessa describe likely applications in geometry and other areas of mathematics.*

The Department of Artificial Intelligence at the University of Edinburgh, under the direction of James Howe, has made the most serious attempts to use Logo as an intellectual tool for learning mathematics in schools. Howe's success has been mixed. Logo has been useful in teaching some topics but not others. Their reports give very interesting information about this aspect of Logo.

*Harold Abelson and Andrea di Sessa, *Turtle Geometry: The Computer as a Medium for Exploring Mathematics* (Cambridge, Mass.: MIT Press, 1981).

THE TEACHER'S ROLE

Another Logo uncertainty—not exactly a problem but a factor influencing much of the use of Logo in classes—is the question of what the teacher's role should be. I have already suggested that many teachers are ill prepared to aid students in learning Logo. But even in the canonical approaches that have come from Seymour Papert and his colleagues at MIT, the role of the teacher is, I believe, uncertain. Many of the examples of Logo used by Papert, quoted in *Mindstorms,* reflect very specialized situations where very small numbers of students are involved with very competent teachers, often from the MIT Logo group. Even in those situations some students learned and others did not.

Some Logo enthusiasts seem almost afraid that the teacher *should* do something. While very competent Logo teachers *do* do something, it is never entirely clear exactly what kind of help, assistance, or guidance they provide. The teacher is not to tell the students the result but to make suggestions—perhaps even give help—that may lead students to the powerful ideas through their own discovery. Often the incorrect impression is given that everyone will learn well on his or her own in environments like Logo if no teachers are available.

LOGO PROBLEMS

Some devotees think of Logo with an almost religious fervor. Seldom is there much criticism of the language, and what there is, is often brief. I should like to give a more balanced treatment, so I will now consider a number of problems associated with Logo in its various applications.

Logo as a Programming Language

In chapter 2, where programming was discussed, Logo was not given great attention. Rather, other programming languages, such as Pascal, were stressed. This was not an accident. Although it has some strong features as a programming language (particularly the way it handles procedures), Logo also has a number of weaknesses. Thus it may not be the best choice as a programming language, particularly when compared to Pascal. However, it can compete extremely well with BASIC, which is a very poor choice for beginners learning programming.

What are the difficulties with Logo? Logo is not a new language. It was intended primarily for learning mathematics and developing powerful ideas, not to teach programming; using it in that fashion is pushing Logo beyond its initial intention.

Logo is weak in at least two areas compared with more recent languages. First, it does not require users to define data carefully. Data types need not be specified, so Logo does not emphasize the importance of data. Thus, it emphasizes the logical side of programming more than the data side. As indicated in chapter 2, both of these are important in modern programming, and should receive equal attention.

Some defenders of Logo have tried to make its lack of concern with data other than lists a virtue. For example, this seems to be the position of Harold Abelson in "A Beginner's Guide to Logo,"* where he argues that not having data typing is an advantage. But his implication that this is done in other languages only because people don't know how to do it better is clearly wrong. Languages developed since Logo do have data typing. It may be that earlier languages did need careful specification of types for compilation. As explained in chapter 2, the necessity of type specification in newer languages, such as Pascal or Ada, is a conscious, desirable design choice, not an accident of the language.

A second area in which Logo is somewhat weak is in control structures. Logo was designed in the days when such inadequate control structures as GO TOs were in use. Some groups using Logo recognize these inadequacies. Currently a new language tentatively called Boxer is being

*Byte (August 1982), p. 88.

developed at MIT to replace Logo. Abelson's article describes Boxer. Logo is an old language that can be improved, although the reasons for this need currently being invoked at MIT are different from the ones suggested here.

One of the features of Logo confusing to beginners, although a powerful tool for an experienced user, is distinguishing between the value of the variable and the variable, leading to an odd use of the symbol ":." I will not try to explain the distinction. But for beginners, it is by no means a trivial one, and it makes Logo a more complicated language for beginners to use. The grammar of Logo could be improved.

Another problem with Logo as a programming language is that it is not standardized, so it differs considerably from one machine and implementation to another. I have seen one of the masters of Logo unable to carry out simple commands in a Logo system that was unfamiliar to him! Logo competes with BASIC as one of the most poorly standardized languages, but at least in BASIC an attempt at a formal standard has been made. Complex programs written in one Logo probably will not run on a different Logo.

Classroom Problems

As suggested, too often Logo has been taught to small groups of students by a highly trained, competent teacher, usually someone from one of the major Logo centers rather than a typical teacher. Hence the question of how Logo can be employed in typical classroom situations must be raised.

Little good material for students exists. Most Logo manuals do not claim to be student textbooks. However, better materials about Logo should appear in the next few years.

The other side of the coin is that most teachers know very little about Logo. Typically when Logo is used today in schools the teacher has learned only the bare rudiments of the language. A week-long Logo workshop is entirely inadequate. Thus only a minuscule fraction of teachers has any conception of Logo's list processing capabilities. Furthermore, most teachers understand little about the philosophy of using the language, either as a programming language or as an intellectual tool. It is often taught, for example, in a rote fashion, with the teacher simply *giving lectures* about how to draw a box, how to draw a triangle, and so forth. This approach allows extremely little of the discovery component. I have seen classes where students enter into the computer only programs provided by the teachers. This is not too surprising, if the teachers have very little knowledge beyond that obtained by reading an introductory manual or going to an introductory lecture or brief workshop.

One result of this lack of student material and teacher preparation is that students often learn the same small amount of material over and over. The problem is similar to what happened with set theory in the 1960s and 1970s. Students learned about sets, unions, intersections, and null sets several times during their school careers. Each time the students "learned" exactly what they had learned before, never going any further. Encountering students who had "learned" set theory about four times was interesting; they didn't want to have anything more to do with mathematics! Likewise, students are encountering Logo superficially. If they encounter it in this manner a number of times, they will be convinced that Logo has no value.

The problems of little good material for students and poorly prepared teachers are not inherent in Logo, but simply represent the present situation. Getting vast numbers of teachers to understand *any* new curriculum development is extremely difficult. Many of the major U.S. curriculum development projects in the 1960s failed completely on this issue; they produced interesting curriculum material but were never able to instruct enough teachers in how to use it effectively. In some cases these programs assumed classroom situations that were impossible to attain in most schools.

Although members of the MIT Logo group might not agree, it is my opinion that the only way that problems of this type can be solved is by developing computer-based learning material, such as that described in the next chapter, that would make Logo almost independent of these school problems and would also make it much more usable in home and public environments.

Needed Research

The last set of Logo problems centers on the fact that little is known about how the language can be used most effectively. In particular, although it was the major example of a "math world," as described by Seymour Papert, outside of the work at the University of Edinburgh, little detailed research has considered how Logo can be used to improve the teaching of mathematics. The Edinburgh group has developed curriculum material using Logo in mathematics, sometimes successfully and sometimes not, in their evaluation. Much additional research, coupled with the development of curriculum material, is needed to determine how Logo and similar languages can be used as intellectual tools in a variety of areas.

BOXER

Boxer, as noted previously, is a language currently being developed by Andrea di Sessa and Hal Abelson at the Massachusetts Institute of Technology. They intend it to be a successor to Logo. Boxer is based on a "spatial metaphor." Each component fits into a *box*. The box can contain text (e.g., for a word processing application), code, and data. It can also contain other boxes. Programming units are identified by giving a box a name, thus establishing procedures. The idea is to have a uniform way for the user to view *all* computer activities, the spatial metaphor of boxes. Boxer has avoided some of Logo's odd syntactical features. So far, however, Boxer has not been used outside of MIT.

Educators should watch the development of Boxer carefully.

ANOTHER INTELLECTUAL TOOL— INTRODUCTORY MECHANICS

Computers can function as intellectual tools in education in a number of environments, not only in Logo. I developed an approach to mechanics over twenty years ago, as my first exploration into using computers in education. My colleagues and I have described this approach many times.* This approach to mechanics is a good example of how to restructure learning when a computer is available as an intellectual tool, specifically applicable to a particular area.

To describe this application for either high school or college physics courses, I assume some slight knowledge of physics. Readers not familiar with physics may want to skim this section rather quickly.

Almost all physics courses begin with the study of mechanics, the description and prediction of how bodies and objects move. The approach almost universally taken is ascribed to Isaac Newton, yet the actual strategy of most contemporary beginning courses of mechanics would be quite foreign to Newton himself; these courses use mathematical techniques from algebra and calculus rather than the geometrical techniques that characterized Newton's *Mathematical Principles of Natural Philosophy.* I am particularly intrigued because this computer direction relates much more closely to Newton's approach to mechanics than to contemporary approaches!

Newton began in his laws of motion with a very specific kind of force, an impulsive force such as a blow or kick. The only effect of forces that must be considered is the reaction to kicks.

With Newton's tactics, what happens where

*See, for example, *Introductory Computer-Based Mathematics,* available in several variants from CONDUIT (Computer Center, University of Iowa). For example, Alfred Bork, Wayne Lang, John Merrill, and Herbert Peckham, *Introductory Computer-Based Mathematics II* (1973).

no force acts is considered first: If the body is initially moving, it continues to move uniformly on a straight line. The blow alters the situation, as pictured in Figure 4.5. In Laws I and II and in the Corollary to Law II, Newton gives a precise method for calculating the effect of the blow.

Although I will not give the full details, it turns out that the kicks or blows correspond to a modern numerical method for solving the Newtonian equations of motion. The Newtonian equations of motion, in our modern point of view, are differential equations. On the computer, differential equations are solved with approximation techniques. The simplest of these techniques, often called the Euler method, is obtained by replacing derivatives with ratios of finite differences. The velocity, instead of being represented by the derivative

$$dx/dt$$

is replaced by

$$\left(\frac{x_{\text{new}} - x_{\text{old}}}{\Delta t} \right)$$

where x_{new} and x_{old} are two positions of the moving object, a time Δt apart. A similar approximation is made for the acceleration. This

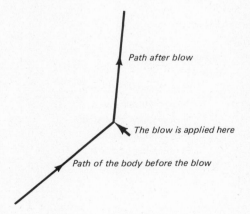

Path after blow

The blow is applied here

Path of the body before the blow

A blow acting on a body in free space.

Figure 4.5 The effect of a blow on a body moving in free space.

method leads directly to the blowlike geometrical approach and thus a very simple way of solving mechanical problems. For the approximation to be "good," the time difference, Δt, must be small.

In this approach, approximations of derivatives as ratios of small quantities, students write computer programs for the solutions to mechanical problems. Chapter 2 contains the set of programs for one physical system using this method, as an example of what the various programming languages look like. Refer to page 30 to see programs in several languages. The physical system considered in these programs is the harmonic oscillator, a mass bobbing up and down on a spring or pendulum, using the Euler approach.

The beauty of this method is that it is very general, covering *any* one-dimensional (straight-line) motion. It extends easily to two- and three-dimensional problems where the motion is no longer restricted to a single straight line. The method applies to any force, and indeed, only one line in the program, the calculation of velocity, refers to a specific force. So the method is entirely general, unlike the methods for solving mechanical problems usually introduced in beginning courses.

These programs all have this structure:

```
PROGRAM MOTION;
BEGIN
      Initialize;
      REPEAT
            NewPositionCalculated;
            NewForceCalculated;
            NewVelocityCalculated;
            NewTimeCalculated;
            PrintPositionAndTime
      UNTIL Time > FinalTime
END.
```

It is difficult for someone unfamiliar with physics to appreciate the value of this new method. The case might be stated in this fash-ion: In the mechanics section, of the typical beginning physics course, students are told that Newton's method or a modern equivalent allows us to determine how *anything* moves. Yet the problems that students encounter, the only problems they are equipped to work, are such relatively trivial problems as masses over pulleys and blocks sliding down inclined planes. Students do *not* see the power of Newton's method and must take it as an article of faith that similar methods can somehow be used for more interesting and more difficult problems such as the motion of planets in the solar system. Indeed, beginning students usually do not see Newton's laws as differential equations at all. More often the differential equation and mechanical methods using it are reserved for intermediate or advanced physics students.

Using the computer as an intellectual tool, the situation changes drastically. Students immediately have a powerful tool that enables them to work difficult problems. The instructor can assign a range of problems workable through computer techniques that would be out of the question in the typical beginning physics class. Thus students can find the orbit of a planet around a sun.

CONCLUDING REMARKS

It should be emphasized again that a tool, just because it is a tool, is not necessarily good or bad. Every intellectual tool must be demonstrated to be educationally useful, to contribute in some way to the learning process.

Educators must be particularly alert for potential problems in using tools with students. My experience has shown that tools can easily be more interesting to the instructor than to students. The instructor's background supplies motivation that students lack. Such materials might work well as long as the instructor is hovering over the student, but in large classes, or where the original developers of the materials are not present, problems may arise. I have discussed these factors in detail concerning Logo, and you should apply similar considerations to *any* use of intellectual tools.

It is essential in all cases to have a good human interface, a convenient way for users to employ the tools. Many early and relatively primitive computer-based intellectual tools, often referred to as simulations, begin by asking students for vast amounts of data, the necessary input to generate some result. In most cases, students at that level have no idea what all the numbers mean, so they are entering a series of meaningless numbers. It is much better in such simulations to start with a set of predetermined parameters, producing interesting results, and then give students control over altering these, presumably one at a time. In any case the question of how the program will appear to the casual user, not the expert, is extremely important.

One great problem with most software—operating systems, languages, computer-based learning materials, tools such as word processors and VisiCalc—is that the systems are very unresponsive to unanticipated user inputs. Thus the student often receives peculiar messages. They may be in cryptic English, such as "error in line 72—syntax error," or they may be collec-

tions of letters and numbers entirely uninterpretable by the novice. Such messages should never occur, but it will take time before better error messages, more oriented toward the needs of human beings, will be widely used. Highly negative language should never be used, as it has unfortunate affective results and discourages students from using the computer.

Although the necessity for associated curriculum development has been mentioned primarily with Logo, the same kind of development is necessary with any of the tools discussed. Tools by themselves do not constitute learning experiences. In fact, users, in education and elsewhere, can learn how to utilize many of our current intellectual tools only in clumsy ways, because of our inexperience in developing user-oriented software. Most of these tools are almost impossible to use without "outside" aid—lectures, books, people. Curriculum development to use tools is an important part of the tool environment in all areas; tools such as word processors can fail miserably if teachers do not develop procedures that work in their classrooms, or do not find such procedures already developed in previous curriculum projects.

chapter 5

Computer-based Learning

● How Many Work Together?
● Aspects of Computer-based Learning
● Examples of Computer-based Learning

Computer-based learning, or computer-aided learning, could, by its very name, refer to almost any way of using computers to aid the learning process. Thus this expression might include all the ways of using computers in education discussed in the last three chapters, as well as the ways covered in this and the next chapter.

Nevertheless, the types of computer usage already discussed are usually distinguished from the uses people characterize by such terms as CAI, or computer-aided learning, computer-aided instruction, or computer-based instruc-tion, considered in this chapter. I avoid acronyms such as CAI because I do not find them useful; they impede reading, particularly by someone unfamiliar with the field. The jargon of acronyms should be banned everywhere!

I would much rather talk about *learning* than instruction, a distinction probably already apparent to readers. A teacher *instructs,* or sets up a learning environment, whereas a student learns. Instruction is useful only if it promotes learning, so learning is the activity that genuinely interests us in the educational process, not teaching or instruction. We often lose sight of this distinction.

Another implication is inherent in the distinction between learning and teaching. Learning can be viewed as an active process, while teaching—from the students' point of view—is often a passive process. The typical teaching technique in American schools and universities is the lecture, where one person standing in front of the room plays an active role while everyone else is an absorber of what is said, in many cases not much more than a blotter. I will emphasize learning both in this chapter and throughout the book.

The expression "computer-based learning" is a little peculiar. We never speak of "book-based learning" or "blackboard-based learning." Nevertheless, in classifying different kinds of computer applications in education, this distinction is convenient.

What is computer-based learning? The term could refer to any way to use computers in learning not covered in the last three chapters. But this seems a bit unfair. The distinctive characteristic of computer-based learning is that students use learning programs that others have prepared.

In a sense, in all computer usage we use programs written by others; thus when we write a program in Pascal, we use a Pascal "translator," a compiler or an interpreter, written by someone else. The distinction is a matter of degree. The person writing the Pascal program *is* writing a program, while the person using a typical computer-based learning sequence is working with a program prepared entirely by someone else. But like all human-created distinctions, this one will fail if pressed too hard.

In computer-based learning, then, students work with programs developed by others. In the best circumstances, the "others" involved in development included a group of highly skilled teachers, knowledgeable about students at the level targeted. (I do not consider in this chapter how the material was developed; that topic is reserved for chapters 11 and 12. Rather, this chapter gives many examples of computer-based learning, stressing the wide variety of possibilities.)

Computer-based learning material is also *subject-matter oriented,* just as books are. Although such learning modules *could* be about computers, they usually deal with other subjects such as arithmetic, reading, science, mathematics, or any other one.

HOW MANY WORK TOGETHER?

One consideration in computer-based learning is that of how many people are actually working at the display, learning from a computer sequence. The assumption that most people have made, and that almost all existing material makes, is that a single person is involved. The exception seems to be primarily with gamelike programs involving two or more people.

Yet in actual usage of computer-based learning material often a group of people are working with the material. Thus if the material is being viewed freely in a library, a group of people is almost always involved. Observations of these groups show that in addition to the learning that occurs directly, because of the student-computer interaction, extremely valuable learning occurs because of student-student interaction. Group usage of computer-based materials encourages a high level of peer learning by getting the learners in the group to talk to each other about the problems involved. Peer learning can be a very valuable educational experience, with or without computers.

A research project currently underway at the Educational Technology Center concerning groups and computer learning indicates that it is often a valuable learning experience to work with other students. Experienced developmental groups are beginning to understand how to develop materials that will behave differently when several people are at the display than when just a single person is there. Thus a cooperative learning process among the students can be emphasized, increasing the level of student interaction beyond that usually possible in a classroom and focusing this interaction on learning problems. Thus the computer can make education more humane.

ASPECTS OF COMPUTER-BASED LEARNING

Computer-based learning units are rapidly becoming commercially available. As I write, dozens of publishers, both large and small, are pursuing this market, electronic publishing, with varying degrees of vigor. But most of the segments available so far are poor, for the field of electronic publishing is still in its infancy. The amount of material available should increase rapidly in the next few years. I also hope the quality will improve greatly, but this is not certain.

Many *different* types of computer-based learning units are available. Although I use the expression "computer-based learning" as if it represented one class of entities, different types of computer-based learning differ considerably in pedagogical goals, in strategy, and in detail. This chapter illustrates this diversity. I will not attempt to develop any elaborate classification scheme for such curriculum material on the computer, although I will delineate types to some extent in describing the various examples. I have chosen the examples to illustrate the wide range of computer-based learning possibilities.

The description of computer-based learning I have given, that the student is using learning programs written by others, is not adequate. The description so far includes such things as intellectual tool applications, for example. In this section I give another model for viewing computer-based learning. This way of thinking about it may be particularly useful for developers, and it is also an effective way for users to view the material.

The model I propose is the model of the tutor. The classic tutorial process involves one

student, or perhaps a very small number of students, and an instructor. The tutorials at Oxford and Cambridge universities in England are one example of this method of instruction. Each student has one or several tutors. Although that student might participate in other kinds of learning experiences, in the classic Cambridge education tutors were, and are, the critical component of the learning process.

In a contemporary university the tutorial process in its pure form still survives in certain situations. Students coming to the instructor's office can ask questions about material. The instructor can then be involved in a one-on-one or one-on-several learning situation. Some instructors will simply repeat the lecture, while others will offer aid in an interactive way, perhaps even querying students point by point to try to find where they are having difficulties. A process of this kind may occur, too, after class in informal get-togethers.

In schools teachers may give some individual attention to students within classes, so again the teacher and student are in a one-to-one relationship. Such attention may, in some schools, occur after the class or after school.

This is the situation that is being duplicated with computer-based learning. That is, an interactive "conversation" between the computer or, better, with the developers of the computer material, and individual students or small groups is being set up. So the tutorial process is our model of computer-based learning.

Computer material must be designed to allow for not just a single conversation between student and teacher but rather an entire set of all possible conversations. The conversation may also have some random components. Since the "computer teacher" has more computational abilities than an ordinary teacher, in the interaction it can use many more mathematical or other details than the human teacher can.

Perhaps the most important difference is that with computer material we have far more chance to "improve" the conversation. The computer-student conversation can get better and better over time as the weaknesses in the program are discovered through testing with students, and as both the interaction and the information presented are improved. Generally, a teacher-student conversation is a single conversation. When the next student comes in, the teacher may have learned something about the process, but it is often hard to quantify exactly what was learned. With the computer's extensive record-keeping capabilities, it is much more possible to improve interaction.

The student-computer dialog allows better graphic possibilities, since the computer can generally draw much better pictures than a professor can on the blackboard. These pictures can depend on extensive calculations, again an advantage over the teacher.

It should be noted that the computer is *not* a workbook; it is highly interactive. Furthermore, it is not programmed instruction because again, many of these features—high interaction, graphics, computational capabilities—are capabilities that are out of the question in programmed instruction.

Given this interactive model of the student-computer relationship, it is fair to refer to computer-based learning material as *dialog*. Dialog is the classic term referring to a high degree of interaction.

EXAMPLES OF COMPUTER-BASED LEARNING

The materials to be described represent some of the best material of their type.

Arithmetical Drill and Practice

One of the oldest uses of computers in learning situations concerned drill-and-practice material in arithmetic and reading. It began about 1963, by Patrick Suppes and Richard Atkinson at Stanford University. Of all computer-based learning material available, this is probably the oldest, most widely used, most widely sold, most widely criticized, most widely studied and tested, and most widely imitated.

The basic notion of the arithmetic drill and practice is very simple. The student at the computer display sees a problem, such as the task of summing two numbers, and types an answer. The student sees immediately whether or not the answer is correct, and the computer proceeds to another problem. Multiple attempts may be allowed. The computer randomly creates the problems, using a series of problem generators, each generating a problem of a given type. The computer presents students with problems of a given type until they attain proficiency, as defined by either the teacher or the program. Students move to increasingly difficult problems, through "strands." The choice of strands is based on available research information on the learning of arithmetic.

The system collects information about student performance. It provides student management information for the teacher in the form of reports on students' progress. Using this information, the teacher can then give individualized attention to just those students who need specialized help. So the teacher's effort can be focused where it is most needed.

Earlier versions of this system worked primarily with typewriterlike display devices, hard copy, while more recent versions use TV-like computer screens. The Suppes-Atkinson material has been improved and refined over the years, yet it maintains essentially the same basic structure it had initially.

Computer Curriculum Corporation in Palo Alto markets this material. Because of the need for the management capabilities, as discussed above and in more detail in the next chapter, it is usually run on small timesharing systems, computers where several students use the same computer. Recently the Computer Curriculum Corporation has advertised it for the Sony personal computer. The computer and the software in the timesharing version are not sold separately, but are leased as a single package. Thus school districts may contract for a certain number of student displays.

This product has been, by far, the most commercially successful computer-based learning material. It is used in schools all over the United States, often for students behind in their arithmetic capabilities, as indicated by standardized tests. This prevailing pattern of use may be largely due to the peculiarities of funding; remediation programs have been funded at the federal level, and therefore the acquisition and use of the drill-and-practice materials have been primarily for these students.

From its earliest days many experimental studies have been based on the use of this drill-and-practice material. As very large numbers of students use it in many different parts of the country, unparalleled possibilities for sizable studies of statistical significance have been available. The impressive experimental studies of the Suppes-Atkinson material are mostly quite positive. Using this material students do improve in grade level a good bit faster than without this kind of help. Little curriculum material of any type, with or without a computer, has been studied so carefully.

Perhaps the most extensive recent study was made by the Educational Testing Service using the arithmetical drill-and-practice material in the Los Angeles schools. This was a longitudinal study, meaning that students were followed over several years. Again, the results were encouraging.

Probably because of the commercial success of the Computer Curriculum Corporation and because the drill-and-practice exercises are relatively easy to program, many companies have imitated this computer-based learning material. These imitations are probably the most widely available of all commercial learning material on computers. Most of the imitations, however, fall short of the management capabilities just mentioned as an important component of the Suppes-Atkinson product. In some cases no information is available for the teacher. The imitators have often made some attempt to add more graphic capabilities than in the original material; but in the examples I have seen, graphic use is not impressive. Rather, it is often at the level of gimmickry. Graphic information is important, but it should aid learning.

Finally, as I have mentioned, this drill-and-practice material, and to some extent all computer drill-and-practice material, has been subject to considerable criticism. Today such materials can be developed with far more interactive tutorial aid, based on careful internal analysis of the difficulties students are having. Some educators feel that drill and practice, while clearly very important in our current non-computer-based education, is not desirable with or without computers. So they object to the arithmetic drill-and-practice material for the computer in spite of its empirical and commercial success. Fundamental philosophical attitudes toward learning and course content are involved in such a dispute. I will not discuss them further, as they go far beyond our concern with the computer.

Sentence Combining

The second example of computer-based learning, intended to improve the style of writing in English for students in grades four to eight, was developed by Irene and Owen Thomas of the University of California, Irvine. It is published by Millicom. The basic purpose of this material is to teach students to build longer sentences from shorter ones by providing practice opportunities. Thus it deals with an important aid to writing, sentence combining.

The material begins by presenting the notion of "describing words," getting students to begin to think about how more such words can be used. A typical early example presented to the student is one with two sentences, such as: "I have a kitten. My kitten is black." The aim is to get the student to see that these two sentences can really be written as a single one.

In this program, the interactive mechanisms are better than usual. The mechanisms for denoting words or locations, such as boxes or arrows, move through the sentences, and the student presses the space bar to indicate a choice. Exercises are slightly more complicated in that the student must change the form of a word—from adjective to adverb, for example—before combining the two short sentences into a single long one. A teacher's guide with auxiliary exercises is available.

Young Children and The Learning Company

Programs developed by The Learning Company are intended for much younger children than are the other examples. Some of the units are intended for preschool children from three years and up, while others are for students of elementary school age. The units are suitable for both school and home.

Most of The Learning Company's material is gamelike and makes effective use of graphics and color. This use of color distinguishes The Learning Company's material; since the current generation of inexpensive personal computers has weak color capabilities, few products use color effectively.

Juggle's Rainbow is the program intended for the youngest children. It introduces such ideas as above and below and left and right and also works on some letters of the alphabet in a series of playlike activities. The two *Bumble* programs introduce notions of coordinate systems, working toward plotting considerations. *Rocky's Boots* is concerned with a gamelike activity for learning some of the ideas of logic, and *Gertrude* expands further on logical thinking ideas and reasoning skills.

Batteries and Bulbs

This program is the first of several developed by Arnold Arons, myself, and Barry Kurtz at the Educational Technology Center.* Stephen Franklin and Francis Collea helped with some modules, and Ruth von Blum and Barry Kurtz carried out the formative evaluation. *Batteries and Bulbs* is part of a series of programs concerned with scientific literacy, raising such issues as what a scientific theory is, how theories are discovered, and the predictive power and empirical basis of theories. These are difficult topics for students, so science courses in both schools and universities often ignore them; in classes where they are covered, they are frequently treated very superficially.

Our primary strategy in the scientific literacy series is to put the student in the role of a scientist, stimulating behavior much like what would be expected of a scientist in a similar situation. Thus the programs have some components of a "discovery method"; the student can gather empirical data, study them, develop hypotheses relating to them, base predictions on those hypotheses, test the predictions empirically, and modify the hypotheses, if necessary. The modules, developed with support from the Fund for the Improvement of Postsecondary Education in the Department of Education, encompass a variety of subjects in science and mathematics.

The *Batteries and Bulbs* program in the scientific literacy series takes average students about two hours; the time varies considerably. Like all materials from the Educational Technology Center, it is programmed in Pascal. The program is approximately 15,000 lines long. (Production strategies for generating this program are reviewed in chapters 11 and 12.)

The program consists of eight submodules, each taking the average student about fifteen

*A. Arons, A. Bork, F. Collea, S. Franklin, and B. Kurtz, "Science Literacy in the Public Library—*Batteries and Bulbs*" (Proceedings of the National Educational Computing Conference, June 1981); NECC-Lausanne, "Learning with Computers in Public Environments" (Proceedings of Third World Conference on Computers in Education; Lausanne, Switzerland, 1981).

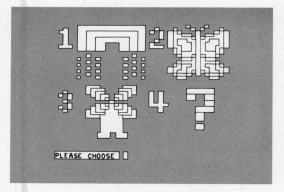 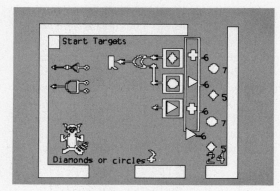

Figure 5.1 *Left:* screen display from *Juggle's Rainbow; right:* screen display from *Rocky's Boots.* (Courtesy of the Learning Company.)

minutes. Students can enter any of these sub-modules from a map, a selection menu, at the beginning of the program.

The first submodule is experiential: The problem posed is how to light the bulb. The student can connect wires in any fashion to the battery and bulb, and the computer faithfully draws these connections. At first, very little aid is given to the student except the visually obvious indication that the bulb fails to light or does light. But the computer records what the student does, and eventually a "tutor" within the program offers assistance to students making little progress.

Although turning on an electric light appears to be a simple task, experience shows that some students, even at the university level, will spend

hours at the program without success when given no help. So it is essential for the program to help students, when necessary. Students cannot be expected to discover the laws of the universe on their own!

In the second module, the students, who have found two ways to light the bulb, are asked to verbalize the results. Users develop some vocabulary (the word *circuit*) and see many examples of possible circuits. The purpose of these examples is to be sure students understand the concepts developed; that is, it checks whether they know under what circumstances the bulb will light.

Learning and testing are combined in a single format, with testing used to guide future learning. Indeed, this combination is a major

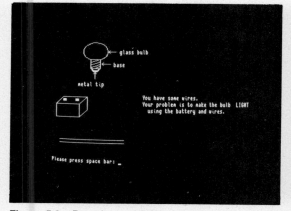 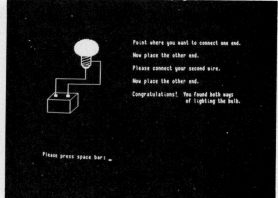

Figure 5.2 *Batteries and Bulbs,* Module 1. (*Source:* Educational Technology Center, UC Irvine.)

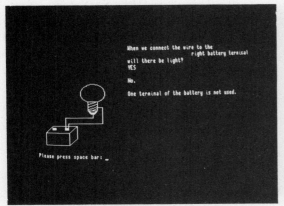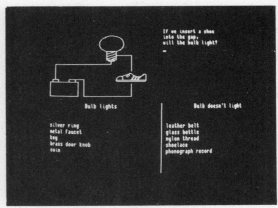

Figure 5.3 *Batteries and Bulbs,* Modules 2 and 3. (*Source:* Educational Technology Center, UC Irvine.)

strength of computers in many areas of education, although it seldom gets much attention.

Later submodules introduce such terms as *current* and *resistance*, but only after students already have mastered the corresponding concepts. The terms are used only in a comparative sense, not in a numerical sense. Thus students say that "the current in this wire is greater than the current in that wire because this light bulb is brighter than that light bulb."

The critical aspect of the *Batteries and Bulbs* program is the development of a *model,* a theory of what happens in simple electrical circuits. The aim of the dialog is to get students to evolve this theory for themselves; we avoid the typical vocabulary-oriented approaches. Words such as *electrons* and *charge* never appear in this computer dialog. Words are introduced only when they are justified by the experimental data, in contrast to many science courses.

In later modules emphasis shifts to prediction, based on the model of the circuit already developed. That is, can students say what will happen in the circuit under certain conditions? The dialog shows that the value of a scientific theory lies in successful prediction.

Readers familiar with recent curriculum development may recognize an intellectual heritage for *Batteries and Bulbs*. Similar curriculum units were developed without using computers in several large elementary and secondary sci-

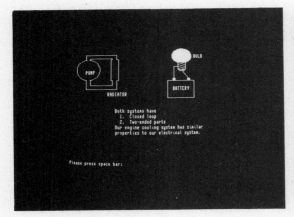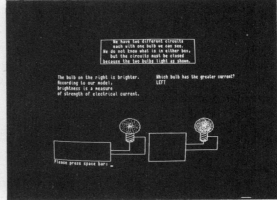

Figure 5.4 *Batteries and Bulbs* on the concept of current. (*Source:* Educational Technology Center, UC Irvine.)

ence curriculum development projects in the late 1960s. Students used equipment supplied in kit form. A curriculum development associated with the new medium, the computer, benefited by borrowing ideas from an earlier successful curriculum development. The original form is quite dependent on experienced teachers and on teachers' being able to provide students with highly individualized attention, a situation that is seldom the case in classrooms. Furthermore, in the earlier instance, teachers, responsible for equipment, had the logistic problems of maintaining and reordering the necessary components, and this turned out to be a time-consuming task. Computers simulate the equipment in the kits, in the science literacy dialogs, obviating these logistic problems. Teachers or students who *do* want to use the kits, however, and have access to them, can still do so, with or without the computer program.

Sophie

Sophie is a program developed by John Seeley Brown while at Bolt Beranek and Newman in Cambridge, Massachusetts. *Sophie* is concerned with fault finding in a complicated electrical circuit. A fault is generated in the circuit, and the student's task is to find it. The program is oriented toward training technicians to locate such faults.

The student can make various measurements, such as checking voltages and currents,

in different places in the circuit. The student can also develop hypotheses as to where the possible fault lies. The program is capable of telling the student if the hypothesis is consistent with the data and, if not, pointing out just why it is not. It can also recommend other tests that need to be made.

Unlike most of the computer-based programs described, *Sophie* uses tactics from artificial intelligence research. It contains a model of the knowledge necessary to carry out the given task, finding a fault in the circuit, and can respond to a wide range of user vocabulary also. Because of this built-in knowledge base, *Sophie* is a much larger and more complex program. It demands a computer larger than today's personal computer, but programs of this kind will probably soon be possible on newer generations of personal computers. *Sophie* suffers from the fact that it was done in a nongraphical environment—only text is output.

Physics Quizzes

The next example was prepared at the Educational Technology Center in 1975; it concerns an introductory physics course. These materials, developed in a timesharing environment, will, we hope, soon be available commercially for personal computers.

The setting is the beginning mechanics segment of the introductory physics course for science and engineering majors, the calculus course. This course is taught very similarly al-

```
>>WHAT IS THE OUTPUT?
THE OUTPUT VOLTAGE IS 11.7 VOLTS.
>>WHAT IS THE VOLTAGE BETWEEN R8 AND Q1?
THE VOLTAGE AT N1 IS 47.6 VOLTS.
>>WHAT IS THE BSE EMITTER VOLTAGE OF THE VOLTAGE
LIMITING TRANSISTOR?
=BASE
=TRANSISTOR
THE BASE EMITTER VOLTAGE OF Q5 IS −0.037 MILLIVOLTS.
>>WHAT ABOUT FOR THE CURRENT LIMITING TRANSISTOR?
THE BASE EMITTER VOLTAGE OF Q6 IS 0.349 VOLTS.
```

Figure 5.5 Interaction with *Sophie*. (With permission from *International Journal of Man-Machine Studies*, copyright 1975 by Academic Press Inc (London) Limited.)

most everywhere in the United States, and similar courses are also taught elsewhere.

As offered the last five years at Irvine, students choose among three different versions of the course. One is a standard course with standard teaching methods. About one quarter of the students select this noncomputer course; I will not describe it further.

The other two versions of the course are computer-based, differing only in content. One has the same content as the standard course, while the other has a different content, using the computer as an intellectual tool as well as in the ways I am about to describe. The two computer courses are self-paced with students progressing at different rates. The course insists on *mastery;* students are not allowed to proceed to the next unit until they have performed more or less perfectly on unit quizzes. Such courses, which usually do not use computers, are referred to as PSI or Keller plan courses.

All the quizzes in the computer-based tracks are given on-line at computer displays. These quizzes, like the *Batteries and Bulbs* material, combine learning and teaching within a single format, but students identify the material as a quiz, rather than as learning sequence. As soon as difficulties occur, quizzes shift to a *learning* mode, often giving very direct help by picking out common errors made by students and responding directly to them. So the aid provided is individualized to the needs of each student.

As students must do almost perfectly, they typically take a quiz more than once, on average about 2½ times. With the large number of students in this section of the course (more than 400), *many* quizzes are given by the computer. During winter 1982 about 15,000 on-line quizzes were given in ten weeks. The same quiz is never given twice, and therefore the instructors encourage students to discuss the quizzes among themselves. A number of factors are selected by the computer randomly at run time to vary the quizzes, but each quiz for a unit covers the same objectives.

One example of an on-line quiz deals with Newton's laws. The problems involve blocks sliding down inclined planes and ropes over pulleys in various configurations; the tactics for solution are often called free body diagrams.

This program begins by asking students if they would first like help. A help sequence is not counted as part of the forty-minute time allowed for quizzes. Students are free to choose help or not. Then the quiz generates a problem, with the computer choosing one of six different types. It chooses the data randomly, within limits specified by the developers of the quiz.

This problem demands two numerical answers from the students. If students have trouble with the first answer, they are first asked to try it again; a calculational or a typing error may have occurred. If the trouble persists, students are then asked again whether they would like a help sequence. The interactive help sequence has several "jumping off" points that are under students' control. That is, students may continue the quiz after a little assistance or may become immersed in a long help sequence. In the second case they either start the quiz over again or work on it another day.

The help sequences are very detailed. They first outline the strategy before they let students pick a mechanical subsystem, a part of the total system, and then they ask students to write the correct equation of motion for that subsystem. Specific help is given in case of student difficulties.

There are 27 different quizzes available in the two tracks, the two different courses available, all concerned with mechanics. The results of each quiz are stored in the computer; management systems to give aid to the student and to the teacher are discussed in the next chapter. The computer also controls access to the quizzes. Thus students who have not completed a quiz are not allowed to take the next quiz. Students who have not passed a quiz after four attempts are told by the computer that they cannot repeat the quiz again until they have contacted the instructor.

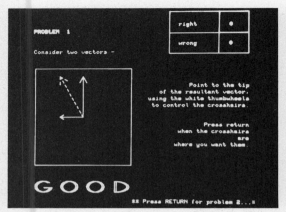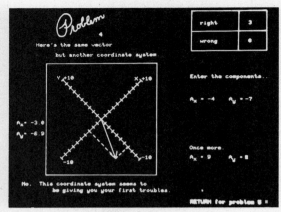

Figure 5.6 Physics quizzes on vectors. (*Source:* Educational Technology Center, UC Irvine.)

A Controllable World for Mechanics

Another program developed at the Educational Technology Center, although still concerned with the introductory physics course and with mechanics, has an entirely different pedagogical orientation from the course just discussed and fulfills quite a different role within the class structure.*

The idea of a controllable world, a term used at the Educational Technology Center for more than ten years, is to provide a student-oriented facility on the computer, a tool that allows students to experiment or even play with relevant phenomena. It is hoped that this play, perhaps structured in some way by the computer or by other learning modes, will develop students' insight about physics; therefore building intuition, through experience with motion, is the main objective. Many formal courses do not help students develop such an intuitive grasp but rather only teach a set of techniques. Similar programs have been called microworlds by the Logo group at MIT.

Since this program deals with mechanics, experiences involving forces with various initial conditions are provided. The program allows students to pick forces, constants, and initial

*This material should soon be available from CON-DUIT.

conditions as well as choose what is plotted. The format is easy to use; students are not asked for large amounts of information at any one time. The program recognizes a wide English and symbolic vocabulary. Thus if a student wants to plot something, words like plot, draw, or graph all work. All the parameters in the equations can be changed, and students can enter their own force laws in addition to using built-in ones.

The most powerful feature is the program's graphing capability. Students can plot any two or three physically meaningful variables against each other and so watch the system develop in time. They can even plot functions of the variables against each other.

In extensive use of this and other controllable worlds we discovered long ago at the Educational Technology Center that although they are very exciting to the professional, they are *not* necessarily exciting to all students in a large beginning class. Used by themselves, they often are entirely inadequate. Auxiliary material, such as workbooks directing students toward interesting cases to study, is essential for controllable worlds to function well in a large class environment. Material developed and tested with only a few students may perform poorly for large groups of unselected students, so it is important when developing materials to test with real student populations. Evaluation is dis-

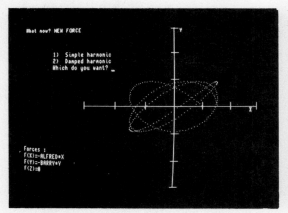 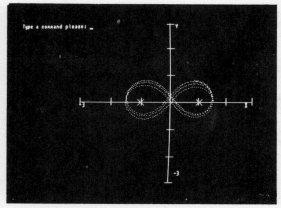

Figure 5.7 A controllable world in mechanics. (*Source:* Educational Technology Center, UC Irvine.)

cussed further in chapters 11 and 12, in the context of developing material.

A Logic Course

In the first example in this chapter we examined the elementary drill-and-practice material developed by Patrick Suppes and Richard Atkinson. Suppes has also been involved in extensive development of college-level courses based on computers. Two particular categories have been emphasized, logic and language. The first of these categories has resulted in complete courses in logic and set theory. The second teaches languages, currently Russian, Old Church Slavonic, and Armenian. These language courses use some of the same underlying strategies involved in the logic course; in particular, they make extensive use of the computer's voice capabilities.

The logic courses are in regular use at Stanford and are the standard ones available to students. Thus, like the physics course, they are essentially fully computer-dependent courses.

The logic course runs on a large timesharing computer, not a personal computer, and makes use of extensive computer capabilities. From the user's point of view, it has two quite contrasting

components. The first component is didactic, teaching in the usual sense. This material is not as interactive as much of the computer material described in this book, but it does involve active use of the computer's *voice*. The main body of the learning material is essentially delivered by the computer as a lecture, with the computer screen often serving as a summarizing "blackboard." Students have the option of repeating sections not understood, and they can also vary the *rate* of presentation. The sound, of good quality, comes initially from a human speaker and is stored digitally in the computer. That is, it is coded in a computer-readable form rather than as sound is normally stored on magnetic tape for tape recorders. This form of storage allows the computer to vary the rate of sound output, without altering pitch, and so lets the student control this rate.

In addition to these noninteractive sections of the material, a second component, highly interactive exercises, occurs frequently. In the logic course these exercises are based on elaborate proof checkers. The student is asked to prove a particular result in logic. The computer is capable of accepting the student's statements and seeing whether they lead to a successful proof and also of offering detailed assistance. The computer can generate proofs to display to the student and can also make suggestions. Both highly formal and informal (typically human) proofs are possible. The techniques of artificial intelligence, referred to in the *Sophie* example, are also used in these elegant proof-checking programs.

Medical Education Involving Computers and Optical Videodisks

The optical videodisk is a relatively new technology that can be combined with a computer to furnish an interesting environment for learning, appropriate in certain situations. It is discussed in more detail in chapter 13, since its applications are mostly in the future. Disks are already available for the continuing medical education of doctors. Because of the content, they are not suitable for general audiences. This computer-plus-videodisk learning material has been developed by WICAT in Orem, Utah. I will describe the first disk prepared: a diagnosis of gastrointestinal problems.

The videodisk allows video sequences, slides, and sound to be part of the computer-based instructional sequence. The sequence is still controlled by the computer, as with the other material discussed.

The program begins by asking the doctor some questions. Several cases are available on the disk, and a case appropriate to that doctor's situation is first picked. The first sequence shown after this is a patient "interview." The patient describes symptoms just as an actual patient might do in a visit to the doctor. Naturally these descriptions are vague, as viewed from the doctor's point of view.

The doctor can then request that various tests be made. In the present version, a multiple-choice format is used, but a more sophisticated version might allow free choice of tests without prompting the doctor. The doctor can prescribe treatment and can make diagnoses, and so can determine the patient's problem and how to treat it. As indicated, several "cases" are available, so the doctor can practice on several pa-

tients. Clearly, this type of practice can have much less in the way of "consequences" than practice on live people!

Writing to Read

The *Writing to Read* program is one of the most ambitious curriculum development programs involving computers yet to be undertaken, perhaps *the* most elaborate. Although the program is not complete, and testing is still going on, it deserves mention. For a program of this size and importance, it has received surprisingly little publicity up to this time (August 1983).

The developer of this program is a retired teacher and school administrator, John Henry Martin. He has been involved in early attempts at introducing improved methods of reading, including phonic spelling methods. The project is supported by IBM.

The basic strategy is that preschool or first-grade pupils should be able to learn easily to type any word they can speak. Furthermore, children who can type a word should be able to read the word. The key is a phonetic way of spelling, not the peculiar spelling of ordinary English. *Writing to Read* is a coherent piece of extensive curriculum development, not an isolated fragment.

The project makes use of both sound and color graphics. The sound is digitized, as in the logic course, and of high quality. The graphics are excellent, as are the arrangements of the screen. But not all the material fully utilizes the interactive capabilities of the computer.

In addition to the computer, other learning resources are used. Typewriters are available to the student, as are workbooks, tapes, books, and a variety of other materials. As a casual observer, I believe that too many different modes of learning may be involved, making the task of managing the program too difficult for the teacher. But only experience will tell. The program is now being tested with 15,000 students by Educational Testing Service.

This is an impressive project, and one that

deserves much further scrutiny. It could be a forerunner of much more elaborate full-scale curriculum development, necessary in the years ahead. It is also significant that a computer company has been willing to fund the project.

These examples of computer-based learning material illustrate the wide range of possibilities. Many other examples of good material also exist. Even more important, our skill in producing such material is increasing.

chapter 6

Management Systems

- Testing
- Sequencing of Materials
- What Information Is Stored?
- Teacher Aids
- Student Aids
- Examples of Management Systems

Computers have been used in learning situations to manage segments of courses or curricula. The primary focus in computer-based management systems is on the computer's data-gathering and data-interpreting aspects. As with other areas of computer uses in education, no one system can be deemed a "typical" computer-managed system. Rather, many variants are possible. Depending on the situation, various features of management systems may or may not be desirable.

At the simplest level a computer-managed instructional system may be no more than a

convenient way of keeping class records, a useful function when class size is large. That is, everything else about the class may proceed in the usual fashion, but the teacher keeps the students' records such as grades in the computer. At a more complicated level the system may provide detailed information and advice to both the instructor *and* students, and possibly to others, about students' progress. A sophisticated computer-based management system may be able to spot students' difficulties and recommend specialized actions to remedy them.

In this chapter some examples of management systems are specially adapted to the Personalized System of Instruction or other systems based on mastery. In such systems the student must master the work in one unit before proceeding to the next unit. So different students move at different rates through the course.

Management systems are often tied to a behavioral view of the learning process that imagines every course to be a series of behavioral objectives and so orients tests toward demonstrating each of the objectives. This is only one possibility for course organization, and management systems can also work for other views of the learning process.

An existing course may need to be modified before it can fit into a computer-managed system. If the course and management system are developed together, then the system can be tailored to the particular strategies of that course.

TESTING

Testing is at the heart of most computer-based class management systems. Tests may be given in the usual manner, not involving computers at all, with only the information about test performance for each student entered on the computer. For example, a score for each test might be stored. Or more detailed information about test performance, such as data about each problem, may be kept by the management system.

Information can be entered for conventional tests either directly (perhaps by giving the test with computer-readable marked sense cards), or the teacher or someone else can enter information about each test. Or, better, the testing may be directly *on-line* at the computer. We have seen in chapter 5, pages 68–69, an example of on-line testing. The on-line test, combined with an effective management system and adequate student assistance, can be an extremely powerful tool in learning, affording many opportunities not available in standard noncomputer testing environments.

In an on-line test the computer typically "constructs" the test, perhaps a unique test for each student. Individual items or questions in the test can take a great many forms. First, they may simply be single questions occurring on every test given. Second, questions may be selected from a *pool* of test items, either by random techniques or by some combination of random techniques and identifiers (associated with each question) for the type of question, the difficulty, or other factors. In this situation, the developers have selected the collection of test items. Third, questions may come from *problem generators,* procedures that generate a wide range of different problems according to specified rules or algorithms given by the tests' developers. I believe that questions from problem generators are the most desirable type, but a mixture of forms may have some advantage.

The notion of a problem generator may be new to some readers, so I will give an example from the physics quizzes already discussed. This quiz presents a single problem to each student, a numerical problem concerning projectile motion typical in beginning high school or college physics. When the student starts the quiz, the computer first chooses randomly one of five different types of projectile motion problems. Fundamentally these types are really all identical, but they have different descriptions and may appear different to the student. Thus one type of problem involves throwing a ball off a building, while another involves a moving car. The computer picks randomly which variables are to be known and which are to be unknown. Finally, the computer picks values of the known variables, within ranges specified by the program developers. The problem generator can provide the full range of projectile motion problems common in beginning physics books; no two students ever receive the same problem.

Another advantage of both pools of problems and, more particularly, problem generators, is that they can serve in testing environments that insist on mastery. In such environments students do not proceed to further tests until they perform essentially perfectly on prior ones. Many essentially equivalent but still different tests are necessary in these cases. Also, since the computer generates tests individually for each student, students can be encouraged to discuss the test among themselves, allowing and encouraging valuable aspects of peer learning.

Several extensive test item pools exist. I am not favorably impressed by the overall quality of these pools in subject areas familiar to me. There are two major problems: It is difficult to ensure the quality of items, and the types of questions in the pools are limited.

Another way of classifying computer test items is by the type of student response needed to reply to the questions. Response types included multiple-choice items, fill-in-the-word items, numerical-response items (typical in science and mathematics), and English-language-response questions. As I mentioned a number of times, I am opposed to multiple-choice tests, which are often referred to by students as "multiple-guess" questions, with or without computers. The major difficulty with these questions is that by looking at a set of possible answers, students can eliminate a few of the possibilities as being obviously wrong and then make reasonable guesses among the others. Much of the extensive "literature" on test taking for students is oriented toward developing such tactics. These tactics subvert finding out what someone knows or learns! Multiple-choice tests were developed many years ago when, with much more primitive computer equipment than we have today, large numbers of students had to be tested. Multiple-choice questions are neither necessary nor in any sense desirable at present and should be avoided in computer-based testing. A number of strategies of a similar nature that do *not* expose all the answers to students are possible and can be used in testing via computer.

One of the major advantages of on-line testing, and perhaps its hallmark as compared to testing without computers, is the possibility of immediate feedback, response, and help to students. This can be at a very simple level, indicating to students whether an answer was correct

or not. Or it might be desirable to provide students with correct responses if their answers are not correct. It may or may not be desirable to reinforce in some way, perhaps visually, a correct response. Finally, it may be desirable to give help, perhaps very detailed help, to students in difficulty. Indeed, it is often possible in an on-line test to identify the student's difficulty precisely and give very specific and tailored interactive aid to the student. In some versatile quizzing systems, these facilities for detailed help can be turned on or off by the instructor.

Where detailed assistance is available and perceptively given relative to students' needs, then tests begin to outgrow the realm of "mere testing" and becomes an important part of the student learning system. It is possible to construct full courses *entirely* based on tests, with *no* didactic learning material separate from the testing environment. The physics course described in chapter 5 is a step in that direction. From the learner's viewpoint the courses would be very different from today's conventional courses. Students would quickly pass over material they already know, not wasting valuable study time. On the other hand, students in difficulty or with background deficiencies would receive very detailed help.

If help sequences within tests are to be useful, they must be more than just a "message" of advice; they should be highly interactive *(not passive)* and responsive to the needs of the learner. These help sequences can be in the best tradition of good computer-based learning. Such help sequences may be needed for each question, with different approaches to learning so that as many students can be helped as possible.

SEQUENCING OF MATERIALS

A function of some management systems is to sequence the materials, either uniquely specifying an order to the course or recommending a particular sequence.

Typically sequencing refers to the order in

which the quizzes can be taken. In some course organizational structures students are allowed to take a quiz only after they have completed certain other quizzes. This is typical in the Personalized System of Instruction, or Keller plan, courses where students are kept on a quiz until they master it. An alternate possibility is to allow students to take quizzes at any time during the course in any order. Or some quizzes may be sequenced, some not. To sequence quizzes, the management system must know the structure of courses and the required order.

I do not wish to suggest whether it is better to sequence or not to sequence course materials. This issue is still debatable. Instructors usually assume some logical sequence is present in the subject, and they structure lectures and textbooks accordingly. That is, they believe that one concept *must* precede another. These same instructors will often feel very strongly, therefore, about sequencing a course in a particular way. This idea of a "natural" or "necessary" sequence is common, so it is not surprising that such organizational structures as the Keller plan require it. Both experimental and theoretical studies suggest that, at least for some students, rigid sequencing may not be desirable. As with many other aspects of using the computer in education, students' decisions will reflect their pedagogical strategies and perhaps the subject area. These decisions typically have little to do with the technology.

WHAT INFORMATION IS STORED?

The heart of most computer-based management systems will be a *student database,* a collection of information stored in computer memory about students, their performance on tests, and perhaps other information. Efficient storage of this information may be a key factor in the effectiveness of the management system. Disk storage is required for an extensive class database (see chapter 9). Floppy disks can present logistics problems, because a database for a large

class may not fit on one disk. The design of a complex database is a job for a professional.

The student information can be entered in several ways. First a class list must be entered in the computer. A computer-readable record of students in the class may already be available from the registrar. In many schools and universities computers help with class registration, so it may be possible to obtain the list of students from tape or other storage media or through the computer itself. In most cases capabilities will be necessary in the course management system for "registering" new students in the course database, those entering after the usual registration period, "dropping" students from the course (with possible retention of their records if desired by the instructor), and changing information about students, possibly because it was initially in error or because of other changes (a woman marries and wishes to change her last name, for example).

A teacher may also want to decide just what auxiliary information about students to save, and a versatile system will allow considerable freedom. Thus it may sometimes be desirable to store student addresses. Or it may be desirable to store results of testing previous to the course, or in a university it may be useful to record the student's year and major. A system that keeps only very limited information may not be very useful.

In addition to student information, a typical management system will also store information about the results of students' tests. The data might simply be overall results, such as recording a pass or a fail or a detailed grade, or it might be very detailed information about which questions were missed or exactly what difficulties occurred within each test.

As mentioned, this information can be put into the computer in several ways. In the case of on-line testing, the computer itself can place this information directly into the database. For off-line testing, on personal computers or not on computers, the results must somehow reach the computer, either through on-line entry of the information or by marked sense cards or forms. Unfortunately, marked sense cards are restricted primarily to multiple-choice tests, which I consider undesirable; it is possible, but cumbersome, to use such cards also for numerical answer tests and for *very* limited free-response testing. If teachers must enter the data, this can be very time-consuming.

A final set of issues about the information stored is associated with security of information. That is, who should have various types of access to the data, who is allowed to enter data, who is allowed to change data, and who is allowed to read the data? For example, while it is clearly not desirable to make it easy for students to alter their own records, the teacher may need to make such changes.

Many methods are used to protect data to ensure that the access allowed is acceptable. The data can be broken into separate pieces (files), and each file can require a keyword or perhaps different keywords for different access types. The data can be duplicated, and the two sources can be checked against each other. The data can be stored in complicated ways, so that only an expert could use it within the proper programs. The data might be coded (encrypted), so that read directly it has no meaning. Again, this is an area for specialists in database design. No information can be made completely secure, but in practice data can be sufficiently protected.

TEACHER AIDS

In this section I discuss the information a management system can supply to a *teacher* about individual students and the class as a whole. The next section considers the student.

It may be desirable to have a facility in the management system for producing on paper, either at regular intervals or on instructor demand, a computer-generated "grade book." Sometimes the instructor needs immediate information about student performance, perhaps in situations where it is inconvenient or impossible to access directly the computer-stored database. In such situations a printed record is valuable.

In addition to storing the initial data itself, the management system may make and store various calculations about the data. Thus it may be useful to store student averages or information about relative rank in class. When it is time for grades, other computations are useful either to determine the course grades or to assist the instructor in the process. One intermediate case would be for instructors to specify a grading structure and have the computer query about each student who is close to one of the boundaries in the grading system. This query could present the complete student record.

A major use of the course management database for teachers is to identify course problems, either problems about the curriculum material or students' problems. In a Personalized System of Instruction or Keller plan system, where students move at their own pace, they can procrastinate and do *nothing* at all. These students are easily spotted in the database, and teachers can offer individualized help to them. Also, students with similar problems can gather together and receive assistance specific to their needs.

Another recognizable difficulty that can be reported to teachers concerns ineffectiveness of the tests or learning material. Thus if all students score very poorly on a particular test, it is a strong indication that either the test is inadequate or the learning material is not sufficient to the students's needs. Since the object of education is *not* to fail students, something must be done to improve the course. Thus the course can evolve by such feedback and be improved over the years.

STUDENT AIDS

Another quite different use of a management system is less common but in some ways even more valuable than the teacher-oriented facilities just described. A good computer management system can supply information directly to *students* to aid them in the learning process.

Some of the student information might be very simple. For example, the management system could provide information to a student

II

FURTHER DETAILS ABOUT THE COMPUTER

The chapters in part II cover a variety of topics. Chapters 7 and 8 are recommended for all readers. Chapter 7 considers the advantages and disadvantages of the computer in education, particularly emphasizing the issues of interaction and individualization. Chapter 8 gives teachers a basis for selecting curriculum material that involves the computer. The issue of standards, of convincing publishers that they should be producing better materials, is important; it is critical that teachers and others who pick material begin to understand the difference between what is good and what is bad.

Chapter 9 is the first of two chapters on hardware. (Chapter 13, which repeats some of the information in chapter 9, looks at hardware from a future viewpoint.) It is not necessary that everyone know all the details of hardware. It is far less important for teachers to know about hardware than it is for them to be able to recognize decent computer-based learning material. However, some knowledge of hardware will undoubtedly be useful for many users of the computer in education.

Chapter 10 considers some of the practical aspects of computers in schools and universities. It considers such questions as where computers are to be located, and who uses the computers.

Chapters 11 and 12 discuss the production of computer-based learning materials. Not all teachers will be involved in producing materials, but some may eventually be doing so. The system discussed is based on the production strategies that have been developed at the Educational Technology Center at the University of California, Irvine, widely used for a variety of learning material employing the computer.

chapter 7

Advantages and Disadvantages of Computers in Education

- Theories of Learning and Curriculum Development
- Advantages of Computers in Education
- Current Disadvantages of Computers in Education

It is important for teachers learning about computers to understand that computers, like any component of modern technology, are neither inherently good nor inherently evil in learning applications. Powerful technological devices like the computer have the *potential* for both good and bad. We must recognize these potentials and try to emphasize the good and diminish the bad, if education using computers is to improve.

Good material is essential for realizing computers' advantages. The computer alone, as a piece of equipment, is of little direct interest in education. Only the development of a variety of educational tools and materials based on sound curriculum principles will allow the computer to be useful in education.

To understand some of the computer's advantages and disadvantages in education, I must talk a little about learning in a more general sense. Learning with computers is first and fundamentally *learning!* Hence to see how computers could serve the learning process, we should review briefly what we know about learning.

Unfortunately, we know less than is desirable. Today's professional literature is full of conflicting notions of the learning and teaching process; probably all of these notions will be judged inadequate in the future. Furthermore, many recent major searches into the workings of the mind have shown relatively little interest in practical questions of learning. Since learning is an important human attribute, it is perhaps surprising that so little is known about it.

THEORIES OF LEARNING AND CURRICULUM DEVELOPMENT

Learning theories can be classified in several categories. None of these approaches is fully adequate and even the classification scheme is almost certain to change. These different learning theories are concerned with questions of how the mind works in the learning activity, but from different points of view. A full neurological theory based on the structure of the brain may be developed in the future, but no current learning theory comes close to being complete; too little is known about brain organization to provide highly useful information about learning theory. Therefore, educators and curriculum developers must work with only partial, incomplete theories.

Behavioral Psychology

Behavioral psychology has played a major role in determining directions of much curriculum development. I will not attempt to discuss all the variants of behavioral psychology. Basically, classical behaviorists maintain that what goes on in the brain itself is, scientifically, *unknowable.* They maintain that humans can only deal with the *stimuli,* the inputs to the brain, and the *responses,* the behavioral outcomes, of the stimuli. Theories of this kind are sometimes called SR theories, emphasizing stimulus and response.

A very influential behavioral approach to learning was B. F. Skinner's work around 1940, teaching pigeons to peck very complex patterns.

Skinner broke the entire task down to a series of small subtasks, rewarded success on the small tasks, usually with food, and, in some situations, punished lack of success.

Programmed learning, with programmed texts, was also very much influenced by this Skinnerian view of the learning process. Behavioral views are often dominant in corporate industrial training programs; the term *instructional design* as used there typically indicates a behavioral approach.

The behavioral approach to curriculum development views a course as a set of behavioral objectives. Success with each is indicated by a test. Very elaborate classification schemes have been developed for behavioral objectives.

Cognitive Psychology

Cognitive psychology takes a very different point of view. While cognitive psychology is not new, recently it has risen rapidly to the forefront of attention, so much so that even learning theorists previously identified as behaviorists now claim to be cognitive in their approaches. While behaviorists argue that what is happening within the brain cannot be understood, cognitive psychologists believe it is essential to understand the "schema" or "frames" by which the brain organizes knowledge internally. One branch of cognitive psychology even attempts to model these activities through computer programs. Cognitive psychology relates closely, therefore, to one field of computer science, artificial intelligence.

Thus far cognitive psychologists have had relatively little effect on actual curriculum development. Many newer developments, such as using computers as intellectual tools, have their roots, in a general sense, in cognitive psychology. But having an idea of how the mind works and having an adequate learning theory are not equivalent. Cognitive approaches are promising but not yet always pertinent in suggesting how to develop learning modules.

Developmental Psychology

Interest has also increased recently in attempting to understand the stages of intellectual development in human beings. Jean Piaget, from the University of Geneva, was a leader in this field. Piaget distinguished the stages of human development depicted in Table 7.1.

Piaget's database—the children he studied—was rather small, primarily his own children and grandchildren. Some researchers disagree with some aspects of his conclusions, either the stages or the student tasks Piaget specified to distinguish among the stages. Piaget wrote little about learning theory itself, and what he did write is often difficult to read in translation.

The general notions of developmental psychology have been very influential in recent years and have even influenced a number of major precomputer curriculum development projects, such as the elementary science material developed at the Science Curriculum Improvement Study (SCIS) at the University of California, Berkeley. Related computer materials have been developed at the Educational Technology Center.

The Learning Cycle

A number of workers have extended Piaget's points of view to explain or aid the process of learning. Robert Karplus, of the University of California, Berkeley, had a most interesting approach, which was used in the SCIS program and at the Educational Technology Center at Irvine. Karplus saw the full learning process or learning cycle as requiring three phases. The first was an experiential phase, letting people play with the phenomena, building up intuition and insight, typically through a series of experiences relevant to the subject area. No attempt at this stage is made to help students to analyze or "understand" the experiences. Raw data and the students' intuition gathered from that data is the only aim. These data may contradict students' existing beliefs.

The second stage in the learning cycle, Karplus feels, is the familiar process of learning

Table 7.1 DEVELOPMENTAL STAGES

Stages	Ages	Characteristics
Sensorimotor	Birth to 2	No internal thinking processes Recognizes different objects
Preoperational	2–4 years	Beginning of symbolic thought Experimenting Egocentric Cannot handle multiple characteristics Has concept of object
Preoperational-Intuitive	4–7 years	More use of symbols Concept of class and relations between classes End of this period—conservation ideas
Concrete Operational	7–11 years	Thought becomes more rigorous Begins to generalize
Formal Operational Transition	11–15 years	Abstract thinking Ratio reasoning Is spontaneously aware of his/her own thinking Classification Making deductions
Formal Operational Achieved	15 years	Can generalize to all situations

ideas as in our usual educational environments. This stage is familiar to most learners, because most courses stress this aspect of learning. In the best programs the student activities in this stage are based on the experiential material just encountered, particularly if that material raises conflicts with the students' earlier perceptions by giving new data not consistent with their earlier mental organizational structures. Because of the emphasis on mental structure, this view is associated with cognitive psychology.

The third stage in the Karplus learning cycle is what to *do* with what is learned. Thus this phase of learning is oriented to applications, to using the knowledge. It can include *testing* also. In the use of the learning cycle at the Educational Technology Center, this testing often leads to further learning material, determined by the results of testing.

Neurological Bases

As indicated, about all that can be said generally, based on current studies of the brain's structure, is that we do not yet understand the brain well. The electrical and chemical aspects of the brain are very complex, and no one is close to relating these aspects specifically to learning.

Research has proceeded much more fully in certain areas than others. Recently, for example, researchers have paid much attention to the effects of severing the connection between the two parts of the brain, thereby obtaining information about the differentiated functions of the two sides of the brain, called laterality. The results of this "split brain" research are complex; roughly, this work shows that for most people the two sides of the brain function differently. Typically, for a right-handed person, the left side of the brain controls, at least partially, reasoning and language capabilities, while the right side of the brain is more concerned with visual information, overall structure, and organization —thus it has what might be called a holistic point of view. This information suggests that

good learning material should use both sides of the brain.

Roger Sperry, the principal researcher in laterality, made the following comments in his Nobel prize speech in 1981:

Regardless of remaining uncertainties concerning laterality, one beneficial outcome that appears to hold up is an enhanced awareness, in education and elsewhere, of the important role of nonverbal components in forms of intellect. Another broadly relevant outcome that derives from evidence concerning familial, mutational, sexual, and other innate variations is a growing recognition of, and respect for, the inherent individuality in the structure of human intellect. The more we learn, the more we recognize the unique complexity of any one individual intellect and the stronger the conclusion comes that the individuality inherent in our brain networks makes that of fingerprints or facial features grossly simple by comparison.*

ADVANTAGES OF COMPUTERS IN EDUCATION

Learners Enjoy Using Computers

The first factor is one that should not be overlooked. In our society, the computer has very high positive motivational value. People of all ages hear about computers constantly in newspapers, on television, in films. Although the computer is not always pictured favorably, for most learners, particularly most young ones, it is presented as an exciting new device. So students are "prepared" for computers, even eager to have contact with them.

In my and my colleagues' long experience in the Educational Technology Center and in my experiences with other groups, I have seldom found individuals who do *not* like using computers for learning, if the use is for more than a few minutes. Indeed, the notion of a machine

Science (24 September 1982), p. 1623.

that "talks back" is very appealing, almost independent of how it is used. This student excitement is often described as if it were linked with some particular mode of using the computer. But my experience indicates that almost *any* way the computer is used, even the most trivial, appeals to many students.

In the field of learning these motivational issues cannot be neglected. Learning many subject areas requires sizable amounts of time and effort. Often it is not easy. Any learning mechanism, such as the computer, that motivates learning, any mechanism that learners enjoy, is desirable.

Many studies of learning indicate that one of the major factors determining how much people learn is "time on task"; a student who spends more time working in a particular subject area is more likely to learn more about that area. So motivational factors, such as the computer, that persuade people to spend more time learning should be emphasized.

Do today's students enjoy using the computer merely because it is new? What will happen thirty years from now, when students have used computers for most of their lives and for most learning activities? Perhaps by then the computer will seem old hat or boring. We cannot tell. The answer depends on the evolution of the computer and on the skill of the developer in producing attractive learning material; it could go in either direction. For the moment, the computer generates very strong positive interest in both classrooms and informal learning situations.

However, in spite of this interest, we have to *attract* student attention, help students to become interested in the learning material. Their interest in the specific material to be studied does not necessarily happen, although an interactive environment highly encourages it. Material can be developed in a highly interactive form, or it can be developed in noninteractive forms that mimic the learning strategies of the older media. Chapters 11 and 12 discuss the questions of production.

Individualization

Most learning theorists, whatever their background, agree with Sperry's comment that learning is a very individualized process. Students have quite different backgrounds and abilities, and they probably differ, from the standpoint of learning, in many ways unknown at present. The time required for learning may also differ from student to student. A central problem in any educational system is how to reach the individual student effectively. This problem is seldom addressed adequately in current educational systems.

Yet, surprisingly, most of the media available for mass education today allow for very little individualization of education. The typical large university environment, where perhaps two hundred students attend a lecture, certainly provides an extremely low level of individualized attention to any one student. Everyone receives the same material at the same rate. A few students may be able to visit the instructor in the office, but the sheer number of people in class precludes this common practice. Indeed, in many large lecture classes the average amount of time available for any one student to receive individualized attention is only a few seconds a week! And often the situation in a class of twenty-five is hardly any better.

A book allows good readers to use it in a slightly more individualized way; they can move from one section to another and refer to other books. Yet many readers do not employ such strategies. And for many less skilled readers, the book is no more individualized than the lecture. In any case, books allow no more than a small amount of individualization.

The current educational structures do achieve individualization in several circumstances. The interaction between instructor and students on a one-to-one basis is an example of how instruction *can* be individualized. But as suggested, this can comprise only a small part of the total learning process. In typical elementary or secondary classrooms most teachers, given the pressure of numbers of students, abandon individualization. While a few very good teachers can provide some individualization in large classes, the burdens are usually too demanding. It is difficult to observe experimentally any differences between a group of a dozen and a group of five hundred or a thousand. Mass education no longer allows individualization.

Even in small-group situations many instructors provide no individualization. On a number of occasions I have seen university students come to the professor's office because they have not understood the day's lecture; in this situation, when working with an individual or a small group, instructors sometimes *redeliver* a fragment of the lecture, as if repetition will increase the student's comprehension. Studies show that many instructors provide far less attention to individual students than they believe they provide.

With good material available, computers can allow individualization responsive to student needs. Student input is analyzed, and appropriate action is taken. This is not to say that computer programs must have thousands of variants. Indeed, experience indicates that in many cases only a few variants are needed for a specific situation. But these few can make a world of difference as to how much students will learn.

Interaction

Most learning psychologists would agree upon another factor with respect to learning: Active learning works better than passive learning. Passive learning resembles drilling a hole in the student's head, placing a funnel in the hole, and "pouring in" the knowledge. This seems to be many instructors' implicit view about lectures. But in this passive fashion, students do not learn as much as they could. Certainly modern cognitive psychologists would argue that internalization of the material is needed and that internalization only comes through active participation of learners.

As Jeremy Anglin states:

> The acquisition of knowledge, be it the recognition of a pattern, the attainment of a concept, the solution of a problem, or the development of a scientific theory, is an active process. The individual . . . should be regarded as an active participant in the knowledge-getting process. . . .*

A useful analogy is the difference between being a spectator or a participant in a sport. Often students in our educational system are spectators who watch the instructor. In a better educational system, they would be participants, active learners. Even the distinction between "learning" and "teaching" involves, from the students' viewpoint, this same active-passive dichotomy. I seldom refer to "teaching," which is an interesting activity *only* if it leads to *learning*.

Interaction is a vague term. What types of interaction am I talking about in computer-based learning? Are some kinds of interactions better than others? How should the computer be used in the interactive process? A good model for interaction is the situation of a small group of students in the teacher's office. A widely known example of an interactive learning process is the Platonic dialog, where Socrates walks around Athens with a group of several students. Socrates is mainly a *questioner;* he seldom presents "information." Thus the process is extremely different from a lecture. Socrates seldom tells anything, but rather asks questions designed to stimulate the students to derive the answers themselves, actively. Students can ask questions too, but this is less common in the Socratic learning process. This approach, which can be closely followed on the computer, might be described as "guided discovery."

I have already raised the question of quality of interaction. Developers of learning units in

*Jeremy Anglin, *Jerome Bruner, Beyond the Information Given* (New York: Norton, 1973), p. 397.

nonactive media such as film often become ecstatic when the computer provides the slightest bit of interactive capability. But those with more experience with computer-based learning material know that not all interactions are of equal value. A situation that sets forth three dense screens of text to read and then offers students the chance to say yes or no, or to respond to a multiple-choice question, followed by further dense text on screens, is *not* an interactive situation, even though students were allowed to interact once. Such educational techniques as multiple choice are definitely weak forms of interaction. In our work at the Educational Technology Center we very seldom use this tactic, even in quizzes, as we consider it an undesirable educational strategy not necessary with computers.

One of the computer's main advantages in learning is its capability to provide an interactive learning experience. There is nothing automatic about this. That is, using the computer is no guarantee of interactivity. Indeed, many poor uses of computers in education impose upon students a passive role in which they make only relatively minor decisions. Most of the examples of computer-based learning in chapter 5 are highly interactive.

Various learning approaches can be measured with regard to interaction and individualization. Figure 7.1 suggests how several different learning methods compare.

Learning Faster

One often overlooked advantage of the computer in education, but one that has some research support, is that students using computers learn in less time. Results in the armed forces suggest that curriculum based on computer-based learning can cut 30 percent from the time students need to learn something. The major advantage comes from individualization. That is, students do not have to spend much time on

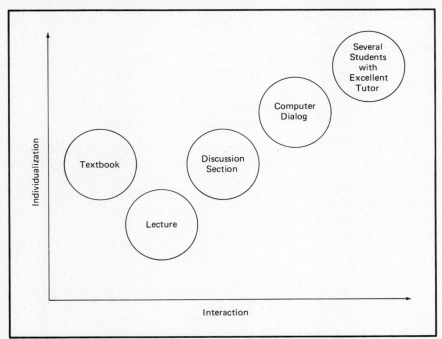

Figure 7.1 Interaction and individualization in various learning methods.

a subject they know when using good computer-based learning modules. Once it is verified that they *do* know it, the program quickly can pass on to other material; so learning is maximized in a way difficult to do in a fixed-pace lecture environment.

Unfortunately, neither schools nor universities have placed much premium on student time. Indeed, a look at how universities are structured leads me to believe that the convenience of the student is one of the *last* things considered! Nevertheless, student time is an important issue, and anything that can increase efficiency, such as the computer, is important. The issue of time to learn is particularly important in training environments where the student is taken off a productive job in a company to learn something.

Visualization

Another important advantage of computers in education, particularly personal computers, is their increasing capability to provide interactive visual information. Graphics are extremely important in the learning process, as suggested by the split-brain research and by common educational practices. Typical college-level science and mathematics textbooks contain about one picture or diagram a page. Teachers frequently use drawings of many types in their chalkboard presentations.

Hence the fact that computers today can provide a remarkable range of pictorial capabilities is important for learning. However, visual capabilities on inexpensive personal computers are not yet fully adequate by any means.

Communications

One potential important advantage of the computer seldom realized today is its capacity to stimulate personal interaction during learning between students and teachers or among students. Although this communications skill is utilized to some extent today, it is still rare in many educational environments.

One possibility for computer-based communications systems is the extensive use of message systems on the computer. In a class using the computer heavily, where communication between the computers (networks) or terminals (timesharing) is available, an instructor can communicate at any time with the entire class or with individual students. Students need not be using the computer simultaneously with the instructor to receive these electronic messages. Rather, they will receive them the next time they use the computer. But not all systems allow this capability.

Interaction with other students—peer interaction—is very valuable in the learning process; computers can serve well in encouraging peer learning in a variety of ways. Material can be explicitly designed for small-group interaction with the computer, with several students working together at a computer display. The computer can assign separate tasks to different people in the group and encourage discussion among individuals. While little material of this kind is available so far, the potential of this technique is high.

CURRENT DISADVANTAGES OF COMPUTERS IN EDUCATION

The major problem with computers in learning is that many of their potential advantages have not yet been realized. Two principal reasons account for this lag. First, as I have often indicated, very little decent material is available now. Currently the purchaser of a personal computer or any computer system will find far less good educational material than is desirable or necessary for extensive classroom use. However, this situation may change in the near future.

Furthermore, only a few teachers in the public school system or universities have adequate knowledge of how to use computers in learning. Hence the machine tends to be misused or not used at all. Such advantages as individualization are not realized, and indeed, sometimes the opposite happens, with the computer serving as a page turner, supplying everyone with the same material.

The management activities of computers, while having some advantages for individual teachers, also have some possible long-range disadvantages. That far more information can be made available about students is a possibly dangerous notion. Educators and developers must closely attend to *what* information is available, *who* has access to it, and what kinds of *controls* exist concerning the accuracy of the information. Even the *volume* of information can present problems for teachers, providing too much material to use in reasonable ways.

This problem is not restricted to education. Indeed, the problem of privacy of information pervades all areas of computing. But it does have relevance to education. While only fragmentary information is currently available in educational databases, this situation will change rapidly.

A number of social problems may be connected with computers in education. Some could become quite serious if not considered and approached rationally. First, home computers are going to be important in education, because more and more learning material will be available. More affluent families will probably acquire computers, and therefore their children will receive the advantages (or disadvantages, if the learning material is poor) of this learning approach. Schools in affluent neighborhoods will also be most likely to acquire computers. It seems unlikely that a poor family—or a poor

school district—will spend money to buy computers and associated educational software. Hence, unless some explicit attempts are made to solve this problem, the educational gap between the haves and the have-nots may further increase because of the computer. While I consider this very undesirable, current education seems to be moving in such a direction. Government action is needed to prevent this situation from worsening.

Another possible sociological problem, often mentioned, is, I believe, based on an overly simplistic distinction. The issue is often phrased this way: In affluent schools, students are mostly learning to control the computer. Less affluent schools use mostly the drill-and-practice materials, such as the Suppes material reviewed in chapter 5. While this is true, the notion of the computer being "good" when under student control and being "bad" if not under student control is oversimplified. Control can come in various ways. This distinction is based on an appeal to emotion rather than a rational consideration of the ways computers can be used in education. The choice of language with emotional appeal—the computer controlling the student versus the student controlling the computer—prejudices the situation. "Control" is a highly subjective concept; I would argue that in all interactive situations the student has *some* control over the computer. Decisions of this kind, choosing the level of student control, demand much empirical evidence before curriculum designers can be reasonably sure of what method is best for learning in each situation. Comparison with other media, such as books, will also prove interesting.

chapter 8

Teacher Evaluation of Computer Materials

- Formative and Summative Evaluation
- Looking Over the Material
- One Example of an Evaluation Form
- Things to Avoid
- Reviews
- Testing with Students

The process of choosing educational units of any type is both important and difficult. Given the vast number of variables in education, which often cannot be controlled, and the large number of students, full-scale evaluation is not simple and therefore usually requires sizable sums of money. But learning modules must be selected.

This chapter is *not* directed to questions raised by a full formal evaluation undertaken by developers (see chapter 12 for a discussion of that topic), but toward a more practical situation, helping teacher, administrators, parents,

and others to judge what computer-based learning material is satisfactory and what is not. I will present some criteria useful for other education evaluation situations, involving media other than the computer, but my primary focus is on good computer-based learning. Note that while few good evaluations of computer-based learning modules have been done, few good evaluations of textbooks, lectures, films, and other learning modes exist also.

If we are to move to a better educational system, it is critical that teachers and others evince an interest in evaluation. Currently much poor computer-based material is being published. Many early products have been marginal or below marginal in quality.

This is not to say there has been no good material. But if educators are to persuade vendors to market quality learning material, we must be able to identify quality material and must *insist* upon on it. Hence it is essential for teachers and administrators to build standards, not just to accept any material because it happens to run on the computer!

FORMATIVE AND SUMMATIVE EVALUATION

In evaluating learning material at any level, the teacher must distinguish between formative and summative evaluation. The distinction is reasonably straightforward, although sometimes difficult to maintain in practice. In *formative evaluation* the evaluator strives to improve the material, either by giving suggestions to others or, as a developer, by altering the learning units and producing a new generation. While a teacher's input to a publisher might or might not be used to improve the material, this *type* of input will probably have the most impact. Hence many strategies of formative evaluation will be useful for teachers.

Summative evaluation is a different matter. The term refers to the evaluation of a finished product, such as a computer program to aid learning, to see if it is effective as educational material. Summative evaluation studies the overall effectiveness of the learning material, and is typically beyond the resources of teachers.

Ideally educators would always prefer full-scale summative evaluations of all classroom materials. In practice, however, good summative evaluations are *very* seldom available. Even the major curriculum projects for the schools that took place in the sixties and early seventies, with large funding, seldom could afford full summative evaluations. Rather they relied primarily on formative evaluations, improving the material through a number of generations.

Full-scale summative evaluation is a difficult process. Probably it should only be done when the materials are "seasoned." That is, they should have had a number of years' use in "real" class situations, with the attendant minor (or not so minor) changes that probably accompany such use. Many projects fail in evaluation because they try a summative evaluation too early. Developers set up optimistic schedules for materials to be finished by a given time, with the evaluation timing dependent upon production schedule; then, unfortunately, because of developmental delays, summative evaluation is undertaken while the materials are still being developed. Hence many summative evaluations do not achieve their goals. In any case, it is not practical for individuals choosing material to undertake summative evaluations. Therefore, other, less formal, evaluation methods are often required.

LOOKING OVER THE MATERIAL

In deciding whether to use, and to purchase, some particular computer-based learning material, teachers must first *examine* the material. That is, the teacher must run the materials, perhaps several times. While teachers are familiar with such experimentation with other kinds of material, computer material presents some specific problems.

The first problem may be that of acquiring the material to look over! Some vendors are reluctant to allow previews of their products. If the material is available, often it is not easy to "browse" through computer units as one browses through a book. Looking over the material can be very time-consuming. In this sense computer material more closely resembles a film than a book. Computer dialogs can be designed to be more flexible than a film, with modular structure allowing easy movement through the program. Teacher information about content can be supplied in print form. But there is no substitute for getting in and spending time *looking* at proposed material. In some cases, the developer may make a "sampler" available, allowing a quick look; but the sampler may not be characteristic of the full unit.

Just looking, with no structure in mind, is not likely to be a very rewarding activity, and hazards a very subjective view of the material. This, unfortunately, frequently happens with textbooks. Instructors browse through a book almost randomly. Their eyes light on a paragraph that appeals or does not appeal, often for reasons having little to do with student understanding of the material. For example, perhaps the material fails to match the teacher's favorite prose format or perhaps the teacher usually approaches the topic somewhat differently. "Evaluations" of this type are often highly subjective, depending very much on an individual's mood at the moment. And they may not be oriented toward the student.

This casual browsing can be surpassed. I suggest that teachers try to answer certain questions as they examine material.

Content

For most people content is the most important aspect of learning material. A major issue with regard to the content concerns the objectives of the material. What educational objectives does it address and how does it go about addressing them? Does the material consider an important educational problem, or is learning the things covered in the material not difficult even in a traditional classroom? Are the detailed approaches presented the most desirable?

The issue of content cannot be too highly stressed. Many program reviews in current magazines do not even question whether the material is something that really needs to be learned or if it is accurate; I recommend that content be the first issue teachers consider. As with many other factors, some alternate opinions might be good. A group of teachers reviewing the module together, discussing each of these factors and arriving at a concensus, would be preferable to a single individual reviewing it alone.

One aspect of content is the *length* of the material. It is difficult to accomplish much in fifteen minutes of student time. Yet many learning programs currently available use short and therefore relatively trivial chunks. A serious topic cannot be approached coherently in so short a time.

Environment

How is the material to be used in the classroom situation? The practicalities of dealing with large classes often cast a very different light on material that is initially extremely appealing to the instructor. Such units can be a complete disaster in larger classes because students lack the instructor's motivation, due to different backgrounds, and because the instructor probably will have little time to work individually with each student. So how to use selected material must be addressed very carefully. Some computer material will work well with one teacher and two or three students, but not in full classes.

In the early days at the Educational Technology Center my colleagues and I developed physics simulations that we found very appealing and that physicists found very appealing too. One such program in mechanics is described in chapter 5. But these simulations sometimes bombed when used in "real" classes. The simulations worked with a few good students or with students receiving the instructor's individual attention while the computer dialog was running; but in classes of hundreds of students, it was impossible to work individually with *all* students. Despite its appeal to instructors, for most students such material was of no use. Students lacked the motivational interests we implicitly assumed when developing the material. They did not know the interesting cases to examine in the simulations, or why suggested cases were of interest, and tended to flounder and quickly lose interest. Only gradually did we learn how to develop and use such material successfully in large classes of beginners.

Material that assumes the teacher must work individually with each student or with small groups can cause problems. Too often I see material being "tested" in groups of three students and two talented Ph.D.'s. The material appears to work brilliantly, but the environment is extremely unrealistic, compared to the realities of schools or homes.

Another problem occurs when the computer is part of a much larger collection of multimedia activities. While multimedia learning is potentially desirable, it often presents tremendous logistics problems for teachers in assembling the necessary ingredients. Teachers may be very unhappy if their primary role is merely one of management, just gathering together all the course components and moving the students from one activity to another. For example, the use of kits in elementary science programs led to severe logistics problems; the kits were critical, but many teachers found it a tremendous chore to maintain the kits year after year, ordering new parts as necessary. So now the use of such science kits nationally is very low; only a small percentage of today's schools use these interesting science modules.

Approach

How does the material approach the content? This is a much more personal issue. As approach often is a matter of individual taste and style, teachers ask if the approach under consideration is compatible with or quite antithetical to the way they really want to work with their students. For example, many mathematics teachers never accepted the "new math" approach. The question is personal, asking whether the material is congenial to the particular teacher. In some cases teacher training material may play a role.

Any one idea, theory, concept, method can be introduced in many ways to learners. Teach-

ers may have strong views about the desirability of different ways of approaching a learning task. Hence it is necessary for teachers conducting the evaluation of a computer-based learning module to check carefully to see if the objectives and approaches used are sound and acceptable to them.

Interaction

In the last chapter I stressed the importance of an interactive environment for students; they should play a very active role in the learning process. This interaction is *possible* on computers. However, a good bit of computer-based learning material discourages students from playing an active role. Teachers should insist on highly interactive material. A simple criterion is the average time between interactions. The *quality* of interaction is also important; multiple choice is an example of low-quality interaction.

Teachers or other evaluators can gather information about interaction by looking carefully at the material. They can ask a variety of questions. Are several types of student input used? Is some use made in inputs of the students' own language (say, English)? Is "pointer" input used? What is the approximate time between student inputs? Are the student responses usually to important questions rather than to trivial questions? All these things can be determined by successive running of the program, but they take the instructor's time.

User-friendly Interface

The term *user-friendly* is related to several other factors discussed in this chapter, the general notion being that the material should exude a friendly attitude to users in both form and content. This includes such devices as avoiding insulting learners because of their problems and designing the program so that a novice with little or no computer experience can easily use it.

But the situation is still more subtle. Students

having difficulty can be encouraged and motivated by careful choice of vocabulary and with thoughtful individualized help sequences. Would that faltering students more often enjoyed such support! More needs to be done for the student in trouble. Thus, in examining new material teachers should, based on their experiences with children, anticipate the *typical* mistakes students will tend to make and then deliberately make those mistakes to see what happens. A user-friendly system will offer meaningful help and motivation to a student in difficulty. I cannot stress too heavily the critical importance of good *interactive* help sequences in computer-based learning material; a verbal repetition of previous material is seldom adequate.

A particularly unfriendly situation occurs when the program simply does not work in some situations. There is no excuse for this. But some computer-based learning modules will work *only* with students who are behaving pretty much the way the developers "want" them to behave. The minimum requirement is that the program, in almost all practical situations, will run smoothly without errors. This does not imply that the program is completely without flaws. Indeed, *there is no such thing as a perfect program.* No matter how much a program is tested, it may break down in some odd situations. Even programs used extensively for many years still have errors. But the program with serious problems should be a *very* exceptional situation. A mistyped letter or a letter where a number is appropriate or expected should never cause a program to "bomb"!

A side aspect of this point, use by novice students, is that students should be given *only* information they need. That is, a student should not be told to answer "yes" or "no" when the question is a yes or no question. The student should not be told to press return if that student already knows to press return. Repeating trivial information that is already known is boring and unfriendly.

An important consideration of a user-friendly computer learning dialog resides in the language used. Language with or without the computer should never be abusive or negative. Don't say things like "No, you dummy." Because someone does not know something *you* know does not mean the person is an idiot! We want to encourage success, encourage the feeling that everyone can succeed, even though some people may need more assistance than others. Careful consideration of language is important in evaluating computer dialogs.

Computer learning units (modules) often use a segment of code several times. In such situations it is desirable within the program to pick a message to be presented several times to the student out of a random collection of possible responses. The choice is made while the dialog is run by students. The teacher should watch for repetitive language while reviewing material.

Another aspect of being friendly to the user is allowing students to make choices on how the material is presented. In our programs in the Educational Technology Center we allow students to control how fast text appears on the screen. Incidentally, we pick a "default" rate, the one the program uses, slower than usual, based on our observation of students.

One point that seems almost obvious, but somehow is often violated, is that in computer learning units the violent instincts in humans need not be stimulated. A vast amount of computer material currently being promoted for classes is almost obscene in its use of violence, with things being killed, destroyed, eaten, hanged, and other unpleasant results. The developers of powerful learning material must have some moral standards; cooperation should be stressed in such material, not violent competition.

Individualization

Another factor discussed in the last chapter again needs to be heavily stressed in examining material. An advantage of computers is that good computer dialogs, interactive programs of all types, *can,* within limits, differentiate between different students and treat individual students differently. But do they?

The degree of individualization in a computer program is difficult to determine in a quick browse through the material. The program must run many times, with many different responses, to show what can happen with different students.

It is a mistake for reviewers to go through computer material *only* putting in *correct* answers. On the other hand, the errors put in should be likely student errors. There is no point in trying to "fool the computer." Answers the teacher supplies should be realistic in the sense that students might provide ones like them; they shouldn't be ones that teachers, with superior knowledge, can think up but that are beyond the capability of almost all students. The curriculum unit is for students, not professionals. Teachers need to be reminded of this fact.

It is beneficial for a number of people to examine the material to determine the level of individualization. The people can compare notes and see to what extent different responses produce different answers. Thus having several teachers run the same material and then discuss it can be helpful.

Graphics

The last chapters emphasized the importance of visual information, usually as a source of information for the learner parallel to textual material. It is relatively easy to determine by inspection if a program is using graphics. In doing this the teacher should keep in mind the pedagogical needs of the average student. What is perhaps harder to determine is whether the visual information relates directly to what is of prime importance. Many programs have very fancy drawings that contribute little to the learning process and so are not *intrinsically* important.

In looking at graphics, reviewers need to constantly ask if the pictures are useful to some type of student. Are the graphics intrinsically important to the learning process?

One very important consideration is to what extent graphics are used in the help sequences. Often material employs graphics as long as the student is proceeding smoothly but gives strictly verbal information to the student in trouble. This is clearly wrong. Many students who have difficulty are those who are weak verbally; they *need* the visual approaches. In reviewing material, teachers should look particularly at how graphics are used to aid the student having difficulty.

Screen Design

By screen design I mean the placement of information on the screen and its arrangement in time, both words and pictures. (I will have more to say about screen design in chapter 12 where I discuss the process of developing computer-based learning materials.)

Screen design is an important factor in the effective use of computer learning units. Readability of material is promoted by putting relatively little text and graphics on the screen at one time, by using much blank space, by time delays before and after critical pieces of text, by arranging text in short sentences, by providing user control over how the text is presented, and in many other ways. The teacher evaluating material should bear these issues in mind.

Sound

Sound can be a delicate issue in a program. First, many teachers will object to having ten computers in a classroom all making miscellaneous beeps and noises. Even with just one computer, the same sounds repeated frequently can be annoying. Thus it is desirable to be able to *turn off* the sound, so reviewers should look for this capability. Particularly annoying are sounds that identify when a particular user is in difficulty; they raise social problems for that user within the class and can lead to destruction of class spirit, unless each student has individual headphones. Yet these negative sounds are all too common in current material.

On the other hand, if carefully used, sound can add motivation. As always, the teacher should consider the possible motivational effects of sound from the learner's viewpoint. Good-quality voice can be very useful in some situations, but it is seldom available.

ONE EXAMPLE OF AN EVALUATION FORM

It may be of some interest to see how a particular organization, CONDUIT, has gone about the evaluation process. CONDUIT's aims are *not* identical to the goal in this chapter—teacher evaluation of the material is the focal point here. CONDUIT's evaluation is for the purposes of deciding which materials are of sufficiently high quality to market. But nevertheless, CONDUIT's approach is interesting.

CONDUIT was initially established by the National Science Foundation to disseminate computer learning material. From its earliest days it has had considerable concern for the quality of material. At the present time it is one of the largest distributors of computer-based learning material at the university level; its products are also usable in secondary schools. Figure 8.1 on pages 101–106 reproduces the CONDUIT questionnaire, which is completed by CONDUIT's reviewers.

THINGS TO AVOID

Just as researchers reviewing computer material can look for definite positive aspects in considering computer-based learning material, they can detect some indications of poor material. Many of these have already been either explicitly mentioned or implied.

Books via Computer

Some developers of computer-based units tend to display books, sometimes illustrated ones, on computers. While this may become desirable at some future time when print costs increase and computer costs decrease, or when new forms of electronic books are developed, at present it is a misuse of the computer to display large quantities of text. Mere display of large amounts of text and graphics on the screen, with no or very little student interaction, is an ineffective use of the medium. Large blocks of text simulate books; books are already available. We don't need computers to duplicate them. On casual inspection it is easy to spot these books masquerading as computer dialogs.

Most developers of student-computer dialogs come from the older pedagogical environments and have already written books. Many tend to handle computers the way they handle books, adding only minimal interaction. Such text-heavy materials should be rejected and designers obliged to develop interactive and individualized materials to better use the computer.

Dense Screens

Dense screens—screens with very little blank space—are a related negative factor. One of my favorite expressions is that "blank space is free on the computer." This is in contrast with books, where the cost of the book depends on the number of pages; increasing the amount of blank space increases the cost. Teachers should avoid programs with dense screens.

Multiple Choice

The *quality of interaction* is one of my persistent themes. A particularly bad type of interaction, unfortunately all too common with and without the computer, is multiple choice, particularly in testing situations. It is a prime example of duplicating a technique from an older technology, neither desirable nor necessary with computers.

PART I:
DESCRIPTION

1. Describe the topics or concepts presented in this package in a few words. (For example: The law of demand in microeconomic theory at the elementary level.)

2. If you can, suggest the title of course(s) for which this material is appropriate. (For example, Elementary Economics, Principles of Economics, Introductory Microeconomics.)

3. Indicate the appropriate instructional levels for use of this package:

   ___ high school
   ___ undergraduate (lower level)
   ___ undergraduate (upper level)
   ___ graduate
   ___ other, specify_____

4. Please indicate prerequisite skills (or courses) required for student use of this package. (For example: Requires knowledge of demand theory in text, ability to graph, and knowledge of how to use a terminal.)

5. Describe the type of computer application(s) utilized in this package.

   ___ simulation
   ___ game
   ___ data base use
   ___ computer-based testing
   ___ drill and practice
   ___ dialog
   ___ problem solving
   ___ integrated program series
   ___ other, specify_____

6. Describe the instructional intent(s) of this package. (For example: To teach the functional relationship between price and quantity demanded. To teach recognition of limiting assumptions about the relationship. To teach ability to estimate demand function for differing commodities.)

Figure 8.1 (*a*) CONDUIT's evaluation questionnaire. (Courtesy of CONDUIT, University of Iowa.)

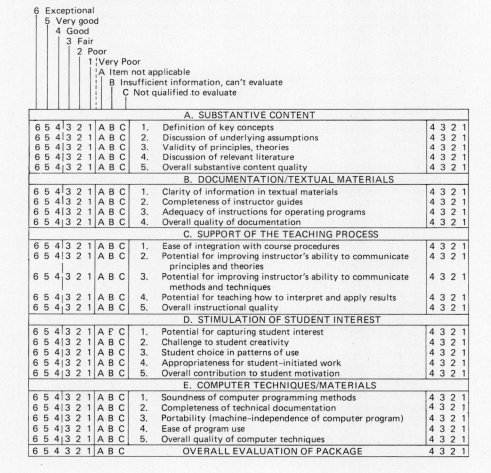

PART II:

EVALUATION

Column 1:

Rate this package on each of the selected characteristics listed below by circling the appropriate number. Please complete this entire column before working on column 2.

Column 2:

Indicate the importance of each feature for this instructional package. Circle the appropriate number.

6 Exceptional
5 Very good
4 Good
3 Fair
2 Poor
1 Very Poor
A Item not applicable
B Insufficient information, can't evaluate
C Not qualified to evaluate

Column 1		Item		Column 2
	A. SUBSTANTIVE CONTENT			
6 5 4 3 2 1 A B C	1.	Definition of key concepts		4 3 2 1
6 5 4 3 2 1 A B C	2.	Discussion of underlying assumptions		4 3 2 1
6 5 4 3 2 1 A B C	3.	Validity of principles, theories		4 3 2 1
6 5 4 3 2 1 A B C	4.	Discussion of relevant literature		4 3 2 1
6 5 4 3 2 1 A B C	5.	Overall substantive content quality		4 3 2 1
	B. DOCUMENTATION/TEXTUAL MATERIALS			
6 5 4 3 2 1 A B C	1.	Clarity of information in textual materials		4 3 2 1
6 5 4 3 2 1 A B C	2.	Completeness of instructor guides		4 3 2 1
6 5 4 3 2 1 A B C	3.	Adequacy of instructions for operating programs		4 3 2 1
6 5 4 3 2 1 A B C	4.	Overall quality of documentation		4 3 2 1
	C. SUPPORT OF THE TEACHING PROCESS			
6 5 4 3 2 1 A B C	1.	Ease of integration with course procedures		4 3 2 1
6 5 4 3 2 1 A B C	2.	Potential for improving instructor's ability to communicate principles and theories		4 3 2 1
6 5 4 3 2 1 A B C	3.	Potential for improving instructor's ability to communicate methods and techniques		4 3 2 1
6 5 4 3 2 1 A B C	4.	Potential for teaching how to interpret and apply results		4 3 2 1
6 5 4 3 2 1 A B C	5.	Overall instructional quality		4 3 2 1
	D. STIMULATION OF STUDENT INTEREST			
6 5 4 3 2 1 A B C	1.	Potential for capturing student interest		4 3 2 1
6 5 4 3 2 1 A B C	2.	Challenge to student creativity		4 3 2 1
6 5 4 3 2 1 A B C	3.	Student choice in patterns of use		4 3 2 1
6 5 4 3 2 1 A B C	4.	Appropriateness for student–initiated work		4 3 2 1
6 5 4 3 2 1 A B C	5.	Overall contribution to student motivation		4 3 2 1
	E. COMPUTER TECHNIQUES/MATERIALS			
6 5 4 3 2 1 A B C	1.	Soundness of computer programming methods		4 3 2 1
6 5 4 3 2 1 A B C	2.	Completeness of technical documentation		4 3 2 1
6 5 4 3 2 1 A B C	3.	Portability (machine–independence of computer program)		4 3 2 1
6 5 4 3 2 1 A B C	4.	Ease of program use		4 3 2 1
6 5 4 3 2 1 A B C	5.	Overall quality of computer techniques		4 3 2 1
6 5 4 3 2 1 A B C		OVERALL EVALUATION OF PACKAGE		4 3 2 1

Figure 8.1 (b) CONDUIT's evaluation questionnaire, continued.

PART III.
SUMMARY ASSESSMENTS

Please comment freely about your assessment of this package.

1. How central is the subject matter of this package to your field?

    ____ critical, absolutely essential
    ____ important to include
    ____ optional, appropriate but not essential
    ____ trivial, not important

    Comment:

2. Is it reasonable to use the computer with this package?

    ____ yes
    ____ no
    ____ not sure

    Comment:

3. Do you recommend the use of this package?

    ____ strongly recommend
    ____ recommend
    ____ recommend subject to improvements (state on next question)
    ____ do not recommend
    ____ why? (Identify strengths and weaknesses):

4. What improvements do you recommend to the substance, program or documentation of this package, if any?

Figure 8.1 (*c*) CONDUIT's evaluation questionnaire, continued.

PART IV:
COURSE USE

1. Have you used this package in course instruction?   Yes   No

    THIS SECTION SHOULD BE COMPLETED ONLY IF YOU HAVE ALREADY USED THIS
    PACKAGE IN TEACHING A COURSE. IF NOT, SKIP THIS SECTION.

2. For each course in which you used this package, please state:

    Course title _____, _____, _____
    Level   _____, _____, _____
    Enrollment   _____, _____, _____

3. Did you find the package easy to implement? _____ Yes _____ No. State the problems:

4. What resources or resource persons were used in implementing this package?

5. Describe student reaction to use of these materials. (Report any attitude surveys, informal reports,
    etc.)

6. Estimate the time (in hours) required:
    1) of an instructor to prepare for course use of this package_____
    2) of a student to prepare for course use of this package_____

7. How many times have you used the package?_____

8. Do you intend to use it again? _____ Yes _____ No

    Comment:

9. Please give any suggestions you may have for successfully utilizing this package in class.

Figure 8.1 (*d*) CONDUIT's evaluation questionnaire, continued.

PART V:
REACTIONS

1. Does a thorough review of this package require experience in class use of the package? ___ Yes
   ___ No. COMMENTS:

2. State any problems you have had in completing this review form, and give your suggestions for improvement of the form.

3. Please indicate the total time it took you to review this package.

   _____   _____
           hours   minutes

4. How many other packages have you reviewed for CONDUIT?
   None _____
   One _____
   Two _____
   Three or more _____

   _____   _____
           Reviewer's signature   Date

   _____
           Reviewer's name (please print)

   _____
           Academic rank or Position

   _____
           University or College

   _____
   City   State   Zip

Figure 8.1 (e) CONDUIT's evaluation questionnaire, continued.

Reviewer_____

Package title_____

PART VI

SUMMARY

Please provide a written summary of your general assessment of the package. Your summary should elaborate your evaluation of the substantive aspects of the material.

Figure 8.1 (*f*) CONDUIT's evaluation questionnaire, continued.

Multiple choice served as a tactic of desperation, when we worked with relatively crude computer equipment and large classes. The problem it was intended to solve was to give exams to very large numbers of students and grade them in a reasonable time. In a few situations, such as national testing, it is still hard to avoid.

"Learned" attempts have been made to justify multiple choice. But even the strongest bastions of multiple choice today realize that it is an undesirable technique in most situations. It is *not* needed in modern computer-based learning material. Good computer-based learning material can be much more responsive to student answers than the multiple-choice technique allows. And with good computer-based learning material, all the guessing aspects inherent in multiple choice can be avoided.

REVIEWS

Reviews of the material under consideration may be available in journals or elsewhere. Unfortunately, reviews at present are of extremely variable quality. In a widely read magazine I saw a review for a new Pascal compiler by someone who had been working on BASIC all his life! Furthermore, the magazines are dependent on the developers of the material for advertis-

ing. An examination of how much material is *favorably* reviewed indicates the basic problem, considering the generally poor quality of much of it. But perhaps there may be a higher standard of reviews appearing.

One possibly bright factor in the review situation is the recent appearance of several independent review mechanisms. One is being conducted through EPI and Consumers Union, which is not dependent on any financial arrangements. However, it is still too early to know what quality of reviews will be forthcoming.

TESTING WITH STUDENTS

So far I have talked about things instructors can do in looking at the material or reading reviews. But it is always highly desirable, whenever possible, to run the material with a few prototype students, perhaps with the instructor looking over their shoulders and playing a completely passive role. Or the teacher can watch the screens on a remote monitor, as students might behave differently with him or her present.

Students do differ from teachers! In evaluating materials this must be taken into account. I have already suggested a number of times that student motivations are *not* the same as teachers' motivations.

Often in the past the net result of the student-teacher differences has been that learning material is more teacher-oriented than student-oriented. Textbook publishers are well aware that, at least in colleges, the choice of a textbook rests entirely with the instructor. In schools the student is even further removed from the choice of textbooks. Hence the book tends to be *aimed* at the instructor or the selection committee rather than at students. A similar tendency already is manifested, unfortunately, in computer-based learning. Teachers should insist that the units be *student-oriented*.

This problem can be overcome if some students are allowed to run the computer modules during the testing phase. Typically in this situation large numbers of students are not necessary, because a formal evaluation is not being conducted. An instructor watching a few students can often gain very insightful information about how the material will work with a larger class. Instructors must not, however, lose sight of the fact that the full class environment may present problems different from those that develop when a few students run the material.

chapter 9

Hardware—The Raw Computer

- What Is a Computer?
- Memory
- Measuring Memory
- Processors
- Chip Technology
- Input and Output
- Graphics
- Maintenance
- Choosing Hardware

This chapter concerns the computer's physical aspect, with particular emphasis on personal computers because of their growing importance in education. Much of this information will apply to any type of computer, large or small; the personal computer is still a computer, differing from other members of its family by its petite size, low cost, and often individual owner. The term *hardware* has come into use for the actual equipment.

You may be surprised that a discussion of the physical components of computers comes so late in the presentation. Indeed, many books about the computer in education begin with discussions of hardware. Yet learning by computer can be compared with learning to drive a car or learning to operate a television set and other kinds of "literacy" useful in our society. Most people who drive cars have only a general knowledge of the car's mechanism, and certainly most of them could not *build* a car! Likewise, for teachers and administrators using computers in education, hardware should not dominate, but should be overshadowed by issues of educational importance. Further, the educational user of computers does not need to be an expert on hardware, so I do not cover everything. Many teachers can either skip this chapter or scan it quickly.

I start with a general functional description of the computer and then proceed to specific details about currently available computers. In chapter 13 I continue this discussion of hardware with emphasis on *future* equipment.

It is a mistake to believe that computers available today are similar to those that will be available in a few years. Computer technology is changing *very* rapidly. New computers are being announced all the time, so a book taking several months to produce can hardly be up to date where issues of hardware are concerned. Remember, as you read this chapter, that this book was written in 1982 and 1983.

WHAT IS A COMPUTER?

Figure 9.1 is a simple diagram of a computer; it shows the computer as having essentially three components. This view of the computer suggests that it is an *information-modifying* or *information-transforming* device. There is an input stream of information, perhaps from several different sources, there is some manipulation or processing of this input, and there is an output stream of information.

The word *information* is to be understood in a *very* general sense, for both input and output. "Information" comes in many forms: text, numbers, pictures, sound. Thus the input might be Shakespeare's *Twelfth Night,* and the output of the processing activity might be a concordance of that work. The input information might be full information about a space shuttle and the output a complete set of predictions about its

future locations. Or the input might be a chest x-ray and the output a patient diagnosis.

Such a diagram for computers can be read in two ways. First, it does represent information and its transformation, as just described. But it can also represent physical devices. The left-hand circle indicates that some physical device, or perhaps a set of devices, puts information into the computer for processing. For typical personal computer use, students usually enter information from a typewriterlike device, while other information, such as the program the student is using or extensive numerical information, may have come from other input sources, such as a magnetic floppy disc.

Output devices are also in the picture. For personal computers the most typical output device is the screen of a televisionlike tube, a cathode ray tube. What appears on the screen can be either textual or graphical material. Output may include sound, text from printers, and information sent to storage devices. Students using computer-based learning material may not even be directly aware of some of the output. Thus, as a student takes a quiz, part of the output may consist of record-keeping information the program is generating for class management.

The third major component is the *processor.* This is the physical part of the computer, the heart of the computer, where the information is *transformed.* A computer system can have several processors.

MEMORY

The diagram of the computer needs further details. Information processors need places to store the information when it is received, need places to store the instructions telling how to transform the information, may need places to store intermediate results, and need places to store the information intended for the output devices, before it goes to these devices. This implies that an essential component of a com-

Figure 9.1 The computer (I).

puter is *memory,* the "places to store information" just mentioned.

So the diagram of the computer might be extended to look something like the one in Figure 9.2. Memory connects mainly with the processors; the two lines show that information can go from processor to memory or from memory to processor. In some computers input and output access memory directly; dotted lines show that possibility.

What is meant by memory, in particular, computer memory? We are borrowing a human term. Computer memory can hold or retain— store—information coded in electronic form. Users must have rapid access to that information to employ it within a fast processor. In today's fast computer memories, the typical access time—the time to retrieve a piece of information—is about a millionth of a second, or a microsecond.

The information stored in memory may be a number, a collection of numbers, a letter, a collection of letters, or anything that can be stored symbolically. If you can store numbers and letters, you can store almost any human product, since from numbers and letters we form our languages. Thus visual or graphical information, genetic information, or sound in coded form can also be stored.

Most computer systems have several *types* of memory. At first glance this might seem peculiar. Novice users may wonder why all memory is not of the same type. First, a trade-off exists

between the memory *speed*—how fast information can be put into and taken out, or retrieved, from memory—and its *cost.* Faster memory costs more money. Modern computers need extensive amounts of memory, so there must be a compromise between speed and cost. Usually we compromise at several stages—several different types of memory are used. A small amount of the computer memory will be fast but relatively expensive. Other memory may be slower and cheaper but more extensive.

A collection of different types of memory or, in computer terminology, hierarchies of memory, is represented in Figure 9.3. Three different types of memory are shown. Although each form of memory could be accessed from input and output devices, here it is connected only to the processor.

In most modern computers fast memory is constructed from electronic "chips." Electronically stored information on the chips can be accessed with electronic speed, around one millionth of a second. When you hear that your Apple has 64K or that an IBM Personal Computer has 256K (never mind for the moment what the K means), it refers to the amount of fast electronic memory.

Almost all personal computers for education also have flexible disk (floppy disk) memory— memory on round magnetic surfaces, currently between three and eight inches in diameter, that can be moved in and out of the machine. This memory is usually more extensive and cheaper

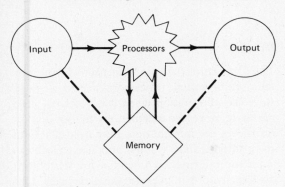

Figure 9.2   The computer (II).

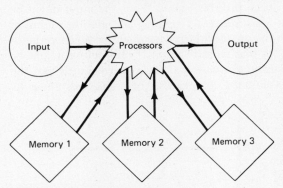

Figure 9.3   The computer (III).

than the fast memory and has the additional advantage that it can be removed from the machine and transported. Thus users can have their own private information, stored in their own disks. Since a floppy disk is inexpensive (currently about $3.00 a disk), it is practical to have a library of disks with your own specialized programs, results, text files, and more. Today's floppies may store from 100,000 to 1,000,000 characters.

A fancier personal computer may have another form of memory, often referred to as a Winchester disk. This "hard" disk, often *not* removable from the machine, is a somewhat more expensive memory, but it has much greater capacity. Its cost per unit of information stored is likely to be less than the cost on floppy disks. "Winchester" is a code name used within IBM when the technology was first developed. While Winchester disks are not common on today's inexpensive personal computers, they are likely to become more common. Other types of memory may be possible too.

Memory is characterized by *addresses,* locations in memory. You can think of computer memory as a set of boxes, like that in a post office. In each box you can store a small amount of information. Each box has an address, needed to store and retrieve information.

MEASURING MEMORY

A number of terms about measuring the quantity of memory are useful. First are the two magic words, *bit* and *byte*. A *bit* of memory is the lowest fundamental unit of memory; it represents a choice between a zero and a one, a location in which either a zero or a one can be stored. Electronically most memory consists of *two-state* devices with two distinct states. These devices must allow quick and easy recognition of one of the two possible positions, conditions, or other ways of showing two states. While for convenience these states are called zero and one, the important fact to remember is that there are only *two* states. For example, one might carry

a positive charge at a given point, with the other a negative charge at the same point. Or two different voltages represent the two states.

I am not too concerned with detailing how the memory is physically realized. In high-speed electronic memory it is likely that voltages store the bit of information. In lower-speed memory such as floppy disks, information is stored magnetically on the disk, perhaps with two directions of magnetization representing the two states.

Another common term in measuring memory size is *byte*. A byte represents enough bits of memory to store a character, such as an *A*, a *Q*, a *4*, or a *+*. In most modern computers a byte of memory contains 8 bits, but some old-fashioned machines have other byte sizes. A *word* is a collection of bytes, usually 2 or 4.

How do you know if somebody is talking about bits, bytes, or words? Usually it is just a matter of picking up the context. Table 9.1 may help to clarify the situation.

When referring to the fast memory of a computer, such as an IBM Personal Computer, one might say that the memory is 128K, meaning (almost) that the computer has 128,000 *bytes* of fast memory or that the machine will store 128,000 characters. Actually, this is not precise, because K really means 1024 instead of exactly 1000 (since computers function in powers of 2, and 1024 is the closest power of 2 to 1000).

Likewise, a modern floppy disk has a storage capacity of perhaps 350,000 bytes. Memory at user level generally *does* refer to bytes, with some exceptions. Some older computers still

Table 9.1 MEMORY SIZES

For	Memory size quoted in	State of the art (1984)
Memory chips	Bits (0 or 1)	16K to 64K
Personal computers	Bytes (characters)	16K to 512K; typical 128K
Larger computers	Bytes or words	Variable

measure their memory size in words, typically four bytes.

Bits as a unit of memory refer to the chips themselves, the electronic components from which the machines are made. Thus 1983 technology for memory employs 64K bit chips, about 65,000 bits, although 256K bit chips have already been announced and demonstrated. A chip with more memory stored on it usually costs little more than a chip with less; nor does it occupy greater volume. Hence the increasing amount of memory on chips has reduced the cost of memory; in going from 16K chips to 64K chips, as the computer industry did recently, the cost of memory diminished (roughly) by a factor of four. While this explanation is oversimplified, it is a good approximation. Several further stages in reduction of cost with current technology can be expected.

PROCESSORS

The processor (see Figure 9.1) is a major electronic component of the computer. A computer may contain more than one processor. A common abbreviation for the processor is CPU, meaning central processing unit, although this is somewhat archaic terminology. The word *central* is left over from a time when computers were gigantic devices, and so there was reason to emphasize the main control processor. Here I use the word *processor*, rather than *central processor*.

What is a processor's function? It is the physical device where the *instructions* to the computer are executed, after the user's program has been translated into computer-understood instruction. Every processor has some set of instructions it "knows" how to carry out, in the sense that these instructions are implemented electronically in hardware.

The instructions processors can directly execute are usually rather simple. They may say "move the information from this location in memory to that location in memory" or "treat the information in these two bytes of memory as

an integer, and add it to the integer information in these two bytes, storing the result at this location." Or they may say "examine a particular number to see whether it is positive; if so, get your next instruction from this location in memory; if not, get your next instruction from that location in memory." Note that the memory may have *both* data and instructions. So the computer can rapidly find either a new data item or the next instruction to execute.

Among a number of basic types of processors, some have instructions that work from a "stack," a collection of numbers or other information, somewhat like a stack of plates. That is, when one removes the top plate another plate comes to the top.

The most common distinction between current processors is the distinction between 8 and 16 bit processors. Older machines generally have 8 bit processors, while recently designed personal computers have 16 bit processors. Eight bit processors are present in Apple II, Atari, most TRS80s, and Sinclair. Sixteen bit processors are available in the TRS80 Model 2000, the Corvis Concept, the Digital Professional Personal Computers, the Apollo, the Sage, and the IBM Personal Computer. In some cases there might be some quibbling as to an 8 or 16 bit processor, so some more details are needed.

What does it mean to call the processor an "8 bit processor," or a "16 bit processor?" Several factors may be involved. First, the *instruction size,* the amount of memory needed to store an instruction, may be 8 or 16 bits long. Second, the bit size can refer to how much information flows in one gulp from memory to processor or processor to memory. Third, the bit size can be the length of internal storage units, registers, in the processor.

Some processors are somewhat in between, having both 8 and 16 bit characteristics. For example, the Intel 8088 functions in terms of instruction size and registers as a 16 bit processor, but works in terms of transfer of data as an 8 bit processor. Machines using a processor of this type are the IBM Personal Computer, the Digital Equipment Corporation Rainbow Personal Computer, and the Texas Instruments Professional Computer.

Typical 8 bit processors are the Zylog Z80, (TRS80 Model 1 and Model 3), the Mostak 6502 (Apple, Commodore), and the Intel 8080. Typical 16 bit processors are the Motorola 68000 (TRS80 Model 16, Corvis Concept, Sage), the Intel 8088 (IBM, Digital Rainbow), and the Digital LSI-11 (Digital Professional). Intel and National Semiconductor have announced a 32 bit processor, but it will probably be a number of years before such processor chips are common. The Motorola 68000 is sometimes referred to as a 32 bit processor because of certain features.

What can teachers and others interested in the role of computers in education make of all this information? The critical aspects for education are that (1) the 16 bit processors are newer and (2) they have some distinct advantages, mostly resulting from their newer technology. They allow the computer to have far more fast memory. Second, they usually have a more sophisticated collection of instructions; 8 bit processors appear primitive by computer standards. As a class, 16 bit processors are much faster than 8 bit processors, because they have been designed more recently and because more powerful instructions are available.

CHIP TECHNOLOGY

The essential ingredient of contemporary computers is the "chip," a large number of electrical components in a relatively small space, usually packed on a flat rectangular structure approximately one-eighth to one-half inch by one-half inch to several inches large.

Each component has two possible states or conditions, indicated perhaps by a location being electrically positive or negative. The notion of the two-state or binary technology is not new, having been used in computers since the earliest days. Binary devices can take many

forms. A mechanical relay, which can be either closed or open, is a binary device. An electric light bulb, if there's no concern about how bright the light is, is a binary device: A bulb is *on* or *off.* Water flowing or not flowing in a tube is binary.

The first useful computers were constructed with vacuum tubes. The jump to transistors in the late 1950s was a major innovation; transistors were much smaller, used much less current, and generated less heat than vacuum tubes. Chip technology is a derivative of transistor technology, but now instead of individual transistors, a miniscule chip may contain hundreds, thousands, or even more transistors and other electrical components.

Although I have referred to "chip technology," a variety of different technologies are involved. Chips can be built in a number of ways. In most, silicon forms the basis of the chip, and the circuit is reproduced on the chip photographically.

INPUT AND OUTPUT

Computers are useless without some human "interface," a way for a person to give information to the machine and to receive information from the machine. The most common input device for personal computers is a typewriterlike keyboard, perhaps with movable keys, perhaps just with areas to press; a few computers are even available with a newer, more rational keyboard layout. The common output device is a cathode ray screen.

Many other types of input and output devices are available. For example, if you use your personal computer for word processing or other paper-oriented applications, then some way of getting "paper" from the machine is important. So you need a *printing* device, perhaps similar to a typewriter, for output.

A range of printing devices is available, with trade-off between the quality of the material obtained and the cost of the printer. Low-cost ($500 to $1000 in 1983) machines are typically dot matrix printers; on these printers, letters are composed of a group of dots. With inexpensive printers, these dots may be readily apparent, lowering the quality of output. A more expensive printer known as a daisy wheel printer (around $800 to $1500) gives output similar to that of a good electric typewriter, with the letters continuous rather than dotted. These printers usually offer more choice of type styles, or fonts. Finally, although seldom used with personal computers today, there are available high-quality output devices, such as laser printers or photocomposition devices. Cost is commensurate with quality and speed. Quality can be comparable with book quality, and many different type fonts are available. In deciding which of these printers to acquire, you must balance your needs against the costs of the equipment.

GRAPHICS

In addition to text, other forms of computer output are very important in education. I have emphasized the importance of graphics in the learning process. Educational computers should include reasonable graphic capability. Before the advent of personal computers, graphics were not always available because of the sizable additional costs involved. While most personal computers have graphic capabilities, the capabilities are crude compared to what is desirable for educational purposes.

In looking at graphics, a number of features must be considered. First, how much detail can be specified in the picture? In most modern systems, pictures are effectively a series of dots on the screen, arranged in rows. If the dots are very close together, the picture appears to be continuous. In this case, resolution is high. If the dots are widely separated, they can be seen individually and odd effects often appear. Resolution here is low.

As an example of an odd visual effect, consider a diagonal line. On a low-resolution screen, instead of getting what looks like a neat straight line, you get a "stair step" effect. This is because the dots change only so often and they stay horizontal on the same row for several dots. The actual effect depends on the angle of the line as well as the screen resolution. Curved lines are also affected.

On today's inexpensive personal computers, typical dot resolutions are about 300 dots in the long (horizontal) direction by about 200 dots in the short (vertical) direction. The "aspect ratio," the long distance divided by the short distance, is often the same as it is on a TV monitor, four to three. More modern systems have better resolution. TV resolution varies from country to country but often about 500 to 600 "lines" (rows) are displayed on a TV screen. High-resolution television monitors in better graphic systems have 1000 or more lines. Vendors' terminology can give a misleading impression of graphic resolution, so you must be careful in interpreting such expressions as "high resolution" or "high res."

The educational user should also be aware of the fact that there can be undesirable interaction between characters and graphics. Thus some systems restrict the characters on the screen when graphics are used, an intolerable situation in most computer-based learning applications.

Another aspect of graphics is the question of color. Again, many personal computers have color, but often it is rather limited. For example, often only three colors are available for any useful resolution. More expensive systems have a wider range of color. Sometimes unfortunate interactions are found between color and the number of characters that can be put on the line; fewer characters per line may be the price of more color. The question of color with regard to characters may be quite different from the question of color with regard to visual or pictorial information.

Personal computers appear to be moving toward the use of a separate processor for graphics or perhaps for graphics along with a number of other input and output functions. Since individual processors are not expensive, this a rational approach. The advent of these special processors plus the declining costs of memory (making it possible to address more dots on the screen) indicates that graphics should be improving, even in inexpensive personal computers. I will have more to say about that in chapter 13.

Input and output on the computer might include other capabilities. For example, sound, both music and voice, is now possible. Music is still rather rare and usually involves additional "boards," collections of electronic components placed in the computer. Voice is available very inexpensively on some small computers using a process that converts speech into digital information. Sound can also be stored magnetically as it is in ordinary tape recorders. Another voice-output technique, more expensive but more versatile, is to represent all the sounds of a language phonetically. These techniques still may not produce speech of the highest quality, but the quality is improving.

MAINTENANCE

An important consideration for personal computers that novices often neglect is *maintenance,* keeping the computer working and repairing it when necessary. A personal computer is a complex device with electronic parts, keyboards, and output mechanisms with mechanical parts. Mechanisms are imperfect; what happens when something does not work is extremely important in both home and school use of personal computers.

In purchasing or leasing a machine, you should inquire carefully about both the initial warranty—what happens if it does not work when you first take it home or to school—and the long-range repair situation. A wise owner budgets for maintenance as a real cost of the computer. A school buying a dozen personal computers without allocating funds for maintenance is inviting serious problems. I cannot stress too highly the importance of carefully investigating maintenance arrangements and al-

locating funds for maintenance before buying any hardware.

You can learn to do some maintenance yourself. Some computer stores have courses in maintenance of a particular computer directed at novices. Or if your school has a sizable number of computers, you may find it desirable to keep extra "boards," the standard building blocks used in the computer, or to hire a maintenance person. This could be cheaper than paying a computer store on a time-by-time basis for repairs of many machines; inquire about costs in your own area to determine the best procedure.

CHOOSING HARDWARE

When you or your school district is ready to buy one or more computers, you must choose among the many different types available. A school district or university probably will choose by circulating a "request for quote," asking for prices among possible sources. A home computer will be chosen less formally. I suggest that the following five steps be followed in making your choice.

First, investigate where you can buy computers and software. Possible sources are computer stores, department stores, other stores (the Xerox store, the IBM store, etc.), salespeople for computer companies, or mail order houses, such as those listed in computer magazine ads. You need a panoramic view of who sells which machines.

Second, decide on your purpose. Why are you buying computers? This step is the most important and the most difficult of all. Many schools and individuals buy machines before fully determining their own educational requirements, because they have started with few specific applications in mind. Don't buy on the vague statement, from a salesman or a current user, that "machine *x* has lots of educational software!"

In choosing the computer, you should be *very greatly* influenced by the learning material currently available on the system. Buying a personal computer in the hope that a lot of material is or will be available, but with no careful investigation of just what *is* available, is a colossal, though prevalent, error. Don't just look at lists of programs, but spend considerable time running programs and choosing ones useful for *your* applications. Thus, if you decide that your major application is word processing, run a variety of word processors available for the machines readily available in your vicinity. You can often do this in the computer stores. Also let some students run the systems, since they are the potential users.

Third, remember maintenance. Check carefully into maintenance arrangements. Don't buy machines that cannot be repaired easily in your vicinity, unless you buy so many that you can do without a few units for a considerable length of time or unless you plan to do much of your own maintenance. Ask your sources for detailed comparison costs on maintenance when you request a quote. You will need to be persistent about this. Salespeople don't like to discuss the notion that equipment needs maintenance! Talk to owners about their experiences with maintenance.

Fourth, look ahead. The machine that you buy must be usable for a number of years. Hence the *current* curriculum material is not the only consideration. You want to pick a machine for which an increasing amount of curriculum material will be available in the future. Crystal ball gazing might help to make good estimates, but there are some good rules of thumb. Pick a *recently developed* machine, all other things being equal, since so little good curriculum material exists on *any* machine. It is a myth that some machines have vast amounts of good material.

You are likely to be better off picking a 16 bit computer because of its newer design. These machines are just at the beginning of their product life cycle. On the other hand, you may get spectacular buys on older machines, and *if* specific educational programs you require exist on those machines, that might influence your choice. Thus, if someone offers you a machine at a quarter of what it cost two months earlier, and you have examined useful applications available for it, you might want to choose such a machine. The stability of the company may also be a factor, but it is difficult to guess who will survive in this competitive business.

Fifth, get recent advice. The information about personal computers I am giving you or that you can get in *any* book is almost certain to be outdated. Owing to the field's rapid changes, books and even magazine articles can be misleading. Your best hope is to *check* the information presented here and elsewhere. Reading computer magazines may help, but they tend to provide more information about older computers than newer ones, and their reviews of components are of variable value. They also tend to go rapidly out of date. The general rule, then, is to be discriminating about all information and to check it through a variety of current sources.

Personal computers vary from country to country. While the computers mentioned herein are available in the United States, different machines, such as the Research Machine 380Z or 480Z or the BBC microcomputer, manufactured by Acorn, are available in British schools and universities. Likewise, in France different machines are available.

This variation between countries is partially due to national policy. A country wishes to support its own industry, so it requires its schools to buy the products of the country. This has resulted in a problem: Important software may not be available because of this nationalistic bias. Thus Logo, useful in many educational situations, was late in getting to Europe, because it was initially developed for computers in the United States.

chapter 10

Practical Issues of Computer Use in Education

- The School Environment for Computers
- College and University Environments for Computers
- Computing Departments
- Who Owns the Computers?
- Teachers and Faculty

This chapter focuses on two issues: first on the question of the computers themselves in schools and universities, particularly their location and use, and second on some issues involving teachers and faculty who use the computers.

THE SCHOOL ENVIRONMENT FOR COMPUTERS

The first issue to be considered with regard to computers in schools is where to physically place them. Their location can be either fixed or movable. A fixed location means that the computer stays permanently in one place, except for rare circumstances. A movable computer may be carried from place to place or it may be mounted on a cart. Mounting computers on carts makes it easy to respond to different needs. Thus, in a two-week period, all the machines in a school can be moved into one classroom as they are needed. Such easy mobility imposes the administrative chore of establishing a schedule and keeping track of where the machines are at all times. Also, they shouldn't be so readily movable that they disappear from the school!

Fixed machines can occupy a variety of locations. For example, they can remain in particular classrooms where it is known that they will be used extensively. They can be located centrally, such as in the school's library or learning center or in special central locations designed just for them. They can even stand in corridors, entrance halls, and other areas, particularly if the school wishes to encourage informal use of the machines. The present tendency is to keep computers in central locations, usually because only a few are available, and they should be accessible to all. Scheduling problems will arise. A teacher who plans to take students to the central location must be certain to avoid other classes appearing at the same time, so administrative control is required.

Like most issues the matters of fixed versus movable machines and location of fixed machines are best discussed among the teachers and administrators *before* the computers arrive on campus. I know of one school where a teacher, deeply involved in acquiring the computers, had implicitly assumed those computers were to be permanently located in her room. She was extremely unhappy when she discovered that despite all of her efforts, the computers were located elsewhere.

Another similar consideration is the number of computers available or how many are to be available for a particular application. This is a financial issue, because the question is how many the school can afford by one method or another. There must be some realistic view of how many machines are required for a particular application. Thus a school that buys computers with the intention of helping its students write better by using word processing extensively is fooling itself if it purchases only three machines for the entire school. Generally computers are more likely to be used effectively in schools that have a well-focused idea of how they will be used than in schools whose strategy is "let's get a few machines and see what happens."

Another factor meriting full advance discus-

sion is the arrangement for maintenance. This involves not only the question of what external or internal agency will maintain the machines, but also the decision process relative to maintenance. For example, suppose a teacher notes that a machine "goes down," or does not work. To whom does the teacher report the failure, and how does that person proceed? Unless administrative structures are well-defined, the machine may remain down for some time. Or maintenance costs may be very high.

Computers enter the school environment for many reasons, and those particular reasons may affect some essential decisions. They may appear because of teachers' demand, because of administrative support, or because of strong parental clamor. This last consideration—computers appearing in school primarily because of the urging of parents who feel their children are cheated of an adequate education if they lack access to computers—is increasingly important in United States schools. It is not necessarily a bad way to introduce computers in schools, but it often requires a special approach. Most parents play less than critical roles in the day-to-day operation of schools, and so schools are unprepared for major parental influence regarding computers. Strong supporters of computers, be they teachers, administrators, or parents, may have very fuzzy notions of exactly what kids are to *do* with the machines when they arrive. So the school, or rather the school plus outside help, may need to provide parents with better information. Similar problems were associated with the new math.

The next issue is how the computer fits into the existing school learning environment. Software of any type cannot simply be dumped into the classroom with the expectation that it will be used. It must fit into the curriculum in some way or other. If it is a small amount of material, the teacher must understand clearly just how it is to fit into the rest of the curriculum. Larger chunks of material can be made to run somewhat independently of the teacher. Instructors can work with some students individually, while others work with the computer material. It is unrealistic to expect a teacher to be able to give sizable amounts of attention to *everyone* in class who is working on computer material.

The classroom situation needs to be considered if the computer material is to be usable in ordinary classes. As I have stressed repeatedly, there is a difference between experimental classes with few students and highly skilled teachers and the real situation in most classes.

COLLEGE AND UNIVERSITY ENVIRONMENTS FOR COMPUTERS

Colleges and universities have used computers in education, often in minimal ways, for a much longer time than schools. Hence many universities already have strong traditions about computer usage. Even more important, very strong power groups within the university are often involved with these usages, power groups that probably don't exist in many schools. Traditional university computer centers often have large budgets, and they are eager to maintain these budgets. The difference in computer organization, such as the existence of long-established centers, is often great between higher education on the one hand and primary and secondary education on the other.

At least three common ways exist for using computers in universities. Unfortunately, many higher education institutions still depend on older "batch" environments, where students have to punch cards to obtain input rather than interact directly with a computer. While it would be better if such procedures no longer existed, examples persist, in some cases for economic reasons. In these systems students must usually go to a location with keypunches, wait in line to get access to them, carry a deck of cards to the input device (often elsewhere on campus), and then appear hours or days later to receive the output. This is tedious and probably will gradually be phased out.

Batch processing has tended to be replaced by timesharing, sometimes on the same computer but often on a different computer. With timesharing each student works at a display, usually a TV connected to the computer. All users "share" the computer. I have said little about timesharing in this book, since my emphasis is on the personal computer. But from an educational user's point of view, the differences between timesharing and personal computers are small.

Personal computers are definitely increasing in postsecondary institutions at present, although there is a fair amount of resistance, particularly from established computer centers that are trying to retain their power basis and very sizable budgets.

For both timesharing and personal computers two environmental strategies prevail. One strategy groups most student access stations in a single location. The alternative provides many smaller locations, scattered over the campus. A few campuses concentrate computers in the libraries, but this situation is relatively rare. Occasionally movable machines on carts are used within a department, particularly in laboratories, but this is not common.

No matter how the computers are grouped, hours of availability constitute an important issue. Again, differences among institutions are great. Some campuses take pride in computers being available for student use twenty-four hours a day, seven days a week, except possibly during an occasional brief preventive maintenance period for timesharing or batch systems. Other campuses, particularly those that are nonresidential, tend to have business hours, with the computers available, say, from 8:00 A.M. to 5:00 P.M. or possibly into the evening, for only five or six days a week. The differences are usually due to finances. In most cases some supervision is needed, if only to prevent equipment from being stolen. Thus longer hours entail more expenses; in some cases these expenses are prohibitive.

Another possibility for college and university systems is to allow use from students' homes, assuming that students have some equipment or that the university will lend it to them. I will say more about this shortly. This method also assumes phone access to the computer in a timesharing environment. Many timesharing systems do provide such access, but the necessary phone numbers are not always announced to students. Students must also have modems to connect the terminal to the phone. On the other hand, some universities pride themselves that students can use their systems from home.

COMPUTING DEPARTMENTS

One issue of importance in schools is the question of how the teaching of computing will be arranged. The typical strategy in schools and universities when new subjects come into being is to create new departments. Some high schools already have computer science departments. They appeared long ago in universities, often as outgrowths of mathematics, physics, or engineering departments. In a few cases they still are part of those departments in universities, generally for political reasons.

There is some question, however, whether a new computer science department is really needed in high school and, if one is needed, what it should teach. Chapters 3 and 5 emphasized that many, probably most, of the uses of computers will occur *within other departments*. I feel it is a mistake for schools to believe that everything about the computer should be taught in a separate computer science department. Even the question of sociological implications of the computer, discussed in chapter 3, might well be taught better by individuals not in a computer science department. Only the programming course, the advanced placement computer science course or some other form, needs a specialist, if it is not offered in a computer-based learning mode independent of teachers. Hence high schools should be cautious in creating computer science departments, separately or within other departments.

WHO OWNS THE COMPUTERS?

Either the students or the institution owns the computer. Until quite recently, in both schools and universities, the institution clearly owned the computers. When the computer was expensive, students could not own one. Yet students often own educational materials of older types. In public schools in the United States, the institution (the school district) almost always owns the books. On the other hand, in universities individual students must purchase textbooks. At all educational levels, calculators are individually owned. Indeed, calculator use developed against the preference of many teachers, but now they are accepted almost universally in universities and in most schools, with resulting effect on the curriculum.

As I mentioned, institutions have traditionally owned the computer. But an institution is a complex organization. While it is true that until recently the university owned "all" computers, the computers might show up in different inventories, rendering ownership functionally different depending on what department in the school is the owner. Thus the computer center itself might be the effective owner, while in other cases the school, college, or department might be the owner. Recently some shift has occurred toward departmental ownership in many universities. Powerful political issues may be involved in ownership.

A few universities now require students in certain curricula to own their own computers: Massachusetts Institute of Technology, Carnegie-Mellon University, Stevens Institute of Technology, Brown University, Drexel University, and Clarkson. Others have announced plans either for student ownership or for very widespread student availability.

Carnegie-Mellon University's plan is perhaps the most interesting. Looking not to the personal computers of today but to the much more powerful ones of the near future, Carnegie-Mellon has signed an agreement with IBM covering the first stages of this project. Plans for the project's curriculum development are as yet uncertain. The eventual student computer will be a very powerful one, perhaps the equivalent of a computer costing about $500,000 in 1980. The university will also construct an elaborate network to make various special facilities (plotters, high-quality printers, large storage units) widely available to students and faculty.

Clearly plans such as these will be widely imitated. A trend toward transferring ownership of computers to students or lending computers to students can be expected.

The problem that arises is how the computers will be used in classes. Many universities assume that the faculty will develop curricula, but this is seldom done. Most faculty have neither the time nor the training to develop the new courses that would effectively use computers. Chapter 14 outlines mechanisms for curriculum development.

As home ownership of computers increases, more people will own their own computers. But the curriculum situation will be even more complex then in the university, as many different types of computers will be involved.

TEACHERS AND FACULTY

As computers come to be used more and more, one question that is often asked is what will happen to teachers and faculty. Will there still be teachers and faculty, or will computers replace them? How will teachers be trained to use computers effectively? This training problem occurs at all levels of education.

At least two types of problems occur in educating teachers about computers. The first problem is in educating teachers about how computers can be used in education. This might be called "computer literacy for teachers," mentioned in chapter 3. The second more specific need is to train people to teach computer science in such courses as the Advanced Placement computer course.

In both these cases it is critical that the computer be used to train the teachers. Teachers should have the opportunity to study from good computer-based learning material.

chapter **11**

Developing Curriculum Material for Computers I

- How Textbooks Are Produced
- Steps Leading to Curriculum Material
- Production Strategy for Computers
- Initial Pedagogical Design for Computer-based Learning Material
- Detailed Pedagogical Design

Not everyone will produce computer-based learning material. But the production process may be of interest to a wide audience. In this chapter and the next I review a process, evolved over fifteen years at the Educational Technology Center, for developing computer-based learning material. I will not give a full presentation of this production system; the two chapters will merely serve as an overview, raising some important issues and sketching the broad outline. More detailed information about this production system can be found in my book *Learn-*

ing with Computers. * Other information is also available from the Educational Technology Center. The quality of materials generated is directly related to the effectiveness of the system.

One system cannot show all possible production strategies. I only comment in this chapter about other strategies for producing computer-based learning materials. Unfortunately, the

---

*Alfred Bork, *Learning with Computers* (Bedford, Mass.: Digital Press, 1981).

present basis of comparison of production systems is weak, coming from very few empirical studies of different ways to compose computer-based learning material. Today's evidence is based on the last dozen years or so when the generation of computer-based learning material has been slowly increasing.

A key to the discussion is that models of curriculum development to follow for computers are fundamentally related to older models for other media. In many ways developing good computer-based learning material is no different from producing good educational films, textbooks, or other learning materials. The emphasis should be on *good*. As will be seen, many of the stages are similar.

I should like to emphasize that developing high-quality curriculum material is a serious, difficult business, independent of the question of what learning media are involved. Producing a good textbook, film, or computer program—good from the standpoint of assisting learning—is *not* a simple process. The notion that someone would be able to acquire a computer and immediately turn out large amounts of highly competent curriculum material is simply not realistic, just as acquiring a printing press does not lead automatically to the printing of large amounts of highly desirable curriculum material.

HOW TEXTBOOKS ARE PRODUCED

To put the development of computer-based learning material in perspective, I will first discuss a process probably well known to many but perhaps not to all readers. It is the procedure in use today for the production of most textbooks. Many variants in this process can be found, but the overall outlines are much the same among publishers.

The textbook comparison is especially cogent, as textbooks are a relatively recent invention in the history of education. The first printing presses in Europe were built around 1450, and textbooks were common in universities by about 1700. As with anything new in education, it took time—about 250 years—to learn how to use the medium. Neither good textbooks nor good computer-based learning materials are produced instantly; it takes more than the technology.

How does the idea for a textbook originate? A writer may contact one or more publishers with an idea for a new book. Or a publisher's field representatives may have heard that someone is already writing a book in an area that might interest the company. Or the company, by market research or other means, may decide it wants a textbook or series in a particular area and so seeks out authors.

In any case this stage entails discussions between the prospective author or authors and the publisher. Usually the author prepares outlines and an analysis of student needs with regard to the topics to be discussed, sometimes in great detail; perhaps they even prepare sample chapters. This material may be sent out for review and then revised. This planning results either in a contract for a book or an author's seeking a different publisher.

Book contracts are generally similar. They assume the author will receive an advance on royalties as well as royalties on sales. A typical figure for royalties on textbooks today is 15 percent of net sales, although all publishers have their own ways of figuring. This possible income from royalties is a major incentive for persuading people to write textbooks; but in practice, the author's income from the book is usually small. Another incentive is status, either within the discipline or in one's own university or school.

After signing the contract, the author begins writing a manuscript for the book, the full pedagogical specification. The manuscript may be reviewed at many different stages. First, the author may send it to friends for comment. The manuscript may even be tried in classes. But the publisher is responsible for most manuscript evaluation and typically sends it for review to a number of individuals, both authorities in the area and those considered representative of the proposed market. Editors employed by the publishing house will also review the manuscript and suggest changes. All this feedback goes to the author, and several such iterations of review and changes may occur.

When both author and publisher accept the manuscript, often with some compromise on both sides, the publisher sends it into the technical production phase. A number of specialists are employed. A graphic designer decides what kind of paper to use, what size paper, how wide the margins should be, how to display the headings, what the typefaces should be, and how the pictures and text should be interwoven. An artist makes any necessary drawings; photographers prepare other pictures. Editors prepare the manuscript for typesetters, working in details such as types of heading already chosen by the graphic designer.

Typesetting, the process of converting the manuscript to formal version in type, is often done in two stages—a galley-proof stage and then a page-proof stage. Most publishers use modern electronic methods of typesetting, and either set the book themselves or hire a composition firm to do so.

After the page proofs are carefully proofread, the book can proceed into the printing process. As few publishers have their own printing presses, this stage is mostly done by outside specialists. After the book is bound, it is ready to market.

Books may be produced using word processors, photocomposition machines, and other technology to bypass paper manuscripts and typesetting, although this is still not common; the process is similar to that indicated.

Many different people with different talents are involved in this process, and considerable cost is involved. These costs include the advance on royalties (a small fraction of the total production cost), the salaries of all the publisher's employees working on the material,

and the fees for external services such as printing.

STEPS LEADING TO CURRICULUM MATERIAL

This view of how books are produced can serve as a general introduction to the preparation of curriculum material, since many of the same or similar features apply to other ways of producing material, including ways that involve computers.

It is convenient to think of the process in five stages. Unfortunately, in a written document such as this, these stages must be presented sequentially even though they do not necessarily *occur* sequentially. Furthermore, a given stage may be repeated a number of times. These are the five stages that will be considered:

1. Pedagogical design
2. Graphic design
3. Implementation
4. Evaluation
5. Improvement

Note that this approach looks something like top-down programming; the overall factors are considered first, and then the details. In later parts of this chapter and in the next chapter I will discuss these stages specifically for the development of learning material for the computer.

Pedagogical Design

Pedagogical design refers to the full process of planning the materials, the planning that precedes any implementation. This stage sometimes is referred to as instructional design. I avoid that term, because it is used very frequently by a group of learning theorists who come from behavioral backgrounds. I want to allow for the possibility of design approaches other than those usually described in instructional design textbooks.

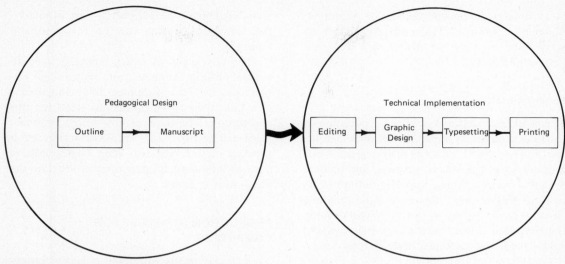

Figure 11.1 The process of publishing a book.

Pedagogical design usually has several stages. First, it includes the early planning of the lesson material, the development of the overall strategy before getting down to details. This overall strategy can result from a variety of methods. Usually the goals and objectives are considered in such early planning. A useful technique is brainstorming in a group.

In brainstorming people are encouraged to generate comments quickly, without much pondering. The first rule of brainstorming is *not* to criticize any ideas presented by others; indeed, there's no reason to worry about duplication of ideas. Criticism comes later. The objective is to generate many ideas for the next stage of the process.

Some analysis of the ideas usually follows brainstorming. Since a group of modules is typically to be developed, this analysis may also classify some of the brainstorming concepts elicited, showing what modules are needed. Here rational considerations play more of a role than during brainstorms, with developers looking for gaps in the proposed approach.

More detailed descriptions must follow this initial start in pedagogical design, producing something analogous to the manuscript of a book. The actual product, the physical form of the pedagogical design, will differ from one medium to another. Thus for film the product might include a storyboard plus a shooting script.

"Script" seems to be a good word to designate the full design specification, regardless of the implementation media. I use the word here with the understanding that a computer-based learning script will be different from a film script or the script for some other medium, because the media are different. An example of a script for computer-based learning is presented later in this chapter.

Graphic Design

The second stage in the authoring process is *graphic design,* which concerns the visual and possibly temporal appearance of the material, its structure in space and time. I have already mentioned what the graphic designer and the artist contribute toward a book's visual appearance. The consideration and sizable budgets allotted to graphic design for textbooks indicate publishers' understanding of its effect on sales. Advertisements and brochures by major computer vendors are another indication of graphic design's importance. These ads are almost always done by very competent and well-paid graphic designers.

Implementation

The most technical aspect of the production of learning modules is *implementation,* which almost always involves a series of specialists. Thus in publishing, typesetters, printers, and binders are involved in technical implementation, while in films cameramen, directors, lighting crew, makeup crew, laboratory workers who develop the film, film editors, and many others play a role. The actual technical activity may be entirely different in different media, but in all cases technical implementation bridges the gap from design to working materials.

Evaluation and Improvement

The three stages considered so far—pedagogical design, graphic design, and implementation— are more or less sequential in most media, although some moving back and forth may occur. That is, some graphic design may be done at the pedagogical design stage, and some additional pedagogical design can be done after graphic design. But the two stages of *evaluation* and *improvement* may occur at many places along the way in the production process and may be repeated several times. Note that they go in tandem. In producing materials developers are, at this point, primarily concerned with formative evaluation to improve the materials for the next stage. The distinction between formative evaluation and summative evaluation is discussed briefly in chapter 8.

An evaluation-improvement cycle generally occurs immediately after each stage of pedagogical design and probably after graphic design also. Competent individuals review the script many times during its development. With a book, the publisher sends the manuscript to

knowledgable people for peer review. Similarly, the script for a film can be reviewed and modified.

In many types of instructional design, an evaluation-improvement cycle may follow implementation. Its nature may differ. In the case of a film, the editing process partially fits this description. The issue of how much improvement can be done *after* implementation is dependent on the medium. With books, little is done at this stage, because after production the medium is inflexible.

PRODUCTION STRATEGY FOR COMPUTERS

Though the details will differ, it is my contention that this same method of producing learning material is fundamentally the most effective to use with the *computer.* Many developers of computer-based learning material would not agree. Rather, more of a "Renaissance man" system has been recreated some fifty times over: a system where one person undertakes *all* the production stages rather than using different specialists for each stage. A large amount of effort has been thrown into development of "CAI (Computer Assisted Instruction) languages" or interactive "CAI systems" whose purpose supposedly is to make it easy for one person to perform the entire process. Hundreds of millions of dollars have been spent in developing such systems. I do not believe that these strategies are successful. At best they can work for limited small personal programs.

The relatively small amount of material of any value developed with *all* CAI languages and systems is a clear empirical indication of the poverty of that approach. I do not believe it likely that large amounts of excellent computer-based learning material will be created using facilities such as Pilot, Planet, Tutor, Coursewriter, Decal, Asset, DAL, or any of the other explicit languages and authoring systems of this type.

For example, Pilot has existed for many years. It has been implemented on many different computers, and it has been heavily promoted for years in ads from major personal computer vendors. But to the best of my knowledge, very little good computer-based learning materials is available in Pilot.

The "Renaissance man" approach, with one person doing everything, is misguided. Most authoring languages and systems lead to trivial computer-based learning material. I'll provide more reasons as I examine the pedagogical design and implementation stages explicitly for the computer.

It is not too surprising that a number of production strategies from other media have been used with the computer. Thus some people try to write what are essentially manuscripts, which leads to poor material. Another approach often used is the storyboard approach. Storyboards are an important intermediate stage in producing films. They show in visual form with a little bit of text each of the sequences of a film. They are not the full story—a shooting script is still needed to complete the details in most filmmaking.

I believe the use of the storyboard as the major instrument for designing computer-based learning material is a serious mistake. It emphasizes the screens alone and neglects the extremely important factor of interaction. An adequately detailed, complex analysis of student interaction cannot be shown in storyboard form, yet ideally programs are highly interactive.

This is not to say that the designers of material for the computer should not draw pictures of the screen—they *should,* particularly when they feel strongly about where things should be placed on the screen. To rely on this as the *principal* mode of representing the information, however, does not lead to material that uses the computer effectively. Material designed purely with storyboards often has many splashy pictures but little else of value; in particular, interaction is weak.

The strategy I propose, used for many years in the Educational Technology Center, is very much like the general strategy for the development of any curriculum material reviewed earlier. It embodies the same five stages: pedagogical design, graphic design, implementation, evaluation, and improvement. It provides for a variety of people bringing different types of expertise into the project. The general outline, however, has been adapted to the particular needs of the computer.

INITIAL PEDAGOGICAL DESIGN FOR COMPUTER-BASED LEARNING MATERIAL

The initial stages in pedagogical design are, to some extent, media independent. That is, a group of people with varied backgrounds is likely to develop specifications for the curriculum units. Brainstorming will generally be useful. The group must include at least *one* computer media specialist, a person possessing detailed acquaintance with computer-based learning, to use the new medium effectively and to keep the specifications within reasonable costs with the currently available computer technology. The initial design group should also include people who have been directly involved in fundamental research associated with *learning* the particular discipline, if any research exists. Thus if the material concerns problem solving, specialists in problem solving should participate in the initial design stage. Good teachers must also be included in this stage.

The product of this stage will be a set of descriptions of the computer modules, based on analysis of student needs. These descriptions may be only one page or a few pages in length, but they should furnish enough details to guide the pedagogical design group toward a reasonable view of what it is to accomplish. That is, the output from initial design becomes the next stage's input.

DETAILED PEDAGOGICAL DESIGN

Detailed pedagogical design is perhaps the most fundamental and critical stage in the production process, for it is in the full pedagogical design specification that the quality of the materials is, to a large extent, determined.

The first guideline is to involve the best possible individuals, working in a *small group.* In the Educational Technology Center we have found that groups of three to five usually function best. We also work occasionally with groups of two. Large groups become debating societies, except when carefully managed, and tend to produce relatively little. Single individuals produce material of lesser quality than groups, particularly regarding the quality of analysis of student input, but naturally the costs are also less.

In seeking the best possible people for the pedagogical design groups, it should be anticipated that they are not likely to be found at a single geographical location. Rather they must be brought together from different parts of the world to work in specific design groups. Usually these people spend only a week or two at this activity. Thus the cost of gathering such a group is within reason. This model is similar to the model used in many major curriculum development projects in the 1960s in the United States. These projects also attempted to assemble the competent people from everywhere.

How are the individuals in the design group selected? Typically, a mix of talents is desirable, and the group must be congenial. One or two teachers who work closely with the proposed target audience should be in each design group. They should be the type of teachers who listen attentively to students and who interact readily with them. That is, a teacher who interacts with learners primarily through lecturing is not likely to be the type of person needed for this task. Researchers will probably also be included in the detailed design groups. And there will be persons whose knowledge of the technology comes through considerable previous experience in producing a wide range of effective computer-based learning dialogs. The group needs mutual and complementary talents, seldom found in a single person. Even if one person has all these talents, that individual will have limited time for production, and so cannot produce all the needed material.

Developing computer-based learning materials is highly intense activity. At the Educational Technology Center our groups work full days working *only* on these activities, usually for brief periods of time such as a week or two, although some have worked only part-time over a longer period. It is best to remove these groups from the usual office environments of students, telephones, computer displays, secretaries, colleagues, and other interruptions. Hence we seek pleasant, isolated environments where the group can concentrate on the task at hand. Guided by the initial design document, we frequently work on full pedagogical design either in the mountains in southern California or alongside pools and Jacuzzis.

Note that in listing the members of the group, a programmer was not mentioned. Our experience in working with programmers in groups has been very mixed, particularly when programmers have only a limited programming background—say a year or two of programming courses but little practical experience in developing complex large programs. People of this type often have a very limited view of the computer's potential, and so produce restricted material. We prefer to give very good teachers great freedom in specifying the material's content and to try to react to these demands at later implementation stages.

After the pedagogical design group assembles, a brief workshop is desirable. For our projects a half-day workshop has been typical, giving participants a background in desirable ways of using the computer as a learning medium, particularly contrasting its capabilities with those of books, video, and other learning modes. In these sessions we do *not* teach computer programming, and we do not teach or use any authoring language or system. Rather we show many examples of computer-based learning, stressing good and bad aspects of how the computer is used.

In the introductory workshop it is important to counteract unfortunate tendencies developers may have. For example, most developers will already be familiar with textbooks, and almost all will be familiar with lectures. So it is important to stress the *interactive* nature of the computer material to avoid booklike or lecturelike modules. In every design group at least one person is already experienced with computer-based learning material, so further "instruction" for newcomers in the medium will occur in the writing sessions.

Remember that the purpose of this detailed design group is to produce the *script* for a learning module, the input to later stages of the production process. This script must give *all* the details of what is to appear on the screen (both text and pictures), how it is to appear, how to analyze student input, and what decisions are to be made based on this analysis. I illustrate the notion by showing two sample scripts; the first is a trivial example to introduce the conventions, while the second is more realistic.

Figure 11.2 shows a sample script in a form used for many years in the Educational Technology Center. This simple example is picked to illustrate how authors specify material. It is trivial and so is *not* shown as a good example of computer-based learning material, but rather to show the tactics for producing scripts.

Figure 11.3 explains the simple conventions for computer scripts. The ingredients may be at least partially recognizable to you. The message "What is 7 × 9?" will be displayed to the viewer on the computer screen. The material in braces, such as "input," furnishes instructions to the coder, in the implementation stage, or comments within the program to make it more readable. The coder may need a variety of instruc-

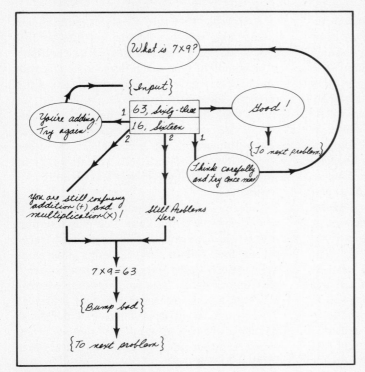

Figure 11.2 A sample script.

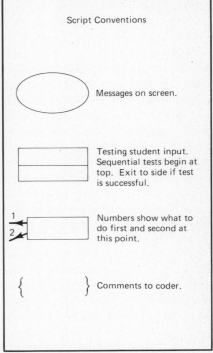

Figure 11.3 Script conventions.

tions from authors, and so these braces are useful for separating these instructions from other specification details. There is nothing magical about braces. They are used in UCSD Pascal, the programming environment used at the Educational Technology Center, as "comment" symbols, so we have adapted them for the scripts.

The boxes down the center of the figure are the tests on student input. These tests occur sequentially. That is, if the first test in the list is not successful, we do the second test. If that is not successful, we do the third test, and so forth. If a test is *successful*—that is, if the string being tested is contained in what the student did type —then we exit the box to the right or to the left, along the line shown going out in that direction. Thus, in the sample script shown, if a student types the correct answer, 63, we reply "Good" and proceed to the next problem.

An important pedagogical point to note about this sample script is that while we look for *likely errors* by students, unanticipated responses must also be considered. A likely error in this case might be that a student, just learning multiplication, does not readily distinguish it from addition. So we look for the possibility of addition, 16, and, if necessary, we explicitly state that addition and multiplication are different. Being able to give immediate feedback in such situations, an important aspect of computer-based learning, makes the computer an effective learning device; in ordinary large classes, it is difficult for teachers to offer such quick help. Highly experienced teachers in the design group can often anticipate students' likely mistakes at a given point, and so these can be incorporated within the program.

In the sample script, students who do add have the mistake brought to their attention, and they can try again to enter a correct answer. It is possible that some students will continue to add the two numbers. Hence there must be some way of distinguishing a repetition of this student input from a first occurrence. We do not want to endlessly point out the same error. The

numbers "one" and "two" on the lines leaving the side of the second box indicate where to go the first time a "match" is found at that point and where to go the second time. Three, four, five, or more inputs occur in some situations, but they cannot occur in this script because we do not allow another input for this student.

Note the lines coming out of the bottom of this set of testing blocks. They imply that we may have tested the student input for each of these two possibilities, 63 and 16, and found nothing recognizable. Unless the items tested in the student input are logically exhaustive, covering every conceivable possibility, we always need to allow for such a "drop-through" case, a student who has put in something completely unanticipated. The pedagogical design group must determine what to do at each point, including this drop-through case. In this script, the first time we simply ask students to try again; the second time we give students the answer.

Remember that this simple example is *not* intended to furnish a "model" of how to proceed when you are unable to predict everything students might type. Each decision of this type should be based on the pedagogical needs of the moment. Thus if the issue is very important, we might want to give extensive help at this point or ask the question a different way or choose other strategies to aid learning. On the other hand, if the issue is relatively trivial, we might want simply to tell the answer and proceed with the material.

Beware! There is a danger in looking at a simple example of this kind. You may interpret this as *characteristic* of computer-based learning material. Indeed many attempts at developing computer-based learning authoring systems have unfortunately been based on simple examples such as this, assuming that they represent how *always* to proceed. There is a tendency, therefore, to develop "templates" that allow one to set up structures such as these quickly and easily, building the logic into the program. But while well-intentioned, these strategies are almost always highly inadequate. Figure 11.2 is given only to show the technique of the script; it is *not a good example of computer-based learning.*

For a more realistic view, Figure 11.4 on pages 132–135 examines a more elaborate section of script. This material is the beginning segment from some material developed jointly at the Centre Universitaire d'Informatique at the University of Geneva and the Educational Technology Center. The subject matter is learning how to use spreadsheets, which were discussed in chapters 3 and 4.

This introductory section determines if a student *can* read a table, and, if not, gives help. This is a fundamental skill for using spreadsheets, so it is a reasonable place to start. The segment shown takes only the first few minutes (or seconds) of the learning process for most students. My main purpose is to illustrate the process, not to show all the details.

Identified at the beginning is the module name and number, the date, and the developers. Comments are in braces. Very little happens on the screen in the initial segments; only seven words appear. The rest is information about timing, delays for readability and emphasis, and information about how the messages will appear on the screen. SPREADSHEET appears in capital letters.

Page 2 is all comments. Several tables are suggested. The one the rest of the material is based on is a bus or train schedule between Geneva and other Swiss cities.

Page 3 specifies the initial screen format. The big box is an outline of the screen. A table area is specified, as well as three "ports," or areas on the screen—a question port, an answer port, and a help port. The names indicate what is to happen at each port. At the bottom we indicate that initially a full table is to be shown, and then part of the table is removed to provide space to place messages. Thus we as pedagogical designers have specified how the screen will be arrayed for this question. The smaller boxes do not appear to the student, but

only identify screen areas for the graphic artists or for the coders.

On page 4 the student is given a question. Several questions are suggested; although only three cities are shown, more will probably be needed.

The input is in the answer port. The boxes down the center of pages 4 and 5 and the messages to each side show processing of the student input. The tests are performed in sequence, down the page; successful exits, with the condition satisfied, are to the side.

The student may be a novice at the computer. The first possibility we check for is that the student does *nothing at all* in six seconds. After each six seconds, up to three times, we give a help message to try to get the student going. The student may not know that we expect something to be input, even though a question appears on the screen!

The next task in the analysis of student input is to identify the student who *has* typed something but has not pressed return. Many students do not know they need to press return. Rather than tell them every time, a boring message, we chose to explicitly seek the situation where the student does not know to press return, at least the first time. Note that the help sequence, line 1 out of the "no return in nine seconds" box, asks another question; we don't assume the student presses return for this particular input. Looking for yes or the equivalent in the subsidiary input must be handled so that no return is required.

The next testing box on page 4 checks for something that is not a number. Students may not be familiar with the typewriterlike keyboard and may need some help. On the top of page 5 we anticipate a likely problem with beginners: Following their typewriter practices, they may use the letter *l* in place of the number *1* or something similar. Note that *we* make the substitution after offering advice, rather than asking the student to do it again. We then come back into the testing loop.

If the student *does* enter a number, three

Spreadsheet – Module I – 19 October 1982 page 1

Alfred Bork, Jean-Claude Courbon, Bertrand Ibrahim, Bernard Levrat,
Gustave Moeckli, Christian Pellegrini, Jean Kydas

Title page, followed by possible "attract mode," followed by possible MENU

{centered on}   Let's look at a
{blank screen}   {delay 1 second.}
              SPREADSHEET   {big letters}
              {delay 1.5 seconds}
                or table
              {delay 3, erase.}

Spreadsheet – Module I   page 2

{Pick and present randomly one of several tables, such as:

Bus or train schedule between Geneva and other Swiss cities
University of Geneva budget, over many years}

{Perhaps only one table initially}

{Task: We determine if the student can read a value from the table.}

{Questions vary with the table. We give one example here.}

Figure 11.4 (*a*), (*b*) Script for introduction to spreadsheets—pages 1 and 2.

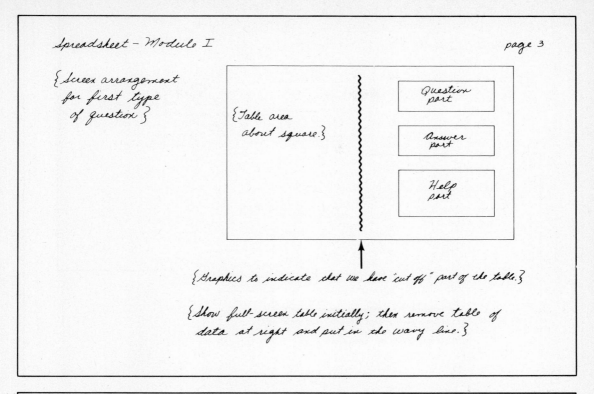

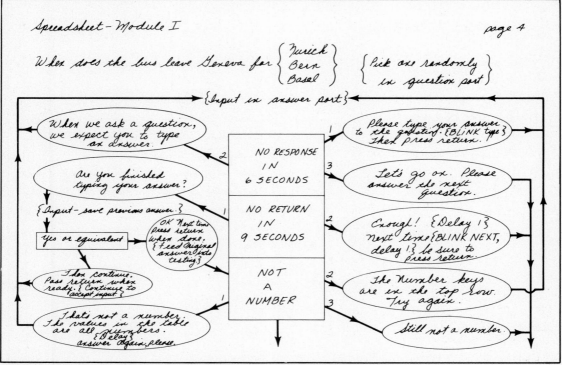

Figure 11.4 (c), (d) Script for introduction to spreadsheets—pages 3 and 4.

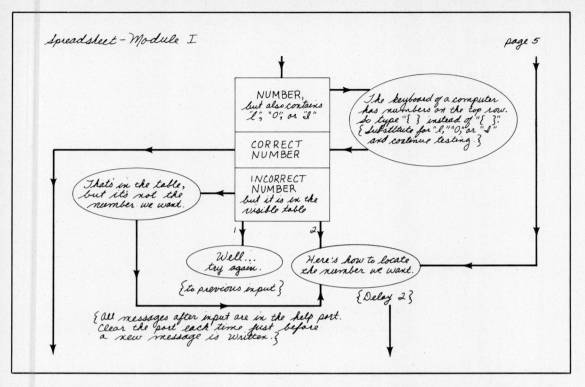

NUMBER, but also contains "ℓ", "O", or "I"

The keyboard of a computer has numbers on the top row. So type "{ }" instead of "{ }". { Substitute for "ℓ,""O,"or "I" and continue testing. }

CORRECT NUMBER

INCORRECT NUMBER but it is in the visible table

That's in the table, but it's not the number we want.

1   2

Well... try again.

Here's how to locate the number we want.

{to previous input}

{Delay 2}

{ All messages after input are in the help port. Clear the port each time just before a new message is written. }

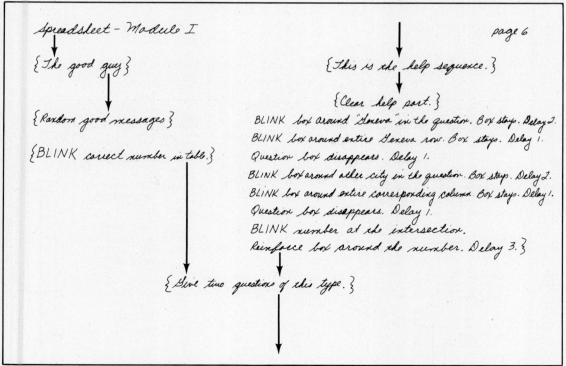

{The good guy}

{This is the help sequence.}

{Clear help port.}

{Random good messages}

BLINK box around "Geneva" in the question. Box stays. Delay 2.

{BLINK correct number in table.}

BLINK box around entire Geneva row. Box stays. Delay 1.

Question box disappears. Delay 1.

BLINK box around other city in the question. Box stays. Delay 2.

BLINK box around entire corresponding column. Box stays. Delay 1.

Question box disappears. Delay 1.

BLINK number at the intersection.

Reinforce box around the number. Delay 3.}

{Give two questions of this type.}

Figure 11.4 (e), (f) Script for introduction to spreadsheets—pages 5 and 6.

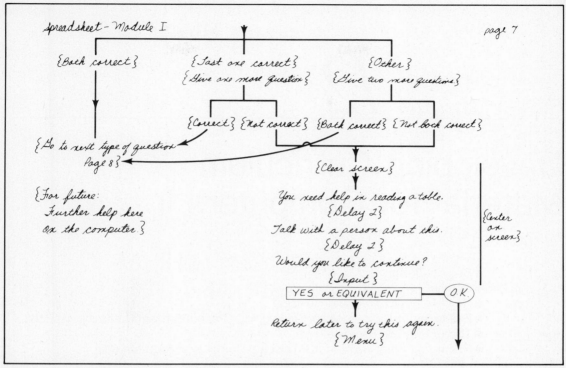

Figure 11.4 (*g*) Script for introduction to spreadsheets—page 7.

possibilities are noted on page 5: The number might be right, it might be *another* number in the table, or it is incorrect, the "drop-through" case. We also specify, in braces, where the messages will appear on the screen, using the ports previously shown.

On page 6 are two sequences, one of a person who responded correctly, perhaps with help, and the help sequence for other people. The help sequence is purely visual, with no text. At least two questions of this table look-up type are presented.

On page 7, we decide what to do depending on the student responses to the two questions. If students answer both correctly, they go to the next question. If they have the last one correct, perhaps because they learned something from the help sequences in the first question, then we offer another table look-up question. If this is answered correctly, they then go on to the next type of question. In other cases we suggest help outside the program. The note at the left suggests that further help may be available later.

I emphasize that this is only a very small fragment of the total program. It shows the details necessary for pedagogical design.

In this chapter you have looked at the initial planning and the detailed pedagogical design. The problem of the production system for computer-based learning material has by no means been exhausted. The next chapter continues the discussion of technical implementation of the script, following the procedures of this chapter.

chapter *12*

Developing Curriculum Material for Computers II

- Screen Design
- Coding
- Review, Evaluation, and Revision
- Estimates of Resources for Developing Computer-based Learning Material
- The Production Process
- Some Important Points for Producing Computer-based Material

SCREEN DESIGN

The next stage in developing computer-based learning material is to design the way it will appear on the screen, both spatially, which refers to the location of the textual and graphic objects, and temporally, which refers to the timing of the material's appearance on the screen.

The pedagogical design group may have specified some screen design, as on page 3 of the spreadsheet script (Figure 11.4). Authors should be aware of the possibilities of screen

design so they can use the screen well. A graphic designer can handle some issues of screen design, and some issues can follow general principles of screen manipulation.

The basic design problem with much older computer-based learning material is that the authors and coders were too much influenced by the design of books and other print material. This influence has mostly been without any conscious consideration of the problem. But the surface of the computer-driven screen is *very* different from the page of a book. It has different properties and different economic trade-offs.

Only gradually have developers begun to understand these differences, and much is still to be learned. But at each stage developers need to ask how the display of information on the screen can aid learning.

I have already mentioned the designer's role in the production of books and films. Graphic designers are also very useful in the production of effective computer-based learning material. Artists who do magazine layout or similar applied graphic work are likely to work well with computer screen design. They must be taught about the learning process and how design may affect learning. Since these artists are seldom programmers, appropriate computer facilities with easily usable software should be supplied to them. Screen designers should work interactively, directly at the computer screens likely to be used for delivery, placing graphical and textual objects, moving them, changing their orientation, until they take the desired form.

General principles for handling the screen in space and time can be suggested. Perhaps of all these principles, the most important is *to have as little on the screen as possible at any one time.* Dense text, some of it representing past history rather than the current student situation, is likely to distract a student who is a poor reader; such a student may be unable to absorb the recently written text that is critical for further learning, if irrelevant text is still on the screen.

Thus the amount of blank space on the screen should be maximized. The way to do this is to display a minimum of information at any one time and to remove any text and pictures not immediately relevant. Modern display screens allow some material to be removed from the screen without erasing the entire screen, and so the screen can contain only current information.

Text need not always start at the left margin of the screen. This booklike technique has unfortunately been built into computer languages. Whereas blank space is expensive in books, and so there is justification for restricted use of space, computer screens have no such financial constraint—*blank space is free!*

Other factors can aid readability. *Short* lines, the avoidance of hyphenation, the avoidance of both left and right justification, keeping natural phrases together on a line, pausing before and after critical words or phrases, and slowing down the text to a pleasant rate for the average individual can all contribute to more readable and more useful text. Text and graphics should work together, reinforcing the information provided.

CODING

At this stage of the production process no running computer-based learning material is available. The next process is to write the computer program to produce code.

As the screen design process may already have entered all the text, coding will primarily concern the *logic* of the interactive process. That is, computer programs that analyze students' input and that make decisions based on that input will be written. This analysis has all been specified in the script during the pedagogical design stage. So the coders work with the script and with the products of graphic design.

Coding, therefore, is related to the conventional programming task, and so it can follow the general principles of programming, as practiced in many application areas. Some features of structured programming have been discussed in chapter 2, and these principles should (certainly) be taken into account in writing code for computer-based learning dialogs.

Programs should have as few errors as possible; the code, for reasons of economy, should be written as rapidly as possible, should be modifiable through successive revisions (some immediately and some later), should be maintainable as obscure errors are found, and should be portable (easily movable to other machines). These goals can be reached by using modern programming structures and environments, using what is known about structured programming and about software engineering.

Before coders start to work, it is important to *plan* the code. Many techniques are available for modern software engineering. Particularly if a number of coders are to work together on a long, complex program, and computer-based learning materials are often long and complex, there must be coordination so each coder knows what others are doing and does not duplicate routines that all need. Eventually all the code must "fit" together. One way to plan the code is by using *structure charts,* diagrams that show the overall structure of the code.

Careful consideration should be given to the programming language and the general environment in which that language is embedded. The environment includes editors and other aids to programming. Modern complex coding is done in relatively few languages. If you notice how the computer industry prepares programs —how compilers, editors, filers, and operating systems are written—you will see that most such software is now written in the structured languages, either descending from ALGOL or PL/I. Probably the ALGOL relatives, including Pascal, Modula 2, and Ada, are the rising languages. The version of Pascal developed by Kenneth Bowles at the University of California at San Diego, referred to as UCSD Pascal, is used at the Educational Technology Center. It has the advantage of running on many small machines and being easily ported (moved) to new machines. It is distributed through Softech Microsystems.

Any language needs amplifying for purposes of computer-based learning. This additional underlying software affects the efficiency of the coding and the case of transportability to other machines. Modern languages allow the use of libraries of procedures (see chapter 2) for such duplication. The weakest aspect of computer languages from the standpoint of computer-based learning material is screen design, the ability to accomplish the tasks of placing material on the screen and in time. Graphic require-

ments are pertinent, as are better ways of handling text on the screen. Procedures can deal with other common needs. Computer-based learning material coders should have libraries of such procedures at their disposal.

Checking the program, reading it, is important. A set of prescriptions for what constitutes a good code should be developed for such checking. But simply having a set of prescriptions will not automatically ensure that they have been adhered to, so inspection of code is essential. Code must satisfy two requirements: It must do what it is intended to do, and it must be good structured code.

Even coders familiar with the language to be used will need assistance before they write adequate computer-based learning material. In the Educational Technology Center we run classes for prospective coders, so they can become acquainted with our underlying software and understand our standards for good code. After some introduction, the students are given small chunks of material to code. We examine the running program *and* the code, emphasizing good programming strategies.

REVIEW, EVALUATION, AND REVISION

One of the major strengths of computer-based learning material is that review and evaluation can occur at many stages along the way, more so than in almost any other medium. The detailed information that can be gathered as the basis for review and evaluation is impressive, again compared to that available in other media. Evaluators can have a very detailed view at each point in the material—a "microview"—of just what is happening with the student, because a good computer-based learning program is highly interactive. But as with any kind of educational material, the more evaluation, the greater the expense. It is necessary in any project to strike a balance betwen extensive evaluation and cost.

Review, evaluation, and improvement of the material can take place at at least nine possible points during the production process. Furthermore, several cycles of review and evaluation, followed by improvement, are often possible for each stage. The possible review, evaluation, and improvement cycles are:

1. Review of design specification
2. Review of detailed pedagogical design as specified in the script
3. Review of the screen design
4. Review of the code design
5. Review of the running version of the computer dialog
6. Review of the computer code
7. Formative evaluation of the running version
8. Peer evaluation of the running version
9. Summative evaluation of the final product

No hard and fast distinction is made here between "review" and "evaluation." Review tends to be a less formal process, conducted within the project itself. Evaluation stages, both formative and summative, tend to involve use of the products outside the project; these stages possibly may involve outside evaluators. For a discussion of the difference between formative and summative evaluation, see chapter 8.

For most of these stages a series of questions might be asked. Some of the questions will occur repeatedly. The groups involved in review and evaluation will differ from case to case, depending on such factors as the intended audience and the funding available.

Review of Design Specification

The first stage in the development process is design specification, one or several pages describing each of the modules to be developed. The design specification is a written or typed document. It can be sent to several people for brief or detailed review. The following questions might be asked:

- Is the design based on the research findings?
- Is the design clear?

- Does the design provide adequate input to the detailed design group?
- Is the design practical for typical student use?
- Is the design consistent with the likely target delivery systems?
- Does the design make use of the computer's capabilities?
- Are there other promising approaches?

These reviews can easily be undertaken outside the project and should involve the same types of people as in the initial design session. The original group, or some subset, can consider the new suggestions and decide which to accept.

Review of the Script

The product of the detailed design groups is the *script*. The scripts, too, can be sent out to review, since they are also paper products.

Reviewers must understand the script so they can "read" it. The conventions of how scripts are written must be explained to the reviewers. It is our experience at the Educational Technology Center that to review a script properly, reviewers need experience in developing such scripts themselves. Attempting to review such scripts can overwhelm someone who has never seen one before. But a person who has designed scripts is not frightened by one. It may be possible to develop computer-based learning material to teach a complete novice how to "read" a script and, therefore, how to comment on it, but I do not know any such program. The material in chapter 11 describing scripts may be sufficient for some.

A few of the questions to be asked at this stage include:

- Is the text clear or can the messages be improved?
- Is it concise? Reviewers should make suggestions for cutting the text.
- Is the text appropriate in level and vocabulary for the intended audience? (This implies that script reviewers understand who the material is intended for. Such information

should be indicated in the design document available to reviewers.)

- Are the messages, the text, *friendly and helpful* to users?
- Can additional visual information aid learners? Particular emphasis should be given to this question, as teachers will often be weak on supplying sufficient relevant visual information.
- Can screen arrangements be improved? Often reviewers may suggest screen arrangements in places where the authors themselves have not. Reviewers should be encouraged to do this.
- Are there any logical errors in the material that would make it impossible to carry out the coding as indicated in the script?
- Have the developers neglected certain cases, indicated in the script by lines that do not connect to anything or by missing lines?
- Have the developers eliminated infinite loops that trap the student, except for trivial intended ones?
- Is the analysis of student input appropriate for the intended audience?
- Are there correct responses that the designers have not indicated in the script?
- Are there misleading or incorrect responses that the program *should* be looking for but that were missed by the developers? Student responses suggesting immediate useful feedback are important.
- Can reviewers suggest additional help sequences or improvements on the help sequences already suggested? The effectiveness of computer-based learning material is dependent on being able to give adequate help to practically all learners in difficulty.
- Can the student-computer interaction be improved?

Review of Screen Design

If screen design is done interactively, with the results of design available only on the computer, the review process must take place at display screens. In this case, people located away from the development site could function as reviewers only if they have similar equipment. Since this developmental equipment for graphic designers may be highly specialized, with special computers involved, most of the screen design review must be internal.

This review stage tends to be neglected. Many of the factors can be picked up at later stages, such as after the program is running. But if screen design can be reviewed and improved, computer dialogs will be improved.

Here are the questions that can be asked:

- Are screens attractive for the intended audience?
- Has ample consideration been given to providing as much blank space as possible?
- Do designers remove unnecessary information, keeping the screens "clean"?
- Is student readability aided?
- Are the text lines short?
- Are natural phrases kept together in text lines?
- Are pauses used after major punctuation?
- Are there pauses isolating important words and phrases?
- Is additional visual or pictorial information possible?
- Is additional visual or pictorial information desirable?
- Does the design make use of such stressing methods as blinking and reverse video?

Review of Code Design

In an extensive coding project, such as those associated with computer-based learning, it is desirable to *design* the code before any code is written. This design might be in the form of *structure charts* or other devices from modern software engineering. These can be reviewed on the same basis as other code design; so experts in software engineering are the desirable reviewers at this stage.

Here are the questions that can be asked:

- Is the code design modular?
- Are each of the procedures or modules of reasonable length?

- Is the role of each module clearly defined within the design structure?
- Are the module names indicative of the functions of modules?
- Are the data structures clearly specified?
- Is it clear what data are to be supplied to each module?
- Is it clear which data are to be global to the entire program and which data are to be restricted to certain parts of the program?

Internal Review of Running Dialog

Availability of the first running material is an exciting stage, an early climax in development of computer learning materials. The design decisions are no longer seen in "peculiar" media such as paper: Their effect can be seen directly at the computer. Often decisions that seem reasonable to the design group are not marvelous when seen on the screen. The project manager and the developers at the development site can run the program many times, keeping notes as to which things need to be improved. This internal review and improvement is likely to occur many times before the dialog is viewed as ready for further testing.

Reviewers could ask these questions at this stage:

- Does the program work in all situations? This can be determined to reasonable probability only by running it many times and trying many different inputs. The reviewer might want to put in "good" inputs, but it is also necessary to try all the help sequences.
- Are the pictures adequate?
- Would additional visual information help the learning process?
- Can the screen design be improved?
- Can the interaction be improved?

Although I list only a few questions, practically every question asked in the earlier stages could be raised during the internal review process.

Review of the Program

This stage is the second important software engineering review process, necessary to ensure the code is readable, modifiable, and transportable. Although I list this stage after review of the running program, both can be done simultaneously. The review principles are those of modern software engineering. Systems programmers familiar with modern programming environments can be the reviewers. The questions overlap those asked earlier with regard to code design.

- Is the computer program readable? That is, can someone who does not know anything about the program find out what the program does and how it does it?
- Is the data specification easy to understand?
- Are the identifiers reasonable? By looking at the names of procedures, data types, and variables, is it possible to get some idea of what those entities do or represent within the program structure? Can better names be suggested?
- Are the procedures—the individual modules —of reasonable size?
- Does the main program clearly show the structure of the full program?
- Are there enough comments so that a new reader knows what the main program does and what the procedures do?
- Are there other comments that might improve the readability of the program?
- Are any features that depend on a particular computer clearly isolated and described with adequate comments to enable someone to recreate them on a different computer? This is particularly critical for transportability. Some system-dependent features—graphics, operating system details, or assembly code— may be essential. These system-dependent features should be kept to a minimum and carefully described with full comments.

Formative Evaluation of Running Version

The critical role of full-scale formative evaluation to improve the material can hardly be underestimated. Formative evaluation involves many students from the target audiences. The questions to be asked are similar to those associated with the internal review of the running program. An important new issue is what students *learn* in using the material.

First, it is critical to test with *typical* groups of students. There might be several cycles of such testing and improvement. While initially the group might be small, consisting of only several students from intended audiences, it is desirable to have several cycles of large-group evaluation and improvement.

Several types of information can be obtained during the formative evaluation process. Some of the information is stored directly by the computer, thus making use of the computer's extensive data gathering capabilities, which are unmatched in any other medium used for learning activities. Other information can be gained through evaluators, specially trained individuals who work with the evaluation process. It is also possible to learn much about how a program works by videotaping student sessions and by peer evaluation, evaluation by teaching experts in the area who have considerable experience with students.

As students use computer-based learning material, the computer can save a variety of information about individual students' progress through the program and it can also generate statistical information on groups of students. First, consider student responses to individual questions. We have a choice of saving *every* student response to a question or saving only selected ones. With large groups, it is not practical to save every response: The amount of data could be overwhelming. Rather, it is better for developers to suggest on the script what student responses should be saved. Often only the responses that could *not* be analyzed by the program should be saved. There is no point in saving student responses for simple yes-no questions or others where the analysis is exhaustive. Each time such a response is saved, it must

be identified with the particular question being answered.

It is also desirable to allow users to make comments, perhaps pointing out places in the program they found confusing or areas that did not hold their interest. A number of strategies are possible. In our programs at Irvine, as one of the "extra services control" features, we allow students to enter comments at any time. These are available later for evaluators to examine.

It is often useful to keep data on paths taken by individual students or by the entire group being tested. These maps of student progress may show where the program needs to be strengthened. For example, if most students end up in many help sequences and few seem to be learning the modules, the learning sequences must be improved.

Learning units are generally designed with the notion that the student will *learn* something. Strange as it may seem, much testing of learning modules does not seem to pay too much attention to what has been learned. What is learned can be determined by giving both pretests and posttests, perhaps built into the computer material itself, in addition to testing during dialogs. Such tests need to be developed carefully with the purposes of the learning material in mind. Pretesting and posttesting are often useful in structuring the learning experience within a dialog, in addition to obtaining information about how the dialog could be improved.

The process of gathering student information is different in different situations. In older developmental activities the computer dialog was almost always available on a timesharing system, with many student stations sharing the same computer; the computer, usually a sizable one, had storage for extensive files, usually on magnetic discs. All student responses, comments, and data on performance could be stored within the machine.

With the advent of personal computers the

storage of student responses has become more difficult, particularly if the personal computers are not networked (connected) to a central computer. If the personal computers are networked —connected together—storage for saving student responses might be available, this situation is still uncommon. The other possibility, not entirely pleasant but workable, is to store student responses on the individual floppy disks, gather them together, and have a master program that removes them from each disk and combines them. Since good computer-based learning material is often extensive, the amount of space available on the disk is likely to be limited; thus student information must be frequently moved from the disks. As networks of personal computers become more common, developmental groups will probably use networking for gathering student responses.

In addition to the computer-stored information, evaluators may work directly with students in the formative evaluation process. They can, for example, observe student performance, by standing behind the students or by checking auxiliary monitors located elsewhere. These monitors, TV-like screens, show exactly what the student is seeing and typing. Trained evaluators can take notes about what is happening and use these for reworking the program later.

Evaluators can also be responsible for pretests and posttests if such tests are not built into the program. Furthermore, evaluators can interview some students who have used the material, looking particularly for motivational and affective issues, values that might be missed by other evaluation procedures. Protocols need to be established so that the interview becomes more than a set of random questions.

Another possible evaluation technique is the videotaping or taping of student sessions. At the Educational Technology Center, we have captured not only the visual and audio information —the discussions that take place within the group running the material—but also the student key pushes. Then the entire experience can

be recreated on two TV screens, with one screen showing the student group, the other screen showing what the students were seeing on the display and what they were typing. Again, protocols can be developed to study the interactions and therefore to suggest improvements. The advantage of this procedure over having the evaluator present is that the tapes can be reviewed over and over from a number of different points of view, even by different evaluators.

Peer Evaluation

Another type of evaluation study can be conducted simultaneously with the formative evaluation of students. Excellent teachers from a range of backgrounds can view the material and make suggestions to improve it. Such evaluation is often referred to as peer evaluation.

In addition to improving the material for student use, this approach will lead to teacher-friendly units, ones teachers will be more willing to assign, and so students will be more likely to use these learning materials in classes. Peer evaluation is simpler and less costly than formative evaluation with sizable groups of students. If some of the teachers are very perceptive, their information can lead to improvement of the material.

Peer evaluators can come to the developmental center or can be located remotely if suitable equipment is available. Questions might be prepared for peer evaluators to consider, or all notes and comments from the evaluators might simply be accepted. Peer evaluation is valuable but should not be the only evaluation strategy used; student use during evaluation is critical.

Summative Evaluation

The differences between formative evaluation to improve the material and summative evaluation to see whether the material is working properly have already been considered. The critical issue regarding summative evaluation of computer-based learning material is whether the evaluation will be based on an explicit set of goals, to see whether the material accomplishes what the developer set out to accomplish, or whether the evaluation will be *goal-free*.

In a goal-free evaluation the evaluators try to discover the effects of using the curriculum units. Unexpected, but nevertheless important, effects having nothing to do with the original intent of the developer might develop. Goal-free evaluations are seldom done, but they can yield very useful information.

Despite pressure to do so, it is probably not desirable to conduct a summative evaluative study until the material has been in use for several years and is in a "stable" condition. Many summative evaluations with computers, such as those conducted at the end of the Plato and Ticcit projects, have suffered because the units were not really finished when the evaluation took place. Under such circumstances evaluation becomes very difficult; extraneous factors can easily dominate.

Summative evaluations may compare several methods for learning the particular subject area. Thus educators' choice of methods will be easier if they know that computer-based modules for learning problem solving are superior to some other approach with general classes and with average teachers.

Comparison studies are meaningful only if *large* numbers of people are involved to rule out random variations. For example, suppose we wanted to compare a computer-based beginning calculus course with the standard lecture–textbook-based calculus course. The standard courses vary enormously, so a comparison with a *single* calculus course taught in the usual fashion is meaningless. Dozens of schools should be involved, half using a "standard" course and half using the computer-based course, to rule out odd variables associated with a particular school. At least tens of thousands of students should be used in an experiment of this kind.

Given the numbers necessary, it is not surprising that summative evaluations are expensive. So they are seldom done on an adequate scale. Much educational research attempts to do such evaluations with smaller numbers, but I personally regard such efforts as misguided, as they do not take into account all the variables that can occur in the educational situation.

ESTIMATES OF RESOURCES FOR DEVELOPING COMPUTER-BASED LEARNING MATERIAL

A common question concerns the *cost* of developing good computer-based learning material. The following outline follows the procedures suggested in this and the previous chapter.

I assume ten hours of material, divided into five two-hour units, developed during a one-and-one-half year project.

OVERALL MANAGEMENT

$1\frac{1}{2}$ year project
Project manager: full time, $1\frac{1}{2}$ years
Principal investigator: .2 time, $1\frac{1}{2}$ years
Secretary, business: .5 time, $1\frac{1}{2}$ years
Code manager (optional): full time, $1\frac{1}{2}$ years
Supplies, etc.

DETAILS

Initial planning meeting
    5–10 people, 3–4 days
    Honoraria, travel, per diem
Review of initial planning document
    3 people, 3 days
    Honoraria
Detailed design groups
    2 hours of material in one week, each
        group; 4–5 people in a group
    5 groups: 20 people-weeks of designers
    Honoraria, travel, per diem
Review of detailed design
    5 scripts, 2 people each, 3 days
    30 person-days
Screen design
    1 person, 10 weeks
Review of screen design
    1 person, 3 weeks
Code design
    1 person, 5 weeks

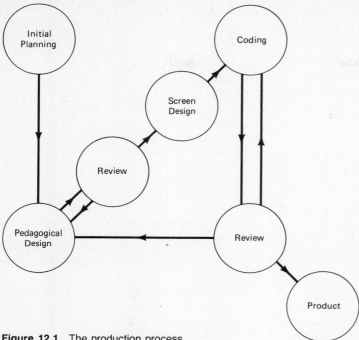

Figure 12.1 The production process.

Review of code design
    1 person, 2 weeks (May be internal)
Coding
    8 weeks for a 2-hour unit, 40 person-weeks
       for 5 units
Review of code
    Usually internal to project
Revision
    3 weeks for each of 5 modules
    15 person-weeks
External formative evaluation and improve-
ment cycle
    5 weeks, 2 people for evaluation
    2 weeks, designers
    5 weeks, coders
Move to delivery machines
    4 weeks, coders, for each machine

HARDWARE

5 developmental computers
2 delivery computers

The type of information just given about costs may seem complex, so it seems desirable to give some other approaches to estimating costs. Another approach is to take a project that has developed a considerable amount of material, determine the entire cost of the project, and then find the cost of each module. For example, the science literacy materials described in chapter 5, with modules typically about two hours long, cost about $25,000 per module for all phases of the activity. This figure is perhaps a little misleading, because the development occurred at a time in our project when we had recently moved to personal computers and therefore were still doing work on some of the underlying software. My rough calculations suggest that the cost of material produced at the Open University in England, mostly not involving computers, is similar. Curriculum material can be developed for less than this, but quality may suffer.

THE PRODUCTION PROCESS

It may be helpful to end the discussion of the production of computer-based learning material with a diagram showing some of the stages. Every diagram of this type tends to be partial, reflecting some aspects of the work but not others. Figure 12.1 shows the major production stages and two review stages, indicating by arrows going back what improvement processes are involved.

SOME IMPORTANT POINTS FOR PRODUCING COMPUTER-BASED MATERIAL

1. Educators must insist on high quality material; it should be highly interactive, not booklike or lecturelike. Such simpleminded tactics as multiple choice should be avoided.
2. Educators must be critical of existing material—most of what is available is junk.
3. The test of any production system is in the quality of the product. Thus abstract arguments about production systems are not critical. Rather, in each case the material produced should be examined.
4. Computers will become more valuable in learning as educators move from strictly behavioral viewpoints to viewpoints that take into account cognitive psychology.
5. Group effort is needed to produce effective curriculum material. Most educators seem to agree with this, but many are still implicitly using tactics that derive from older nongroup strategies.
6. Authoring languages and systems should not be used in the production of computer-based learning material. In most cases they lead to uninteresting or trivial material. However, authoring tools can be useful in the coding process.
7. Far more experimentation in the development of computer-based learning material is needed. The best curriculum production systems can undoubtedly be improved.
8. Educators' strategies need to be future-oriented, particularly toward the large-scale production that will be necessary in the next few years.

III

THE FUTURE

A book that examines any aspect of computing should attempt to anticipate future developments. In this respect, education is like any other area involving computers. To plan only in terms of today's situation, to think of computers as they are today, can be disastrous. While considering computers in learning, persons who fail to think about the future will soon find their work outmoded.

I cannot overemphasize the highly dynamic technology of computers, in all likelihood a technology now only in its infancy. Development is very rapid in terms of software and in terms of future computers. New computers appear frequently, and facilities, languages, operating systems, and production systems for generating material all change.

Change is particularly critical for developers of computer-based learning material. Such developers often start with *today's* equipment and software in mind. By the time they finish, that equipment may no longer be in the forefront; newer computers may allow a better approach. The reasonableness of proceeding to second-guess possible hardware and other developments will occur only to someone fully alert to the dynamic nature of computing.

The two chapters in Part III concern different aspects of the future. First, I consider the future of the software and equipment that may be used, particularly developments affecting education. In the last chapter I look at profound changes that may occur in the future of education through the uses of computers.

chapter 13

Future Computer Equipment

- Evolution of Chips
- Memory Chips
- Processor Chips
- Future Software
- Auxiliary Technology for Education
- New Technologies

The computer as a machine—the hardware—is evolving very rapidly at present, with no sign of a slowdown. The development of computers, particularly personal computers, may even continue to gain momentum.

During the last several years a rash of new personal computers, or microcomputers, was announced. Some of these were simply rehashes of older machines, but many are genuinely new, using newer chip technology. Many new technologies are being tried, and the Japanese computer industry is now speaking of the "fifth generation" of computer hardware, due about ten years from now. Experts may disagree about the exact form of future computers, but they agree that computers will continue to change and improve very rapidly.

EVOLUTION OF CHIPS

In looking at the evolution of chips, the basic ingredients of today's computer, four factors might be considered: the size of chips, their cost, their speed, and their complexity. Often new generations of chips are little different in size and cost from older generations, but they have more components. The size of the complete chip package is often determined by exterior connectors, convenience of handling, placement into sockets, and the need for occasional removal for replacement. Although several sizes of chips are in use, the variation is not great.

The cost of each chip tends to remain about constant, but the cost is dependent on the volume of production. The cost to *design* a new chip is large. If only a few chips must bear this cost, those chips are very expensive. If, on the other hand, the design costs can be spread over hundreds of thousands or millions of chips, the cost per chip becomes small.

Speed increases with chip evolution. That is, the amount of time to execute an action continues to decrease as chips evolve. Usually an increase of this kind accompanies a change in technology. Within a technology any changes in chip speed are usually more modest.

Increases in complexity bring the greatest change in the evolution of computers. A chip stays about the same size in cost, but it *does* much more. That is, its vastly greater number of components render it capable of more activity than its predecessors.

Because of the increase in chip complexity, a chip's *effective* size and cost go down. That is, with more on a chip, the cost per component and the size per component go down. Now some personal computers are no bigger than a small typewriter keyboard, while earlier computers occupied large rooms. So the overall size of computers has gone down, even though the size of the individual chip does not change drastically.

One limitation on chip size is the speed of light. Light, and therefore electricity, has a limiting speed, which may seem enormous. For light to move one meter takes 5 nanoseconds, or $\frac{5}{1,000,000,000}$ of a second; electrical signals are similarly limited. Speeds on the order of nanoseconds are obtainable in computer circuitry at the present time, so the physical separation of chips and components on chips may be an important factor. As speeds become even faster, the major limitation will be the distance between components close together on a single chip. The problem of interconnecting chips is also a limiting factor. Distances between chips should be as small as possible so the time electricity must travel between them will limit the speed of the computation as little as possible. Multilayer chips are a modern approach to this problem.

MEMORY CHIPS

In this section and the next I look again at two types of chips, memory chips and processing chips. Other types of chips are found in modern computers, such as those controlling input and output devices and those associated with network interfacing. Memory and central processing units are fundamental, and their evolution has much to say about the way the computer as a whole will evolve. Chapter 9 discusses memory and processing unit capabilities; some material will be repeated here, for the sake of completeness.

At present much computer equipment is delivered with 16K memory chips. That is, the chips have on them 16 times 1024, or 16,384, bits of memory; each bit is a binary choice, equivalent to being either a 0 or a 1. More recent designs involve 64K chips, which are fast becoming the new standard. 256K chips have been announced, both in Japan and in the United States, and further progress can be expected. The memory chips tend to stay roughly the same size and cost when undergoing these changes, so the cost per bit will decrease steadily in the future.

Memory capacity in personal computers will increase, in the sense that we will get more memory for the same amount of money. For a while the cost of memory—the cost of a bit—was going down by 50 percent *a year*. That rate is probably too high to maintain, since starting production on new chips is a lengthy process. But more compact computer memory costing less per bit can be expected in the future.

Personal computers demonstrate this. The older generation of personal computers mostly had 48 to 64K bytes *maximum* memory. The new generation of personal computers has much more memory, often going to 512 bytes. This is not just a question of the cheap cost of memory. It also concerns the newer processing units.

PROCESSOR CHIPS

Remember that the processor is the seat of action for the computer. It is the unit that fetches the commands in the program, acquires numbers or other data from memory needed to execute the commands, and then performs the desired operation, perhaps returning the result to memory. The computer can then proceed to the next command. If the command is a branching operation, the processor will pick another command elsewhere in the computer memory.

A processor on a chip is inexpensive, typically costing only a few dollars. So computers can be built with more than one processor. Some processors might be specialized to particular tasks, such as graphics. Or several processors might be devoted to the main calculation. Or the processors could be used alternatively with different software.

It is in complexity that processing chips differ most. A number of measures of this are used, one being the complexity and size of instruction—the space in memory the instruction occupies, as discussed in chapter 9. Another is the amount of memory that the processor can address. Many newer processing unit chips such as the Motorola 68000 and the Intel 8086 and 8088, use complex instructions. This increase in instruction size implies a much wider range of different types of instructions, so an operation can require *fewer* instructions and therefore be much faster. These processors can manipulate more data in a single instruction. A second implication is that the larger instruction size typically allows the processor to "address" more memory; personal computers using modern in-struction sets can have vastly more memory attached (the amount depends on the details of the chip and also perhaps on the marketing choices of the developer).

The processing chips also relate to the size of the data paths—the gulps, so to speak, in which information is transferred between memory and processor unit and vice versa or in other channels. This distinction is clearly seen in the Intel 8086 and 8088, which both use 16 bit instruction sets. In the 8086 the data paths are also 16 bit, while in the 8088 data paths are 8 bits. The computer will take longer to carry out an instruction on the 8088 than on the 8086, because more accesses to memory may be required.

Many newer processing chips also have *some* memory on the chips themselves. They may also have other circuitry to control input and output devices or for networking to other computers or clocks. If enough of these additional capabilities are present, we speak of a "computer on a chip" or perhaps a computer on a set of chips.

Chips will increase in capabilities. Already 32 bit chips have been announced by Intel and National Semiconductor, and the Motorola 68000 has some 32 bit aspects. New large computers mostly emphasize 32 bit technology, so it is not clear that microcomputers need to surpass that. Soon more very complex computers on single chips will be available. Soon personal computers will have the same processing capabilities as almost *any* computer.

Those who develop only for current technology may find their courses and curriculum primitive, because the new technology available when the course is ready has advanced to the point where much more complicated things can be done. A developer of computer-based learning units must keep one eye on the future.

FUTURE SOFTWARE

We will now look at some prospects for future software, primarily for personal computers.

Application Software

A much greater variety of application software, including educational software, will be available in the future. Some of these application-oriented programs will be designed for other purposes but may prove useful in education. The continual development of computers, particularly for the home market, assures us that learning units will be more and more available.

One interesting aspect of this software is that it will become more self-standing, not relying on external learning devices. If you want to use a spreadsheet today, you either read an introductory part of the manual, attend a class, or get a friend to teach you. Manuals and classes will probably vanish as software engineers become more skillful in developing programs that are completely self-teaching. In such a program a student with no previous background can quickly begin to use the application software in a sophisticated fashion. The bare beginning of such user-oriented programs can be seen already, but we have far to go.

Operating Systems

Much discussion concerns the future operating systems that will dominate small computers. The operating system is the underlying software that "runs" all applications.

Several operating systems are available on several personal machines, and they are often mentioned as "standards" for future small-machine operating systems. The first is the CP/M operating system, primarily available on computers with the 8080 or Z80 processor, but also now on some of the newer 16 bit computers. The second is the DOS system, made popular on IBM personal computers. The third is the UCSD Pascal system, developed at the University of California, San Diego, by Kenneth Bowles. This product includes not only Pascal, but a full operating system of editor, filer, and other necessary features. The fourth is the AT&T Bell Laboratories Unix system, developed initially primarily for larger computers

and now being widely touted for the more advanced small computers.

Of these systems, the easiest for an ordinary, nonprofessional user is the UCSD Pascal system. It exists on most personal computers. The Unix system, at least in principle, can take on a different appearance for different users, with different operating system commands. But the "native" Unix operating system is not easy for a novice user to learn, and few Unix-based interfaces are easy for the nonexpert to use. Unix has been primarily promoted through computer science departments, where it is a powerful tool. Few of its powerful features, such as pipelines and the notion of subdirectories of files, are of direct help to novices. Nevertheless, Unix has considerable momentum, and the developers of many newer machines have announced that they will provide Unix or Unix-like operating systems; a few are available in 1983.

It is commonly believed that using the same operating system on a number of computers will automatically speed the ease of transferability. However, the operating system is only one factor affecting transferability, typically not the major factor. The way the code is written, as discussed in chapter 11, is usually of greater importance.

Languages

In the future new programming languages will be developed. More and more emphasis seems likely on the features of structured programming. Concepts that were previously part of the operating system will become part of the programming language. Thus Ada, a new programming language receiving considerable attention at present, contains the notion of *packages* of code and data. Such packages make it possible to adapt the language for special purposes. In older languages such groupings, if at all possible, were typically done through the operating system.

The use of Pascal as a programming language is increasing rapidly, and seems likely to continue in the future. Its main competitors are related languages such as Ada or Modula 2. Modula 2 is a product of Niklaus Wirth, the developer of Pascal, while Ada was developed through a series of procurements from the United States Department of Defense.

Some people believe that since BASIC is already commonly available on personal computers, it will continue to be a widely used beginning language. Other people, including me, are very much worried about BASIC's flaws as a programming language, particularly from the standpoint of structured programming (see chapter 2). At present, BASICs differ on different machines, particularly beyond the simple features. The new proposed BASIC standard differs considerably from existing BASICs, and so far, outside of Dartmouth College, I do not believe that any BASIC follows the full new standard. Indeed, it is questionable why the standard form is still called BASIC, after undergoing so many changes. There is also a growing belief, mentioned in chapter 2, that BASIC, as currently presented as a beginning language, creates severe problems for those who wish to continue work with computers. BASIC is easier to implement on very small computers than newer languages, but as processing units develop and more memory is available, this feature will grow less important. I predict that while the use of BASIC may not have quite peaked, it will undergo a definite decline within a few years.

Automatic Programming

"Automatic" programming systems are another type of capability receiving much discussion today, even though few practical examples can be exhibited. These systems purport not to use any language at all, but usually proceed with a series of queries to the user or some non-procedural description of the program. It seems very likely that more such systems will be developed and that eventually some may become important, particularly for specialized applications. At present, particularly in such fields as computer-assisted learning, the weaknesses of

automatic programming systems do not allow a full range of capabilities. It is not clear how soon automatic programming will compete with powerful general-purpose languages.

Programming Environments

Programming environments are likely to take on increasing importance in the next few years. That is, programming languages will become less important than the question of how to use them and the various auxiliary tools that enhance their usage. The task of interest to programmers is *not* just to use Pascal or some other language; the task is to write workable, modifiable, transformable programs. The total programming environment—the editors, the programming aids, the debugging aids, and other facilities of this kind as well as the languages—will become of increasing importance in the period ahead. The development of Ada has particularly emphasized programming environments.

Expert Systems

The use of artificial intelligence techniques, such as expert systems, has potential for improving education. Expert systems attempt to capture and use the rules experts use in a given discipline. But so far extremely few computer-based learning units use expert systems, so it is not entirely clear how they will compete with other material. Of the programs listed in chapter 5, only *Sophie* and the Stanford logic course employ the ideas of artificial intelligence. Expert systems provide a promising set of techniques for education but one that, in spite of its publicity, has yet to show that it can live up to all of its claims.

Advanced Production Systems

Improved production systems, going far beyond the system described in chapters 11 and 12, can be expected. One possibility is that the computer will be able to "read" the scripts; therefore much of the input, and even much of the programming, will be done automatically. Systems of this kind are only being thought about and will take years to develop successfully. However, they will receive impetus as more computer-based learning material is produced.

AUXILIARY TECHNOLOGY FOR EDUCATION

So far, in looking at either hardware or software, I have discussed primarily the computer itself. But a whole range of technological developments, mostly associated with input and output, enhance the computer's educational role. In this review of auxiliary technologies, I group them roughly in order of *time*. That is, the first items are already available, though not on all machines and not necessarily at prices reasonable for educational applications. Later items look toward the more distant future.

Voice Output

The first auxiliary technology to discuss is *voice output*. Some quite inexpensive units, such as the Texas Instruments Speak and Spell, already provide recognizable but not perfect voice output at modest cost. Devices for voice output exist for some computers, but most personal computers still have no such capability.

Voice output can be accomplished with at least three different technologies. First is regular (analog) sound recording, perhaps on magnetic tape, as with everyday tape recorders, perhaps with playback control by computer. The second method is digitizing of voice (converting it to a binary form), storing the digital information, and reconstituting the sound by the inverse process. The third speech-output method is creating speech with phonetics. In this process any word is broken into its fundamental sounds. Several "print-to-voice" systems use this technology.

Quality of output speech declines as one moves through these three technologies, but versatility increases. In most systems digital and phonetic speech still has a "computerese" sound, different from human speech. All these forms of voice output should improve steadily, however, and become more common.

Print-to-Code or Speech

One interesting kind of hardware that already exists but is too expensive for most educational use is the "print-to-code" device. These devices, such as the Kurzweil reader, *read* in a somewhat literal sense. That is, a *book* can be placed into the reader and the machine will change the book into internally stored character code, the usual computer form. The machine can read many different typefaces. The original versions of the Kurzweil machine, designed for the blind, then converted the characters into spoken language using computer-based phonetic techniques, so that the device would read books aloud. But variants also exist in which the spoken part is bypassed, so the device is used as a fast way of entering already printed material into the computer without human typing being involved.

Music Output

Another important accompaniment to computer-based learning material, rarely available today, is background music. Film makers have long understood the affective value of music. Such music output devices as are available for computers are seldom available in learning systems. But as this type of output improves, it seems likely that it will be more common in learning activities.

Display Technology

New display technologies may influence the development of learning activities on the computer. Some of these new approaches either modify the common cathode ray tube (the TV tube) or replace it with an entirely different device. Two new recent television sets from Japan, both small, hand-held ones, reflect such strategies. One from Sony modifies the TV set so that the beam travels mostly at right angles to the screen. The second employs a flat screen technology developed by Panasonic.

A number of flat liquid crystal screens have already appeared in small computers, such as the portable Epson, Texas Instruments, NEC, and Radio Shack computers, which weigh only 3 or 4 pounds. Liquid crystal technology is widely used on watches. Some stereo amplifiers also use it. While no commercial computer is available with a liquid crystal screen as large as a TV screen, perhaps one will be in the not-to-distant future.

Flat screen technology may go far beyond current possibilities such as liquid crystal. Thomas Standish, one of my colleagues at the University of California, Irvine, feels that in the future a large roll that looks like cloth will be available to computer users. The user rolls out as much as wanted, say, a piece 4 feet by 6 feet, and then tacks the piece on the wall. That then becomes the computer "screen."

Another approach that has received attention but is still not practical is holography. The aim is to provide displays that are truly three-dimensional, not just two-dimensional. Another three-dimensional technique used in some expensive computer graphics equipment involves a vibrating mirror; the mirror vibrates rapidly enough to show different parts of the object at different times and so gives an effective three-dimensional view.

High-Quality Text Output

Presently most inexpensive printing devices available for computers are based on dot matrix printers. The availability of higher quality hardcopy devices is essential for certain types of educational applications, particularly those requiring print material that will be exchanged with others. Thus for word processing to realize all of its important educational applications, inex-

pensive, high-quality hard copy devices are needed.

These devices should be simple; the current daisy wheel printer, with its tricky changing of wheels, is too complex. Putting ribbons in cartridges helps. Further human engineering will lead to inexpensive machines that use very high resolution dot matrix characters, with color. Another possibility would be inexpensive ink-jet printers, which spray ink on the page to form dotlike characters. The ink-jet technology is not new, but it is still being improved. Laser printers might also drop in cost.

Greater External Storage

The amount of information that can be stored affects what computers can do. With more complex programs, more storage at a variety of levels is needed. The increasing use of Winchester-type technology and its likely increased application to personal computers has been mentioned in chapter 9.

One current trend is the movement toward smaller, more dense disks, both removable floppy disks and fixed disks. Sony and other vendors recently marketed smaller disks, between 3 to $3\frac{1}{2}$ inches, containing the same amount or more information than the larger floppies. Auxiliary storage will, like other storage, rapidly continue to become less expensive per unit of storage. Both the medium itself—the disk—and the recording and playback units will grow more compact. As fast memory continues to diminish in cost, there may even be less need for disks; we are already using RAM disks using fast electronic memory to replace disks.

Networks

The ability to connect computers—to network them—through a variety of strategies is very useful in certain educational applications although not in others. For example, a management system associated with quizzing, as discussed in chapter 7, benefits from personal computers able to send information occasionally to a database containing student records. Networking might provide student access to very large or rapidly changing databases. Furthermore, networking eases the evaluation of computer-based learning modules, particularly the gathering of data. Networking can connect either local or remote computers.

Several local networking strategies are available. The oldest one mimics, to some extent, the older timesharing systems, with each personal computer connected to a larger central machine that has sizable storage capability. Occasionally local machines send messages to other computers or facilities through the central machine. Several other strategies go under the name of local networks, the most well-known perhaps being the Ethernet, developed by Xerox Corporation and also promoted by Digital Equipment Corporation and Intel. The Ethernet requires no central machine. Personal computers are on the net, perhaps some with extensive storage for large databases and other facilities such as high-quality fast printers. In such a networking arrangement any computer can communicate with any other machine.

Networking of all types is being very much affected by newly developed technologies. Thus fiber optics, which are coming into widespread use in the telephone network in many countries, may be very useful in high-speed local nets for computers. For distant networking, satellites, reflecting a signal off a space station 22,000 miles above the earth, are becoming more and more a possibility. With satellite transmission arises another interesting feature: The distance between the sending and receiving stations is no longer of much consequence—a few thousand miles on earth are small compared to the 44,000 miles in space the signal must travel.

It is not clear which of the competing network technologies, local or distant, will dominate the future. The Ethernet idea and other local networks have developed slowly. In the future I foresee greater use of local networks in education, and probably also use of more distant networks. However, communication costs will continue to be a problem for distance networks.

Graphics

It might seem strange that graphics is on this list of future developments; today almost all personal computers have graphic capability. Nevertheless, *improved* graphic capability is a needed dramatic change in personal computers, with very important consequences for education.

Current graphics available in inexpensive computers are relatively crude, inadequate for some learning situations. First, the resolution—the number of addressable points on the screen—is insufficient for some educational applications. In inexpensive personal computers at this time, resolution is still less than that in ordinary television sets in the United States; and American television sets have a poorer resolution than newer standards permit elsewhere. Increasing the graphics on common personal computers to TV resolution will be the first stage. It is a matter of memory and processor speed. But reaching TV resolution is not enough.

The next graphic problem with current displays is a lack of a full spectrum. Having three colors is almost tantamount to not having any color whatsoever! Modern systems may restrict colors peculiarly when it comes to mixing text and graphics. For example, using colored letters sometimes results in fewer letters across the screen and the prohibition of concurrent color graphics.

Only limited animation is possible with today's personal computers; the full animation ideal in many educational applications is not available.

A great difference in color, animation, and in other aspects of graphics should come with special processing units, built just to drive the graphic capabilities, now becoming available. When coupled with additional memory, these processors, which are just beginning to appear, work independently of the "main" processor, the one executing the user program. They will allow better color and better resolution in addition to other capabilities such as animation.

Characters

If the inclusion of graphics on a list of future auxiliary technologies surprised you, the inclusion of characters such as letters may surprise you even more. That they were not one of the first items mentioned, and therefore are farther in the future, may seem peculiar too.

While all current personal computers display characters, in most inexpensive systems the *quality* of the characters is abysmal. In the early days of computers the objective was to use the minimum information required to represent a character and still have the character intelligible, because space for storing the character shape was very limited. The critical question was, could one tell an *A* from a *B*. Obviously this is a retreat from the sophisticated use of characters for printing that has developed since 1450. A book designer has a choice of many typefaces and sizes, with each letter carefully formed and prepared. The typefaces composed of dot matrix letters, letters built up of collections of dots, would have been intolerable in print even in Gutenberg's time.

Better characters correlate with better resolution, already discussed under graphics. If more detailed information can be put on the screen, better characters are possible. Some systems, such as Star, Lisa, and Apollo, do have better characters, with choice of letter fonts; the systems are mostly imitative of the Xerox Alto system developed at the Palo Alto research laboratories.

Future systems are likely to have improved characters, offering users a wide choice of character fonts and sizes. Furthermore, newer systems may well allow authors to design their own character sets. A few such systems are available today.

Videodisks

The videodisk is an exciting new technology in computer-based education. Among a number of approaches to storing video information on phonograph-like disks, the one most promising so far for educational use is the *optical videodisk,* in which a laser reads the information stored as "pits" in tracks. Typically today's optical videodisks contain half an hour to an hour of television material. The major videodisk market at the present time is for movies for home use.

Disks can also store sound, either directly in two television sound tracks or in compressed form. It is also possible to store code—computer instructions—on the same disk, with all of these components under random control, but so far disks mixing visuals and code are rare.

Most commonly, each turn around the disk is one TV picture. Thus if the beam stays in the same "track," the effect is that of a slide. Most videodisk systems allow the user to hold at a given slide or to move slowly through the disk in either direction as if it were a collection of slides viewed on a TV screen. A half hour of video contains about 50,000 slides. Thus the disk allows full multimedia computer-based learning material—video, slides, voice, and code —on the same disk.

Small internal computers drive all today's optical videodisk players, but these computers are of limited capability. The real educational strength of the videodisk emerges when it is combined with an *external* personal computer, with all the capabilities available today.

What are the educational implications of the videodisk? Imagine the kind of interactive computer learning materials discussed in this book, particularly those in chapter 5. Imagine that at some point in the learning sequence the instructors want students to see a video sequence, or perhaps slides, or to hear something. The videodisk player under computer control could show them. The program might then question students further, then either show the video sequence again or proceed to some other information. Thus segments of film could elicit much interaction, in contrast with current passive film and video uses in education. The possibilities are exciting.

Unfortunately, today these educational possibilities are mostly still on the designing boards. Although the notion of the combination of the videodisk and the computer—the intelligent videodisk—has been around for years and equipment is available in several forms, few viable educational examples are available. On the contrary, much educational use of videodisks with computers is poor, ignoring either the capabilities of the computer (the interaction is of very poor quality) or the capabilities of the video medium (ineffective use of visuals). The most interesting intelligent videodisk sequences I have seen are the medical education materials developed by WICAT, described in chapter 5.

While I see very interesting potentials for the computer-videodisk combination, these potentials are only slowly being realized. Far more development and far more experience with students is needed. Eventually, the question will be to choose in what circumstances to use a computer alone and in what circumstances to use a computer plus videodisk. In some areas intelligent (interactive) videodisks will have no advantage and in other areas their advantages will be considerable. It will take some experience to properly use this powerful combination. Digital Equipment Corporation markets a computer-videodisk combination, the IVIS system.

I anticipate no heavy use of the intelligent videodisk in education in the next ten years. The major problem is finding sufficient funds for trial development of learning material and for later full curriculum development.

Voice Input

While voice output was mentioned first, and many technologies for it are already available, the ability of computers to interpret human speech is still primitive.

I must qualify this statement. Certain types of voice input are practical today. They involve *discrete speech,* wherein the speaker pauses noticeably after each word. Many of these systems involve "training" the computer by the user's repeating the same word over and over again while the computer "identifies" that user's speech pattern. Without additional training, the computer would not recognize another person saying the same word.

It will be difficult to move from this very limited situation of discrete speech, which is of little use in educational environments, to the type of computer input that accepts normal human speech from any speaker. Many major research projects are investigating speech recognition for more general purposes. Among many important applications not directly concerning education is the example of preparing a document, such as a letter or book. The first draft of this book was a typescript of the tape from a small tape recorder transcribed at a word processing machine. In the future a writer may talk to a word processing machine to get the first draft. But this concept is futuristic, not likely to happen quickly!

While different estimates appear in the literature, speech input may not be available in low-cost systems in the next ten years. Major research efforts are addressing the issue. The difficult problem in identifying speech, a pattern recognition problem, is made more complex because there is no obvious way of dividing sound into words.

Brainwave Input

Brainwave input to computers, the last auxiliary technique considered, sounds to many people like science fiction. Yet to some extent, from the computer's point of view, it differs not too greatly from speech input. Both cases deal with a very complex pattern recognition problem. From the human point of view the patterns are very different—sound waves in the air versus brain signals with electrically recorded patterns. If voice-input techniques become highly successful, similar techniques may apply to brainwave input. So in the future all the input to the computer may very well come through *thought!*

The idea of brainwave input has occurred frequently in science fiction and other literature, even in educational contexts. For example, in his book, *Education and Ecstasy,* George Leonard discusses OBA—ongoing brainwave analysis.* It is limited, however, to distinguishing an "I understand" and "I don't understand" sensation from the learner. Recent studies of brainwaves at the University of California, San Diego, triggered when a reader encounters an unfamiliar word, seem related to the brainwaves needed for OBA. But there is still far to go for full practical brainwave input for educational use. Problems of privacy might become important too.

NEW TECHNOLOGIES

In this chapter I have reviewed a number of technological developments concerning computers and related equipment that seem important for future educational computing applications. But the specific technologies mentioned are not the only ones that will be important in the future. What currently appear to be minor technologies may become extremely important, and as yet unimagined technologies may develop. It may well be that the most critical hardware and software developments for the future of education have not even been mentioned! Thus researchers are already discussing "molecular chips" with organic molecules as their basis. We can be sure, however, that dramatic change will continue to occur. The computer technology is young and vigorous.

*George Burr Leonard, *Education and Ecstasy* (New York: Delacorte Press, 1968).

chapter *14*

Computers and the Future of Education

- Current Problems in Education
- There Will Be Computers!
- Extensive Curriculum Development Involving Computers
- What and How Will Learners Learn?
- Environments
- Teachers
- Students
- Visions of Learning

It seems entirely fitting in the last chapter of the book to dwell on where education is going, both with and without computers. I am particularly interested in educational futures involving computers.

In looking at the future I must speculate; it is important to speculate about computers in education because of their possible great impact on our educational system. Because of so many current possibilities, and because of the technology's rapid evolution and the likelihood of change, likely major effects must be carefully considered.

I have emphasized the rapidly changing technology time and time again; I believe it is impossible to overemphasize its importance. Many teachers and administrators who think computers in education have reached the *end* or are near the end of a long process are nowhere near the truth. This is the *beginning* of the use of computers in education. All of us have much to learn about this process. The first lesson should be to approach the future with a great deal of humility; we should be prepared to explore.

In spite of this need for humility, I start with a very rash prediction that even goes beyond proposals from many of the staunchest believers in computers. I believe that computers, although little used in education at present, will eventually become the *dominant delivery system in education at all levels,* from earliest childhood through the schools, community colleges, and universities, through adult education and also through training activities within companies. The pedagogical advantages of computers augmented by continually decreasing costs and increasing capabilities will ensure their dominance.

I begin to explore the future of education by examining current problems. This input plus the background on the future of computer hardware and software from previous chapters provides the basis for later considerations.

CURRENT PROBLEMS IN EDUCATION

All levels of our educational system are currently in very serious trouble. As my main experience is within the United States, I shall restrict comment to those systems. But friends elsewhere, plus my own observations of other systems, suggest that the problem may be worldwide. The case for the problems in American education has been made many times in the past few years.*

First, it can be argued from a variety of evidence that there is a decline in *quality* of American education. Supporting statistical evidence comes from national examinations, including the Scholastic Aptitude Tests and the National Assessments. Discipline problems in American schools at all levels are obvious to almost every visitor. Students' negative attitudes reflect similar attitudes about education in the general populace.

The financial plight of schools is becoming more and more an issue. American voters seem niggardly regarding any expenditures of public funds, with schools suffering particularly harsh treatments. School districts have closed schools, teachers' strikes are numerous, and teachers in areas such as science and mathematics leave the field altogether for more remunerative and gratifying jobs. Schools of education are graduating very few secondary science and mathematics teachers, and so more and more people hired for those positions possess minimal qualifications.

Students complain too about the quality of university education. The problems are particularly bad in certain disciplines. Thus currently computer science departments cannot hire the faculty they need. Therefore many qualified applicants are refused admission to university computer science departments. Computer science faculty often fill the gaps by recruiting people from the community. In some regions this procedure is reasonable, but in other areas it results in deterioration in quality of the courses. When the chairs of major computer science departments meet, they dwell upon this topic. But no adequate solutions are forthcoming. Similar problems exist in engineering. Though these problems have been well described in reports from the government and elsewhere, these reports have had no substantial effect. *Global Stakes,* by James Botkin, Dan Dimencescu, and Ray Stata, considers university problems and their negative effect on our future economy.†

Coupled with all these difficulties is the tendency of education to "dig in" and attempt to avoid change. The educational system is very conservative. Teachers and faculty considering educational issues are often indisputably conservative, resisting any significant changes.

Furthermore, instituting changes can be suicidal. I have recently witnessed an interesting example in a large university beset, as are many universities, by serious financial problems. The reaction to economic trauma has been to weed

---

*I would particularly recommend to readers a report prepared for the Secretary of Education by the National Commission on Excellence in Education, *A Nation at Risk* (Washington, D.C.: U.S. Government Printing Office, 1983).

†James W. Botkin, et. al., *Global Stakes* (Cambridge, Mass.: Ballinger, 1982).

out almost every distinctive feature of that university, even though these unique features had elicited considerable national recognition. Most faculty and administrators come from the "traditional" areas, so these disciplines have the political power in the university. If an area in which the university might excel is not common in education, it is likely to be cut. In a few years this university will have only conventional departments, with nothing to distinguish it from five hundred other universities around the country. If at that time the issue becomes the closing of campuses, by minimizing its distinctions, this university has made itself a prime target for closure. This example is by no means isolated.

To a certain extent, the problems and the challenges of securing quality in education stem from the large numbers of students. In a democracy everyone should be educated to the highest standards. Education is expensive where large numbers of people are involved; resources decline and the public's negative feelings toward the educational system increases. Existing means and resources are inadequate to meet these needs.

Many parents are aware that something is wrong with the educational system. Increasing numbers of parents around the country are attending workshops about computer-based learning and other uses of computers in education. These parents are worried about their own children's education in their local educational systems.

Yet other teachers and parents may be unwilling to admit that the educational system is faltering to the extent I claim. Many are complacent about these problems. I can only urge such people to study the situation in more detail.

THERE WILL BE COMPUTERS!

In seeking ways out of our current educational difficulties, the paths seem few. The current situation, with concurrent declines in quality and resources, allows few opportunities. Parents and educators can aspire to greater resources for education, but this seems extremely unlikely. Furthermore, it is not clear how such resources would be used even if they were available. The various reports suggest directions, but these are often either inadequate or difficult to implement.

Often computers *are* suggested as the solution to our educational difficulties. Computers are becoming increasingly known in our society, reaching into all areas and eliciting tremendous publicity and attention. Some people consider computers to be a panacea, a solution to all types of problems. Others see that the computer *could* improve education. So it is not surprising that parents often recognize the potential of computers and lobby for computers in schools.

It is remarkable that even the current severe financial limitations on schools do not preclude their purchasing computers rapidly, perhaps even more rapidly than is good for them, given the current paucity of good material and teachers prepared to use computers effectively. Atari, for example, has advertised the fact that the Miami-Dade school system acquired over four hundred of its computers in a single purchase. While there have been many similar large purchases, access by all students is still limited.

Both "good" and "bad" factors imply that computers are likely to be used more and more in school systems and in all other educational environments. The good reason is that computers *can* effectively aid students to learn, interactively and with individualized attention. Developers know how to design materials, through a careful design process with full testing such as the process discussed in chapters 11 and 12.

Another factor, repeatedly stressed, is that computers will continue to decline in cost and increase in capability—or, more likely, both. Whether computers are competitive financially today can be argued, but in the future computers will unquestionably be the *least expensive way* to establish a new educational system. Computers will provide the economic system of choice for almost all types of learning activities, given rapidly declining hardware costs and increasing costs of other learning modes.

Another economic factor is also extremely important in considering the greatly increased role of the computer in education. Computer-based learning material is rapidly becoming a big business, with many older companies, such as publishers and computer vendors, investing funds in developing computer material and many newer companies springing up for just this purpose. I will have more to say about these companies later.

All this is not to imply that there will be nothing but computers. Teachers, books, and films will often be coupled with computers in new learning material. Computers will not supersede other educational delivery systems overnight. It takes time to change education. A Carnegie Commission study (primarily concerned with universities) called "The Fourth Revolution—Instructional Technology in Higher Education"* predicted that the years from 1990 to 2000 would be a period of rapid introduction of computers into higher education, with computers common after 2000. That report, only a few years old, is remarkable in that it predated personal computers and so referred to older computer technologies. Therefore, its prediction is perhaps a little conservative. A similar time for widespread computer use may be appropriate for other parts of the educational world. So it can be reasonably expected that the next twenty years will be a period of great change and tremendous turmoil in education.

Many questions arise. I have frequently emphasized that as yet little besides primitive computer learning material is available. Massive curriculum development efforts, in which whole curricula are developed through school systems and universities, are needed. But how can this expensive curriculum effort occur? Who will do

it? How? How will it be financed? Who will distribute it?

Other important questions can also be raised. How will this change affect our institutions? We tend to expect institutions to continue indefinitely. But will they? Or will we have new forms of education, new educational institutions? Will public institutions or other schools become more important or less important in education? Will the home become more important in education? How will schools be organized, if they continue to exist?

I will not give definitive answers to all these questions. But I will consider some possibilities.

EXTENSIVE CURRICULUM DEVELOPMENT INVOLVING COMPUTERS

The types of computer-based courses needed to improve education will not be developed just by tinkering with existing courses, adding a few pieces of computer material here and there. Existing courses were developed with a certain range of learning media in mind, learning media based primarily either on books or lectures. (Films, audiovisual material, and slides still play only a minor role in most existing curriculum material.) Good courses will not result from minor computer additions to those designed fundamentally for other learning modes. The computer is a new and unique device, and its effective use in learning demands rethinking the curriculum profoundly, area by area and course by course.

Is this type of rethinking possible? How can it be done? Several precomputer efforts of nontrivial magnitude can be mentioned. In the 1960s and the early 1970s extensive curriculum development was undertaken in the United States in secondary school science and mathematics. This was to some extent a reaction to Sputnik, a dramatic event that stimulated the United States to demand better education in science, mathematics, and technology. The National Science Foundation, the Office of Education, and private foundations provided signifi-

*The Carnegie Commission on Higher Education, *The Fourth Revolution—Instructional Technology in Higher Education* (New York: McGraw-Hill, 1972).

cant funding. Biological Sciences Study Committee, Physical Sciences Study Committee, Project Physics, Chem Study, Chemical Bond Approach, the Madison Project, School Mathematics Study Group and other curriculum development groups are well-known. The list is long. About $50 million was spent in such curriculum development over approximately twelve years; perhaps ten times that much was spent in attempts to retrain teachers.

This development came to an abrupt halt in the early 1970s. Rather oddly, the halt was due to one course, a sociology course for ten- to twelve-year-old students called "Man, A Course of Study." The science education program within the National Science Foundation never recovered. All curriculum development, which had been very extensive, stopped. Funds for science education started to decrease, particularly as reflected as a percentage of the entire National Science Foundation budget. These funds ceased entirely in the first year of the Reagan administration, but they have been recently reestablished.

It is interesting to note in light of my earlier comments about public feelings toward education that this drastic cut elicited almost no newspaper or magazine reaction. That is, the press did not think it worth reporting to the general public. Only now, in 1983, is there renewed interest in science and mathematics education, due to all the recent reports on the state of our educational system.

So at one time the United States was willing to support a very large curriculum development effort and an even larger teacher training effort. At the beginning of this effort workers were naive about how to develop materials. Sophistication increased in these projects. How ironic that the funds ceased to exist when researchers were really learning how to use them! A number of other countries were able to profit from the experience of the developmental work in the United States. Thus in the USSR there was a massive redesign of the mathematics and science curricula during the 1970s.

The Open University in the United Kingdom presents another interesting example of massive curriculum development efforts at the higher education level. The Open University is a learning-at-a-distance institution; students work mostly at home, using very carefully developed learning sequences. Sizable amounts of money are spent, perhaps a million dollars, developing *each* course. The principal learning mode is print material. Television programs are produced as part of courses, but they play a lesser role than originally anticipated. Study centers, with tutors, are available throughout the country. A few courses also use computers, but so far this is a minor delivery mode in the Open University.

While not so obvious, a third example of major curriculum development merits attention. The development of *existing* curricula in most schools in the United States was quite different from the large-scale developments in the U.S. and the Open University. About four textbook series dominate the field of mathematics in the first through sixth grades in the United States. The production of such textbook series are major curriculum development efforts. Similar situations exist for most education in the United States.

The development of these series can be examined (see chapter 11). In almost all cases commercial vendors provided the impetus and the funding, and their efforts can be monumental. Several publishers have been willing to quote approximate costs to produce a first-through sixth-grade mathematics series. Three series averaged about $5 million each, a small amount on a per-student basis. That is not to be viewed as a firm figure, because the companies do not keep comparable data; what to charge to development and what to charge to marketing also can vary. But the figures provide a likely order of magnitude. These companies were willing to risk sizable amounts of money in the hope of capturing a large segment of the primary mathematics curriculum market. College textbooks cost less, but again the publisher must invest a large sum of money before a book is actually sold. Textbook publishers are responsible for development of most curricula now in use at all levels of education in the United States.

Therefore it is of great interest to note that many of the major textbook publishers, and many minor ones, are now actively investigating or beginning to market computer-based learning materials. Such companies as Scott, Foresman & Co., Science Research Associates, Random House, Addison-Wesley, McGraw-Hill, Harper & Row, and Harcourt Brace Jovanovich are vigorously pursuing computer-based learning. In some cases they already have extensive catalogs of material, although typically it is material they neither developed nor commissioned but that is already available from other sources, primarily schools and universities. Regardless of the overall poor quality of this material, at present the total financial effort put forth by the publishing houses is very impressive. The amount of funds devoted to computers, while still small compared with the total developmental budgets of these companies, is growing rapidly. In many cases the impetus has come from high-level management. The more these companies perceive increasing interest in this market, and the more companies begin to clarify the current uncertain nature of the market, the more they will become more interested in investing in curriculum development involving computers.

Furthermore, in the current market, textbook publishers are unlikely to increase profits by increasing their share of the textbook market: Today's competition is strong and the status of conventional education is declining. But the computer presents an entirely new "game" in which the situation might change entirely. A new computer-based learning publisher or a small textbook publisher might become a major publisher of computer-based learning material. A medium-size textbook publisher might become a large publisher of computer-based learning material. A large publisher might increase its share of the educational market.

Given these possibilities, it is not surprising to see that both major existing textbook publishers and new companies have become active in developing computer materials. Nor is it surprising to find that these companies are fearful of future uncertainties, whatever their current policies may be. Each company must ponder how much money to invest, what areas to work in, what types of computer emphasis to pursue, how to market the material, with no established tradition or experience to provide guidelines. All these uncertain areas lead to great turmoil and discussion within each company.

Publishers, new and old, are not the only group with a possible future financial stake in marketing these new learning materials. Perhaps even more important are the companies that manufacture and sell computers. These companies want to increase the sales of their computers, and, particularly for the home and school market, they see that educational software can be an important stimulus to purchase their equipment. Further, educational software itself is a possible new source of profit for computer companies. So it can be expected that at least some of the major companies, such as IBM and Digital, will make major investments in developing computer-based learning materials.

Anyone concerned with the future of education cannot feel entirely happy about the increasing commercial interest, for it implies dangers as well as opportunities. Although many companies sincerely want to improve education, they are even more dedicated to increasing their own profits, as they must be. Hence their decisions may not always lead to the best educational material. We as educators must work with them, trying to convince them to promote quality of material.

A real hope for the future is for the United States government to resume at least partial sponsorship of educational improvements, perhaps collaborating with commercial companies and foundations. As the problems of education become greater, and as more and more new efforts are undertaken, it seems likely that sizable government funding will again provide for curriculum development. International cooperation is also a good possibility. Combined efforts with industrial training groups may also occur.

Other types of dangers and problems could also arise. One worrisome problem already present is that only more affluent students may access the computer as a learning device. This problem is likely to increase in the next several years, as U.S. Title money for disadvantaged students, which has often supported computer programs, vanishes.

So we can expect to see more and more commercially available and marketed material for computers in education in the United States and other countries. But what will or should education for children and adults be like when computers become the dominant educational delivery device?

WHAT AND HOW WILL LEARNERS LEARN?

In the previous section I discussed some problems associated with the sizable curriculum development needed to use the computer effectively in education. I barely touched on the most critical problems. What is to be learned in all these new computer-based curricula? You may have assumed that I have been discussing the *same* courses you are already familiar with, the same content. But this is not necessarily the case. The computer may lead to new and entirely different modes of learning in our society, and these modes of learning may affect not only *how* we learn but, perhaps even more profoundly, *what* we learn.

First, even if there is little change in content, the computer allows entirely different ways to *organize* courses. The classical lecture-textbook way to learn in our schools and universities is by no means the only possibility. I have mentioned the possibility of test-driven courses, where the tests become the courses' major learning material. In strategies of this kind, the student begins

a particular unit *immediately* by starting a test in that unit. The test may review some necessary background and then may proceed with what is expected to be learned. As soon as students are in difficulty, the computer shifts perhaps imperceptibly from a testing to a learning mode. Often this learning covers exactly the difficulties the student is having. The tests themselves embody all or almost all of the learning material. This is not to say that students could not use books and other learning modes, if they desire. But the tests would be the focus.

This is not the only new way to organize courses. Indeed, these ideas can be combined with others, such as those of the learning cycle (see chapter 7). Once computers are allowed to play a major role in education, educators may want to organize courses very differently than they are organized at present.

This still leaves the more difficult issue of whether there should be substantial changes in content. The educational system is to a large extent an accident of history, as with all human endeavors. It is not clear that the way we do things is necessarily the best way.

One set of factors leading to changes in content is the influence of the computer itself, the role it will play in society. Should people be taught long division, given that it will soon seldom be done by hand? Considerable time goes into teaching long division in the fifth and sixth grades, and the "new math" tried valiantly to change the way it was taught. The rote procedure used today is seldom understood, yet much student effort and time goes into learning this procedure. Does anyone *need* long division in the age of calculators and computers?

But long division is only the tip of the iceberg! What about adding and multiplying fractions? What about differentiation? What about definite and indefinite integrals? The symbolic mathematics computer packages already allow differentiation and integration, and although these packages are not yet in common use, their use will increase. Current curricula from first grade through graduate school teach people many strategies that, in the near future, humans will perform with the aid of computers.

Sometimes it is not the computer alone that makes the difference; integration is a good example. Up until recently evaluating an indefinite integral involved some guessing. Students learned a series of possible procedures to use, but these did not guarantee that the integration could be carried out or indeed even that an integral existed within the functions the student was familiar with. But several years ago, partially because of the needs of symbolic mathematics, a decision procedure for determining whether any expression had an integral, within a given class of functions, and for carrying out the integral, was found. Guessing is no longer necessary. With sufficient computer power, this procedure makes symbolic integration an easy process.

An even more radical position can be taken. Given the possibility of voice input, will anyone need to *write,* in the physical sense, in the future? That is, will writing become essentially an unnecessary art, if there is always at hand a simple device that will accept speech? Or, perhaps going further along, is there any need to teach *reading?* As mentioned, devices such as the Kurzweil reader may allow all reading to be done directly by computers. I am not suggesting that we immediately abandon the teaching of reading and writing. But as more and more powerful tools become available on the computer, allowing us to take over more and more of the routine aspects of human endeavor, very difficult questions will have to be answered concerning the nature of the curriculum. New and powerful intellectual tools imply new ways to learn subject matter and perhaps even entirely different subject areas.

Although I can hardly expect to give complete answers to these difficult problems, some clues about the future can be discussed. First, some ways of working are critical in human endeavors. Thus everyone must be able to develop insight and intuition into every area they work in. If you wish to win a Nobel prize in a particular area—say, physics—you will not succeed by solving routine problems, no matter how complex, with routine techniques. The researcher needs insight, the ability to know which problems are the critical ones and thus which problems to tackle. Years ago, Richard Hamming from Bell Laboratories made amusing speeches called "How to Win the Nobel Prize." Hamming pointed out rightfully that what most people were doing in science couldn't *possibly* win a Nobel Prize because it was not interesting enough! It's only if researchers pick the interesting problems and directions to work on that they can hope to make really creative developments. So developing such insight and intuition will continue to be a major problem, and all our curricula must take that into account.

A subset of this problem has to do with the ability to make quick estimations, whether with simple addition or multiplication of fractions or the results of carrying out an integration. That is, a student must be able to look at the results and say, almost instantly, if the result is reasonable or not. Our current educational systems do a poor job of teaching quick estimation, a type of "intelligent guessing." Indeed, students are often misled by the educational system to believe that guessing is somehow evil. Polya said a long time ago that we *must* teach guessing!

Many interesting issues can be raised. Can *all* of education be restructured so that the student works only with a whole series of very powerful intellectual tools designed to aid learning? This is the vision of the future that Seymour Papert gives us in *Mindstorms.* But I believe this is too great a jump from the current situation and rests on too narrow a base—Logo—for us to assume that it is possible. We can only try various experiments and see to what extent we will still need structure and to what extent students will be able to proceed on their own with these powerful tools. All education is a balance between freedom and control; both play a role. It takes insight to win the Nobel Prize, but it also takes discipline. I am not convinced that tools alone will supply that discipline for most people.

ENVIRONMENTS

The next issue concerns where learning will take place in future educational systems dependent on computers. A number of possibilities need to be considered: schools, public places, and home.

Schools

In the next few years the number of computers in schools will continue to increase rapidly. If many new schools were being built, their architecture would be altered to provide for the advent of computers, with specific rooms allotted for computing and wiring for networking computers. At present in the United States, however, few schools are being built. School population has been declining, so that many school districts find they have more space than they need. Demographic data indicates that this trend will continue for a few years.

As schools are used less, available rooms may be converted to computer facilities. Computers may be kept in learning centers, in individual classrooms, or they may be movable, on wheeled carts. As more computers are present in schools, there will be less need for such mobility. Secondary schools tend to group computers by discipline, and it seems likely that classes for teaching programming will be laboratories containing numbers of personal computers.

The major problems in schools for many years will be the lack of sufficient teacher preparation for using computers and the lack of first-rate computer-based learning material. A vigorous, well-supported federal policy could ease these problems.

Public Places

The second possible location for computers is in public places such as libraries, shopping centers, airports, and train stations, although there are few current examples of learning computers in these locations. This situation is likely to change significantly.

The library is already an important learning location. Public libraries are weak in the United States at present because they have suffered seriously from the same unwillingness of citizens to pay taxes, and therefore support good institutions, that has affected schools. Libraries too have been trying to alter, to some extent, their image as a "book" environment. Many public libraries also lend tapes, records, and other audiovisual material. So computer-learning material fits naturally into the library environment.

Several experiments have put computers in libraries. An example is Computertown USA, which now has a number of sites in the United States and abroad. These public environments teach some programming, and they also help people who are shopping for a computer and want to try a number of different ones. School districts or groups of school districts have set up similar facilities, many intended just for teachers, but some having a broader clientele.

The Educational Technology Center has developed material recently for use in public libraries; see the description of *Batteries and Bulbs* in chapter 5. This use is like conventional library use of books, in that computer learning units in libraries compete with books to aid learning. Just as any book in a library could aid some learner, any good computer material should also be in the library for a learner's use. That computers are used so little in libraries at present is due partly to the dearth of good computer-based learning material, partly to its being a new idea that will take time to become established, and partly to libraries' current financial problems.

Computers will also be used in other public places. Shopping centers, airport lounges, train stations, and other public gathering places should have computers containing, among other things, educational materials. The computer facilities in Sesame Place, now in Philadelphia and Dallas, and soon to be elsewhere, have a small—though perhaps growing—educational component. Besides having an admission charge, Sesame Place charges people (mostly children) to use the computer. The developers, Children's Television Workshop and Anheuser-Busch, intend to develop additional facilities elsewhere. Undoubtedly others will develop similar facilities, making educational access to computers more common.

Computers are also being used in public learning centers, particularly in commercial learning centers being formed independent of any school district; the number of such centers is likely to increase. Control Data Corporation has set up such centers, though they are still rather expensive for the general public. But the idea of public learning centers, using cheaper computer technology, has good commercial possibilities. One such center in my area sells time on Apple computers and runs courses, mostly teaching programming in several languages. While most people at this center seem to spend their time playing computer games of little or no educational value, this does not have to be the case. Much of the programming being taught in such public centers suffers from the problems enumerated in chapter 2.

Issues of quality of the educational experience will obtain here. It is not clear how to persuade public learning centers to reinforce quality when they can market shoddy wares. But if the standards of teachers and parents can be raised, the learning centers should improve also.

Homes

The relatively new idea of computers as home appliances, something needed in a home, is gaining favor rapidly. Furthermore, Sinclair and Commodore, among a number of small computer vendors, seem to see the home market as their *principal* market, judging from recent advertising. Both Texas Instruments (no longer in the home market) and Commodore are said to have sold over one million machines in 1982. Projections suggest that the number of computers in homes will increase rapidly. As with school computers, the capabilities of these computers will also increase rapidly; currently many home computers have minimal capabilities, but better machines such as the Coleco Adam and the IBM PC jr. are beginning to appear.

The people who will contribute to this increase are *not* the ones who have been buying home computers. Many sales of home computers have been to *computer hobbyists*. This parallels the distinction between people who buy short-wave receivers for tinkering with the electronics and people who buy radios to hear the news or listen to classical music. Members of the first group are hobbyists, whereas those in the second group are employing a home appliance. That home computers have been geared to hobbyists is evident from the fact that it is easy to open them and add chips and new electronic boards. This ability to make internal changes is not possible in other home appliances, such as radios, television sets, washers, and stoves. Recently some computer manufacturers interested in the home market have been moving more toward packaging characteristic of home appliances.

As the appliance market for the home develops, computer gadgets will have to *behave* like appliances. No one buys a refrigerator intending to hook it up in various ways to perform various tasks. Refrigerators always come *prepared* to do certain tasks. Similarly, many people who will buy home computers will have no interest whatsoever in programming. They will buy computers to accomplish some purpose important to them—playing games, writing letters or papers, keeping financial records, preparing income tax, getting financial advice, keeping personal notes and data, engaging in learning activities. More and more *applications*, the software, the things the machine can do, will determine the home computer market, as vendors are only slowly realizing. At the moment they are still primarily selling hardware, in spite of the lessons offered by such highly successful software products as VisiCalc and word processors. These highly successful software products, including educational ones, will be major determining factors in the battle for the home market; eventually the company that takes this seriously from an investment point of view will dominate.

Education is among the commodities to be supplied for the home market. Some learning materials developed for schools will also be important in the home market. The inverse phenomenon will also arise—marketers will realize the importance of software and therefore develop educational material *specifically* for the home market. Some of this material, but not all, will often trickle down to the schools. Home computer applications could quickly become an important area for development of educational materials, eventually "wagging the tail" of educational development, determining what educational products will be available.

Thus the home computer may well become the primary influence upon the educational systems of the future. This change in the focus of production will in turn lead to many changes in educational practices. For example, the home material will certainly not depend on live teachers' efforts, since no teachers are available in homes. So the role of the teacher in future learning activities may well be affected by this movement of learning to the home. Motivational factors will also be critical in the home market, so the learning products will have to be good at holding users' attention.

I can go a step further. If more and more computers appear in homes, homes may become a *major site* of education. That is, some or all of what currently happens in schools may occur in the home environment. This may be one of the most dramatic consequences of the use of computers in education.

It seems unlikely that all current functions of schools will move to the home. One school function, not to be underestimated, is the babysitting or custodial role: Schools remove children from homes for a period of time, relieving parents of

responsibility. Many parents, for one reason or another, find this desirable. And other roles of the school, such as teaching children to get along with other people, will be difficult to move to the home.

A distinct possibility, perhaps even a likelihood, is that *some aspects* of current school learning will move into the home environment in future educational systems. Voucher systems and similar proposed strategies could very much accelerate the shift of learning to the home; with such systems, some educational funds would go directly to parents to use whenever they desired. The voucher system would deal a heavy blow not only to public schools but also to private schools that are promoting it, expediting commercial dominance of the educational market. If education suddenly is worth lots of money, beyond the money for books, commercial forces such as Sears, Roebuck—to pick a random example—may plunge into teaching, primarily in the home. While schools, public and private, would not necessarily disappear, their role would change greatly.

As more and more education does occur in the home, another interesting effect will occur. The fact that the computer is being used in home instruction will mean that parents can assume a greater degree of control of their children's education, if they wish to. Not all parents will welcome this, but some will consider it a distinct improvement in the educational system. From a national point of view the consequences may not be entirely desirable.

Since the child is working at home in these situations, the parents can even be *actively involved* to the extent they wish. The experience of the Educational Technology Center with public library material shows that we frequently did get parent-children combinations working together on the library computers—something that happens very seldom in the typical school situation, where, although a parent may help a child, both do not generally learn together. Computers in libraries and homes will make this much more practical. Education based on the use of personal computers may become more of a family activity.

TEACHERS

What will happen to teachers in the educational future? What are some of the possibilities? My experiences with beginning physics courses via computer are relevant. Since teaching that course, I have been able to consider how my role changed from my role in a traditional course. If I had taught a beginning physics course in the standard fashion, I would have given a series of lectures. In the physics-via-computer course, I used some lectures, because some students expect them, but they were not of central importance; they contributed less toward learning than did the computer-based exams, with their extensive help sequences. This is not just my opinion; students concurred year after year in questionnaires.

To characterize my role in the course, I would say that I shifted from functioning primarily as a lecturer to functioning primarily as an individual tutor for students in difficulty. The system required students who did not pass a quiz after four attempts to consult me. The students *could not* take additional tests without seeing the instructor. (Other students *could* see me, and sometimes did.) As fifteen tests were required, a student might appear a number of times during the quarter. Always my task was to determine the cause of the student's difficulties; even with all the learning resources available the student had not learned. I worked frequently with individual students or with small groups in my office. I was effectively the court of last resort, the teaching-learning device students could appeal to when all else failed.

Since I was working one-to-one with students, my task was to boost them sufficiently to successfully pass the computer quizzes. I enjoyed the additional advantage of seeing in detail where the learning material was weak; by determining where many students had difficul-

ties, I was often able to improve quizzes by adding help sequences, particularly in the first year or two when the Educational Technology Center still had ample funding to continue course development. This is a nonstandard teaching role, and I found it much more interesting. However, not all my colleagues would agree. I have heard distinguished researchers say, particularly in universities, that it is a waste of their time to work individually with students.

In elementary and secondary schools, a shift in the teacher's role toward solving learning problems not susceptible to other learning resources available to students can also be anticipated. In this situation instructors continue to have a role to which they are accustomed, helping students. Teachers will do this on a much more individualized basis than in today's classroom, playing a different role for different students. Self-pacing also renders the teacher's life more interesting. As each student is at a different point in the course, with different problems, repetition is avoided.

An obvious effect in the elementary-secondary arena is a new type of teacher who teaches *about* the computer. This new subject area takes on importance because of the societal roles some students (but not all) will assume after leaving school. This new teacher role will be important, but it will probably reach a plateau. Presently it is often not explicitly recognized. That is, a teacher of mathematics, of science education, or anyone claiming some computer knowledge teaches programming. But this area is likely to become structured as are other disciplines in the school system, with specialized teachers. As previously mentioned, finding competent teachers will be very difficult—and impossible in many school districts. I emphasize again that *most* use of computers in education should occur in the standard courses. (See chapter 3 for more discussion of this point.)

The exact role of teachers who are teaching in a subject matter area in primary and secondary schools will be determined by newly developed curricula, some involving extensive computer use. Undoubtedly as computers begin to increase in usage, various competing strategies will be available, with less uniformity than at present. The rational approach would rely upon large-scale testing on a national or international scale to determine which curriculum approaches are most successful. This testing will be a difficult and expensive process; "success" can have many meanings, and such testing is probably not feasible politically. So it is unlikely that it will happen, except in a few situations.

The major problem associated with any new curriculum development has been to train teachers, in this case to teach programming, computer literacy, the intellectual tool use of computers, or the computer-based learning use of computers. Teacher training has always been an Achilles' heel in curriculum development. Major curriculum developments, such as the elementary-level new math, failed in large part because of the inadequacy of teacher training. Other problems also contributed to failure of such major curriculum projects, but inadequacy of teacher training to change teachers, in spite of major efforts in this direction, was striking. When new math was introduced, with extensive training and new curricula, most teachers proceeded to teach the "old" math.

Many people seem to think of preservice and in-service training as the model for teacher training, with the expectation that schools of education or other institutions will offer such training. However, with the school population declining or static, the number of teachers trained afresh is unlikely to be large. In-service training is likely to be inadequate for the problem, given the number of teachers and their widespread locations all over the country.

Furthermore, from the school system's point of view, training teachers to teach about computing may have undesirable consequences. Because of the shortage of computer programmers, much more remunerative and interesting jobs will attract teachers highly trained in computer science. So it will not be easy to train teachers adequately in programming and keep them as teachers. The task may be easier for other uses of the computer.

Thus the nature of the job market will inhibit successfully training teachers to teach programming competently. While salaries could be adjusted to reflect demand—areas with few teachers because of high demand outside of schools would pay more—a drastic change in salary scales would be required. Such a change, often suggested in studies such as "A Nation at Risk," seems politically difficult if not altogether impossible. Because of the shortage of science and mathematics teachers in high schools, a few schools already have some salary differential, but the trend will spread slowly if at all.

The best choice is to develop curricula requiring relatively little recurring input from instructors. Teachers can be trained by computer-based learning material! The large numbers of teachers needing training constitutes a strong argument for use of the computer. All other solutions suggested appear to me to be entirely inadequate.

STUDENTS

I hope you feel something of a crescendo in the issues discussed in the last sections. Environments are less important than teachers, and teachers are less important than students. (Curriculum does not fit well into such a linear scale.) An educational system should be directed toward student learning. This is regrettably not always the case within our current systems. But it is fitting to conclude a review of future factors by imagining the students' point of view of what education is likely to be.

Schools, curricula, teachers all exist for students. The object is for students to learn. This must not be forgotten in any consideration of the computer in education. Too often the learning system and curriculum units are organized for the convenience of the instructor or institution rather than for the benefit of students. Students should be able to exploit their maximum capacities, to have powerful skills. The educational systems should prepare students for profitable and enjoyable lives. Interaction and individualization are key factors in these goals.

Will students see future educational systems as *better* than present ones? And will careful observers of education consider the heavily computer-dependent learning systems of the future better, in some sense, than current systems? An affirmative answer would be reassuring, but the crystal ball is cloudy.

The educational system of the future may be *worse* than the present one. Every powerful technology, including the use of computers in education, can be good or bad, as I have noted frequently. The courses and curricula developed for computers and the teachers using that curricula determine the future, not the computer. Nothing ensures that computers will be used successfully to *improve* learning.

Imagine, for example, a highly totalitarian society where computers could by rote indoctrinate students to support that society. Educators need only look at controlled restrictive societies such as those pictured in the Soviet writer Eugene Zamiatin's *We,* Orwell's *1984,* and Huxley's *Brave New World.* In *We* the educational system is computer-dependent in the sense that teachers have been replaced by teacherlike robots. They provide a highly controlled educational system to match the very controlled totalitarian society. In *We* computer-run education is a major weapon for suppressing individual freedom.

But totalitarian education is by no means the only alternative of computerized learning. By contrast, fortunately, through the use of the computer we can realize our goals of individualized learning for each student, letting all students learn at rates suitable for them and making education an active and enjoyable process for each student. In the light of our many problems today, the computer can lead us to a better educational future.

How can we help determine this future? Even with so complex a situation, each of us can work toward a better educational system and by

so doing very much increase the possibilities. It is up to us as humans.

VISIONS OF LEARNING

I want to conclude on the theme that you should develop your own views of what you would like education to be, your own *vision of the future of education.* It is critical in a time of great change that we have such visions. We cannot proceed to work in a piecemeal fashion, simply reacting to each development hastily as it appears. Rather, we need to have coherent long-range views of what we would *like* the future of education to be.

Remarkably few such visions are in the literature of education, with and without computers. One would think that establishing major goals toward which learning should be evolving would be an important theme. But it is not popular to be visionary in academic circles.

We offers such a vision of the future of education, but it is a bad vision, an undesirable future for our school system. Likewise John Hersey's *The Child Buyer* offers another extremely undesirable technology-based mode of education.*

There are, however, some positive and desirable views of education. George Leonard's book, *Education and Ecstasy,* suggests a system that, while not ideal, has many interesting features. Two chapters portray a school of the future, a school just after the turn of the century. (It seems unlikely that Leonard's school could be realized in such a short period of time.) The chapters are in the form of a visit of parents to see their children in school. Children go to school starting at about age three and in about ten years have the equivalent of a university bachelor's degree.

Leonard's school has two completely separate parts, reflected in the two chapters. In one he presents the knowledge-based components of

*John Richard Hersey, *The Child Buyer* (New York: Knopf, 1960).

education, where students learn not only about two plus two and differentiation, but about more difficult tasks such as how to solve problems. In the other part of the school Leonard addresses the sociological components of learning, students learning to live with other students and with themselves.

I will not give a detailed discussion of the sociological part of the school. Much socialization occurs in small groups, with a variety of techniques derived from modern encounter-group philosophies. The knowledge-based components of Leonard's school all take place in the knowledge dome. Students entering this attractive building are greeted by a circular array of large three-dimensional color holographic displays, going all around the outside of the room. Each student, carrying an identification box, goes to an unused display. The computer has a complete set of records of exactly where that student is, a full management system. When a student sits down, review in various subject areas may precede new material. The material is highly interactive computer-based learning material. Each student will be doing different things. Some interaction between students is encouraged—neighboring displays interact with each other.

There are no teachers in Leonard's knowledge dome, although there are many teachers in the sociological part of the school.

Leonard's school has one interesting feature already mentioned in the last chapter. Each student wears a small cap, and that cap is designed to pick up brainwaves. With this Ongoing Brain-Wave Analysis, the system is able to know, moment by moment, whether a student understands or doesn't understand what is happening. This becomes another ingredient to feed back into the computer-based learning material available in the knowledge dome.

Although Leonard's knowledge dome is in a physical school, everything that is done in the dome could be done now almost anywhere in the world. That is, students could be in their own homes, for example, and they could be provided with the learning capabilities available in the knowledge dome. Leonard's system leads easily to a system in which part or all of the knowledge-based components could occur in the home. Indeed, some other views of the future of education portray similar learning in home environments. Leonard has written another future-oriented view of a school in the May, 1984, issue of *Esquire*.

My purpose in discussing George Leonard's vision of the future of education is not to argue that it is the only vision. I think it is a friendly vision, leading to an interesting system, provided good curriculum material is available. In bringing it to your attention, I wish to stress the *importance* of vision and to stimulate your imagination. The computer is almost certain to lead to major changes in education, as I have argued throughout this book. Whether the changes will be desirable or undesirable will depend much on the visions that each of us can develop and on our seriously working toward those visions. Decisions made within the next five to ten years will probably affect our educational system for a much longer time after that. If we are to make the right decisions, we must have strong visions.

Index

Italicized page numbers refer to material in tables and figures.